WRESTLING
WITH THE TRUTH

Wrestling with the Truth

PV Sage Publishing, LLC
pvsagepub@gmail.com

First Edition: April 2022
10 9 8 7 6 5 4 3 2 1

979-8-9855283-0-5 - paperback
979-8-9855283-2-9 - hardcopy
979-8-9855283-1-2 - eBook

To book Robert L. Shegog or Nicholaos Kehagias as speakers, contact pvsagepub@gmail.com

www.wwttrobertshegogstory.com

Editor: Suzanne Gochenouer, www.TransformationalEditor.com
Cover Design: Angie at www.fiverr.com/pro_ebookcovers
Cover and Author Bio Photos: Alex Kun, alexkun926@gmail

Disclaimer: This is an autobiography. It reflects the author's present recollections of experiences over time. Some events may have been compressed, and some dialogue recreated.

The publisher is not responsible for the contents (or maintaining) of websites that are not owned by the publisher.

Printed in the United States of America

Contents

Dedication

This book is about the loves of my life, both the abstract and the physical. The abstract resides in the achievements of the teams and the wrestlers. Death shattered my physical loves. I wish I had a love story like my grandparents. They were married for over fifty-four years and died only six weeks apart. I was blessed to know my great-grandmother, who was born a slave, and regret that I didn't ask more about her life. It amazes and gratifies me to have the opportunity to examine our family line in this book.

In wrestling, we learn the motto, "Strong enough to stand alone." This statement glorifies individual victories on the mat. But it fails to recognize that with each win comes from the support of numerous loved ones. These individuals sustain us off the mat in good and bad times. I would not be at this point in my life without my mother's guidance and love. Amanda L. Shegog was a single parent who set strict standards for her children. Family and friends who stepped in to raise me knew her rules. Those standards received reinforcement from my coaches; Bart Kruse, Floyd G. Marshall, James K. Houston, Ken Kannegieter, Bruce Gilbert, Jare Klein, and my scoutmaster, Truman L. Barnes.

A famous Nigerian proverb states, "It takes a village to raise a child." That village includes people outside your family. People often refer to honored folks as aunts and uncles, cousins, or brothers and sisters. The closeness led to the phrase, "My brother/sister from another mother."

While we invite people to be part of our village, not everyone has our best interest in mind. I have paid attention all my life, hoping to emulate only those who create excellence in themselves and others. "Bad things happen to good people," yet good people must continue to strive toward their dreams and passions.

Robert L. Shegog, 2021

Foreword

For nearly ten years, I pestered my high school wrestling coach, Robert Shegog, to write his autobiography. He never said no, only laughed and suggested that his life was not something others wanted to learn about. I respectfully disagreed.

Coach Shegog, as we still call him today, is one of the oldest living people with HIV. He received his diagnosis in 1986, five years before Magic Johnson. Treatment and outcomes during this time were so poor that contracting the virus was a death sentence. Coach Shegog lost numerous loved ones to the virus and he suffered multiple bouts with the often fatal opportunistic pneumonias.

Yet he persisted. Driven by his passion for wrestling, he got back on his feet so he could be there for the team. HIV had to wait because Coach Shegog had unfinished business. He needed to make sure his students were on track with their classes, able to graduate high school, and ready to continue their postgraduate pursuits. He knew everything about his kids and made sure they knew nothing about him. They never knew when he was sick. They never met the man he loved. They never knew he had to abstain from some critical wrestling moments to be with his dying partner.

He knew coaching wrestling wouldn't have been an option had people learned the truth about him in the 1980s, 1990s, and possibly in the 2000s. He lived a lie and did so for the sake of his students. For my sake. I recall my fourteen-year-old self as a freshman in high school and wonder, "Would I have been mature enough to join the wrestling team if I knew the truth about my coach?" It brings tears to my eyes because I know there's a good chance that I would never have wrestled had I known. I would have missed out on all the life lessons, so much character building, and who knows what kind of life would have resulted. I wouldn't be surprised if many other students had similar feelings.

That is why in October of 2020, I strongly suggested once again to Coach Shegog that he needed to tell his story. Only this time, I offered to write it for him. After weeks of internal debate about whether he wanted to open up to the world, he finally agreed as he realized what telling his story could mean to people. Writing *Wrestling with the Truth* has been a true labor of love. Helping this man, who did so much for thousands of students, is one of the highest honors in my life. I hope you read his story and feel the same life-changing inspiration that I, and many others, were privileged to share.

Nick Kehagias, 2022

My Life Passion

NO FEAR is a wrestling expression often seen on T-shirts. Although meant to inspire wrestlers to do their best, the statement is misleading. We all experience fear. It is how we control or direct our fear that makes the difference. In wrestling, some fear losing, looking bad in front of friends and family, or failing the team. Fear can be a great motivator, but it can also lead to missed opportunities or destructive behavior. This book addresses the fear I experienced—being prohibited from following my passion simply because of who I loved.

My name is Robert Lee Shegog, and I found my life's passion early. I began a life-long love affair with wrestling. As a high school coach, I taught the sport for nearly thirty-three years. Not the scripted spectacle you see on TV but the unpredictable sport that takes place on a two-inch-thick mat. Opponents, equal in weight, are put to a test of pure grit and determination. There is no hiding, no excuses. It's all about how well you prepared and executed. You can attain the highest glory or face the deepest despair.

I love this self-challenge, and I still get an adrenaline boost every time I coach, let alone think about wrestling. However, I believe I would not have been allowed to coach, would never have fulfilled my passion, if people knew the truth about me.

On the surface, people see a tough wrestling coach who happens to be Black. When I retired in 2006, I was one of only five Black head wrestling coaches in Arizona. Yet that statistic only scratches the surface of the experiences that shaped me and got me to where I am.

These are my stories. Many important people to me encouraged me to share them. But did I want to open up? Did I want to be vulnerable? Is telling my life story a form of vanity?

I was hesitant at first because, as a young child attending church, I learned that pride goes before a fall. We practiced humbleness, making it hard to accept a compliment or a gift. When Nick suggested the book idea nearly ten years ago, I resisted. Over time, I realized such behavior leads to tearing down one's self-esteem and the deprivation of natural joy. Every day, loved ones remind me that my life has meaning and reason. So, I said okay. I'm ready to tell my story. This book is a record of my passion and purpose. It captures my truth.

·_·· ——— ···_·

CHAPTER 1

The Early Years

I am a Thanksgiving baby, born November 24, 1951, in Buffalo, New York, the youngest of four children. My older brothers were three and two years older and my sister Orpah, not Oprah like the TV host, was one year older. Three, two, one, and then me.

We lived near a garbage truck storage yard. The memory of the smell permeates my nose to this day. My father was a hard worker who held multiple jobs. He worked at the steel mill, drove an independent cab with a medallion certifying him to operate in New York, and was an amateur photographer with his Polaroid camera. That camera provided the only photographs many Black families had of their special occasions.

He did quite well financially and even owned multiple properties. Unfortunately, he was also controlling, and some of my early memories involved regular yelling between him and my mother. During these arguments, they told us kids to go to a bedroom. Immediately after, I would hear yelling and bumping on the walls. I didn't see it, but I assumed he beat my mother and threw her around.

When I was six years old, my mother found out that my father had a child with another woman. A year later, she finally had enough of the cheating and abuse and packed our belongings. She even threw away the curtains. I'm not sure why, but my guess is that it was one last way to stick it to my father. Her brother and her uncle met us in Buffalo, New York, and took us to Albion, Michigan. Here, we lived with my grandparents and aunt.

Albion was a smaller town of about twelve thousand people. Following the Civil War, Blacks started the Great Migration to northern states. It was common for them to find employment on the railroads, in factories, or as domestics. My grandfather, Grandpa Kemp, the son of a woman born into slavery, came from Alabama to work on the railroads. He traveled a lot for his job, weeks at a time, north through Chicago into Michigan. His sister moved to Albion, inspiring him to settle there as well. Grandpa saved his railroad money and bought ten city lots outright for fifty dollars per lot in the 1930s. He began growing wealth and establishing himself in Albion.

Like my grandfather, other Blacks throughout the country were attaining wealth. Black-owned businesses were plentiful and did well. A model of that success was evident in the Tulsa, Oklahoma, neighborhood of Greenwood. This predominantly Black area of town flourished to the extent that it became known as Black Wall Street. You'd think that wealth would lead to prosperity and peace. Instead, the opposite happened. Once again, Black Wall Street became an example, this time in a horrific manner.

In 1921, the infamous Tulsa Race Riots unfolded. White mobs murdered nearly three hundred Blacks and burned numerous homes and businesses. Airplanes were even used to deploy Molotov cocktails in what was one of the earliest recorded uses of planes in a domestic conflict. Now, close to one century later, one-hundred-seven-year-old Viola Fletcher, a survivor of said riots, is still awaiting recognition and justice for an event nearly forgotten by the world.

After my grandfather purchased his land, he farmed and rented out part of it. Growing up, we had all this land, and each person—parents and children—was responsible for maintaining their segment. We also had a chicken coop. Between the poultry and our garden, our needs were always provided for, so we never really went hungry. When I was growing up there, you knew it was going to be a nice day in Albion if you smelled manure. The odor meant the cows were out grazing.

Tradition at the time was for families to build houses near one another, and my grandfather shared this aspiration. Ironically, none of his five children decided to build houses there.

Our church was Pentecostal, based on strict rules and a literal understanding of the King James Bible. We attended about eighty-five percent of the events, and our lives revolved around the three sermons per week, on Tuesdays, Fridays, and Sundays. Service times rarely changed. One exception was when the high school basketball team made the state playoffs. This should give you an idea of the town's priorities.

For the holidays, all the kids recited poems or bible verses from memory. I remember my poem from when I was seven years old.

"What are you looking at me for? I didn't come to stay. I just came to wish you a Merry Christmas day."

My cousin Mark, a little younger than me and incredibly smart, recited the entire Matthew 27 chapter with a bit of assistance from his mother. At twelve years of age, he delivered the Gettysburg Address from memory during our town Memorial Day celebration. Everyone knew he was destined for great things, and he eventually became a lawyer. We were good kids, wanting to please our parents and do good within our church and community.

My father traveled from Buffalo for occasional visits, and we wrote to him periodically but my memories of him are limited. He was a veteran and always seemed to spend a significant portion of his time at the Albion Veterans of Foreign Wars playing bingo. Because he wasn't around that often, I mentally adopted father figures in the community—uncles, wrestling coaches, and my Boy Scout leader.

My mother, however, was my top role model and the main person I wanted to please and never disappoint. She was more of a father figure to me than my actual father. I always respected her and learned early on not to make her tell me twice. She was tough, working as a domestic for wealthy patrons during the day. "Domestic" was the term used for housekeepers in the 1950s-60s. At night, she went to her job as a nurse's aide at the county hospital.

It wasn't easy for a single mother to take care of four kids, but we always had everything we needed. We grew our own food on my grandparents' land, raised chickens, sold our extra veggies to neighbors, ate fish from the river, and were endlessly resourceful.

Eight people lived in the house, and all the boys slept on the living room floor. My grandfather used a wood-burning stove to heat the house. He often heated bricks in the fire, then placed them under our sleeping bags to keep our feet warm. We didn't have central heat, so this was the way we kept warm in the cold Michigan winters.

Our house had no indoor plumbing. During the day, we used an outhouse. A big, round chamber pot sat next to our bed at night. I have a picture of my sister Orpah sitting on it, perfectly expressing what it means to be "on the pot." I had that photo blown up and planned to hang it on the wall for her sixtieth birthday. Unfortunately, she died one week before that milestone.

Growing up packed close to each other in my grandfather's home made us very tight-knit. We shared everything and always felt much loved. After we'd been there two years, my mother was able to rent a house the next street over. Buying a house was not an option for a woman at that time because she needed a man to sign for her at the bank. Being a divorcée meant it was extra hard.

Eventually, we moved into a house owned by a man named Edward Jones. There was no way my mother could afford to pay the standard rent, but Mr. Jones was romantically interested in her. There is a soul song by The Commodores about a beautiful woman described as a brick house. My mother was a brick, strong, loyal, and supportive. She did not drink, smoke, or hang out in undesirable places. The big drawback was that she was a divorcée with four kids. That didn't stop Mr. Jones. While he owned the house he rented us, he lived and worked in Muskegon, Michigan, a two-hour drive from Albion. He would make that drive sometimes twice a month to spend time with my mother.

My mother paid what rent she could, and Mr. Jones was okay with that, even showing up to help us however he could. He helped so much we started calling him Uncle Eddy. Our home was about five hundred square feet, including a living room, one bedroom, a kitchen, and a bathroom. The boys all slept in the bedroom while my mother and sister slept in the living room. This was a step up from my grandparents' residence. No more outhouses, no more pumping water, and no bathing in a big metal tub with the subsequent dumping of water out back.

When Uncle Eddy visited, he made repairs on the house. After some time, he decided we needed a new house. So he built one, enlisting the help of his cousins and an uncle who lived in South

Bend, Indiana. They traveled to Albion and worked on it almost every weekend. When finished, the house had a full cement-block basement, three bedrooms with closets, a large kitchen, and a living room with a stone fireplace.

Uncle Eddy took the family on the only real vacation we ever had, to Mackinac Island. He asked my mother to marry him. She made one mistake… she asked us. We children said no, thinking, *He's not our father.* We hoped our real dad would return to the family. As we grew up and left home, it became very clear we were wrong. Uncle Eddy married another woman in Muskegon. When Edward Jones died, my Uncle Robert arranged it so my mother could purchase the house. Uncle Eddy treated my family more than considerately and was very caring toward my mother.

Now we were safe and happy. A stable home, such as ours, is part of the foundation for a successful life. Some of my classmates moved several times, were evicted from their homes, or lived with different extended family members. My mother kept us together in one home. Most of the town's Black families lived west and northwest of downtown. Our residence was on the south end near the Kalamazoo River. That prompted students at school to refer to my siblings and me as the river rats. The water was so close that a person on the street out front could throw a rock to the riverbank. The nickname went away as we grew older, except for mine. Some of my classmates refer to me as RAT to this day.

Albion was a segregated city with Black neighborhoods and schools with the exception of Dalrymple Elementary School, which I attended. Dalrymple was a mix of Blacks, Mexicans, and Whites. And I had friends and interacted with kids from these different backgrounds, which significantly influenced my attitude toward race.

Because my mother worked the night shift, we were home by ourselves a lot. But we never were without oversight and we never felt alone. She talked to the neighbors and told them that nobody was to go in or come out of the house after ten p.m. In addition, she routinely stopped by the police department on her way to work and asked if they could patrol past our house. It seems like an odd request these days, but the police department obliged back then.

That didn't stop my sister, truly a wild seed and very independent, from trying to sneak out. One night, my sister convinced me to go with her so she could see some guy.

"Why me?" I asked.

"Because I like him, but I don't yet know him well," she said.

Against my better judgment, I went along, knowing we'd be in big trouble if caught. As was the norm in many parts of Michigan and the Midwest, houses in Albion were not fenced in, making it easy to traverse the adjacent backyards until we reached the neighboring street. While we sneaked through the yards, somebody yelled at us.

"Where are you going?" Our neighbor, Mrs. Ridley, was standing on her back porch.

Stunned, we turned around and ran right back home.

Having the town watch over us was both a blessing and a curse. Concerned citizens kept us from doing stupid stuff, but they also knew our every move. Sometimes someone would stop us and ask, "Aren't you a Shegog?" Or "Aren't you Amanda's child?" Occasionally, they would give us a ride or some other assistance. The townsfolk learned early on that my mom was fierce, and they often used the threat of contacting her to keep us in line. On occasion, however, those same neighbors saved us from our mother's quick and focused punishments.

One such punishment occurred on my first day of fifth grade. It started when the other kids made fun of a morbidly obese teacher as she walked down the hall. I think she might have had a thyroid condition. They kept yelling out the name of a popular dog food. She chased after the kids, unable to catch them. Even though I was innocent, I too ran— right into the restroom. I jumped on the toilet and closed the door, hoping to hide. Within moments, through the crack between the stall door and wall, I saw our teacher gasping as she entered.

Oh no, I thought.

She walked toward my stall, opened the door, grabbed my arm, and dragged me to the principal's office.

Soon after, my mother arrived. The principal began to explain that I was yelling the name of a dog food product at the teacher.

I knew I was innocent, so I interrupted him yelling, "But I didn't do anythi . . ."

Smack! My mother immediately slapped my face into the block wall only a few inches from my head.

"You will not interrupt your principal when he's talking," she said.

I kept my mouth shut, in shock, holding back tears. I could feel that my right front tooth was loose. Blood began filling up my mouth. I tried swallowing the blood for fear of angering my mother by crying or spitting it out.

The principal noticed a rivulet of blood exuding from the right side of my mouth.

"Mrs. Shegog, your son is bleeding."

Without hesitation, she said, "He'll live."

I eventually made it to the dentist and got my tooth repaired. That pain was not my only punishment. When I got home, my mother firmly scolded me for being in the wrong place.

"Get out of my clothes! You don't own anything in the house. Everything you own belongs to me!" I was in my underwear, lying across the bed. My mother grabbed her leather strap and whupped me, saying, "If you ever act out in school again!" She wore out my cookie that day.

For the next few years, on the first day of school, my mother escorted me to all of my classes. I begged her every year to stop, but my pleas fell on deaf ears. Finally, at the beginning of my sophomore year in high school, she felt I'd had enough and let me go alone. Although she wasn't in the classroom, I could still feel her presence as the kids teased me.

"Hey, Shegog, where your mama?" They had gotten used to making fun of me every year.

And when the teacher asked a question, I would hear my mother's voice in my head saying that I better raise my hand and answer.

Moments like these kept me from misbehaving and gave my mother a reputation for being strict. Just the threat of teachers calling our mother was enough to get us to change our behavior. She gave her phone number to each teacher, saying, "If he gets out of line, call me." She wanted to make sure I started the year on the right foot and to put a little fear in the back of my mind.

Fear of my mother lasted well into adulthood and wasn't just isolated to us kids. Even the administrators felt our pain at times. One example revolved around senior ditch day. I really wanted to go, so I ditched for the first time ever, and made it to the lake with my friends. It was a fun time, but not without this nagging worry in the back of my mind. I knew my mother would not give me a dismissal note the following school day. I bit the bullet and confessed to Ms. Johnson, the principal's secretary, before classes started the next day. Without hesitation, she wrote me the required excuse because she knew the wrath that my mother would bring. Mama never found out, and I was okay with that.

All these experiences taught me valuable lessons, including the understanding that actions and words matter and that I would have to pick each of them very carefully. My mother maintained discipline with a mix of strictness and support from her family and church. From the church, two lessons helped define me to the core. One, when angry, I should think before I react. Two, if slapped on one cheek, I should turn the other one.

Those lessons came into play when I had to write my first multi-paragraph essay in sixth grade. The topic was "What I want to be when I grow up."

In the early 1960s, Albion had only a few examples of Black professionals. There were a few Black teachers, one Black policeman, and one Black city councilman. Most of the other Blacks worked in local factories, in the service field, or in small businesses like salons, barbershops, landscaping, or trash hauling. But it wasn't long before that started to change. My uncle, Robert Brown, owned and operated a welding company with nearly one hundred employees. Eventually, Black doctors and administrators moved into town. However, teachers were the largest group of Black professionals in Albion.

I enjoyed school. So naturally, I wrote about being a teacher. The teacher returned my paper with the written comment: *You need to be more realistic.*

That hit me like a brick. I was so angry. Though I enjoyed learning, I was not the best student. My penmanship was subpar, I came from a poor family with no college history or funds, and people, therefore, assumed I could not be a teacher. Despite my anger, I used my early church lessons, evaluated the situation, and turned the other cheek. I made a commitment to prove the teacher wrong. I told myself that I wouldn't let anyone tell me what I could or could not do. I was going to make my dream happen despite what others thought. That would not be the last time someone judged me by my color and family history.

In our neighborhood, there were about thirty to thirty-five Black kids and we often met at each other's family homes. We played ball in the street, ran around vacant lots, and even walked to school together. Occasionally I'd play in an adjacent White neighborhood with three boys—Danny, Mike, and Ricky. Bill Stoffer, another White boy, remained my friend until he died at the age of sixty-eight. Bill never left Albion, but he served multiple terms as mayor and contributed greatly to the city and college. Growing up, I had friends of many different backgrounds. It felt natural to me.

But having White friends made me a liability at times. In the early 1960s, my family drove to Alabama to visit my grandfather's side of the family. They always left me in Albion. When I asked my mother why, she answered, "Because you have too many White friends." She worried that I didn't know how to talk or act around Southern

Whites. The story of Emmett Till was still fresh in everyone's mind, and she did not want me to experience the same fate. When I was older, I did make a trip to Alabama with my family, only to have her watch me like a hawk.

In Alabama, the social divide between Blacks and Whites was striking. My older cousin, Lenn Reid, reminded me of how we were often called "Northern Niggas" or "pickaninnies." We couldn't just do what we wanted because there were always rules separating Whites and Blacks.

In public swimming pools, Whites had earlier swim times than Blacks. It was often the case on sweltering days that they continued swimming well into the time set aside for the Blacks, leading to the Blacks being unable to swim that day.

We couldn't even travel without rules about where we could stop to eat or sleep. The Green Book, officially known as "The Negro Motorist Green-Book," directed our travel plans. It contained the addresses of Black-friendly gas stations, restaurants, and hotels to help with safe travel across the country.

These were only a couple of the many Jim Crow practices where separate was not equal.

Even in Albion, it wasn't all rainbows and butterflies. I noticed the racial tension as I grew older. Remember those three White friends, Danny, Mike, and Ricky? One day they all beat me up for no reason. That was the first time I realized I was different because I was Black and that the difference came with rules, even in my hometown. Nowhere was it written in stone, but Blacks sat on the balcony at the theatre while the Whites claimed the seating on the main floor. Blacks were discouraged from buying homes in certain White neighborhoods.

Even securing a business loan was more difficult if you were Black. One of our neighbors found this out when he tried to open a roller-skating rink in downtown Albion.

There were four K-6 elementary schools. Two were all White, and two were mixed. I went to one of the mixed schools, Dalrymple. At the seventh-grade level, all the kids went to one school. All the upper grades were in a three-story building with a full basement. The basement and first floor were the junior high, while the second and third floors housed the high school. Despite the mixed classes, there was still separation by race in social activities and in the cafeteria. This division led to continued tension and eventually spilled over in high school as the occasional race-based fight. The lack of diversity in homecoming queens and the lack of African-American studies classes or clubs were some of the issues that triggered racial fights or riots. The tensions culminated in trouble numerous times, but one moment in particular stands out.

A Black student named Al Armstrong, who was very smart, wrote poetry and reported for the school newspaper, decided to read a poem for the talent show. He read one written for his girlfriend, who happened to be White, titled "If you could feel my Blackness." That was not what he read during the auditions. Otherwise, he would not have been allowed onstage. When the predominately White student and parent audience heard his poem, they were infuriated. Immediately, they verbally and physically attacked Al. The outnumbered Black students rushed to Al's aid and defended him against the White audience. Even after that night, the school and community continued their ridicule of Al, who was eventually suspended. Al never came back, and few people ever heard from him. The rumor is that he moved to be with family in Alabama, although I can't imagine his circumstances were much better there. Al's story is not uncommon and remains a sad reminder of what can result from racial tension.

꙳

But our town was also able to rally together at other times. Albion had a small Class B (between nine hundred and a thousand students) high school, yet we often advanced to the state level in various sports and other activities. Blacks, Whites, some Hispanics, and even Native Americans participated together in cross-country, cheer squad, debate team, newspaper, and wrestling. That bit of diversity did make Albion a special place to grow up. We had problems, but we learned to get along with other cultures inside our community. The wrestling team was a family. That family influenced my actions, career goals, determination, and core values. My school days in Albion prepared me well to move on to college.

Higher education was more than an expectation at Albion High School. Prior to high school, all students were tested, then classified as general or college prep. There were core classes everyone had to complete for graduation, and the college prep classes were intense. For example, the cutoff for an A was ninety-three percent. A score of seventy percent meant you failed.

Our community supported education to an extreme, and our town reaped the rewards. Each year, Albion High had a group of four or five National Merit Finalists or Semi-Finalists. One time, an Albion student changed the wording of a poorly written Scholastic Aptitude Test (SAT) question to answer it correctly. In response, the national testing body sent the school administration a letter congratulating the student. At Hartland High, where I would later pursue my first teaching job out of college, the school and community went wild if they had a single National Merit Finalist. But in the town of Albion, educational excellence was matter-of-course.

The focus on education shared throughout my entire family extended to my first cousins. Dropping out of school was unacceptable. We were expected to go to college or learn a trade. My family consisted of the Shegogs, Browns, and Kemps. I was the first to go to college, being one of the oldest but not the smartest of the cousins. We were supposed to behave, excel, and do our best. This fact was never more evident than when my oldest brother tried to challenge my mother's rule.

My oldest brother got held back in sixth grade. At the time, there was no guarantee that a student would progress to the next grade. Students were required to demonstrate they had learned the stipulated material before advancing to the next level. Social promotions did not occur, and therefore it wasn't uncommon to see junior high kids with significant facial hair. When my brother started his senior year, he was eighteen years old. He decided that he was now a man and withdrew from school on his own say-so.

Ms. Johnson, the principal's secretary, notified my mother. Mama didn't yell, which scared us younger kids even worse. Instead, she went into my brother's room, boxed up his belongings, and put them on the curb. Unfortunately for him, it rained that day.

When my brother got home later that night, expecting to sleep in his bed, he instead discovered everything he owned outside. His clothes, pictures, and other items—all ruined by the rain.

He complained to our mother, "What about my stuff?"

She calmly replied, "But you're a man and take care of your own stuff. You can't live here anymore."

He pleaded, "Give me a few days."

"No, you're a man. You figure it out."

My mother then turned to us and said, "This is what happens when you drop out of school."

After that, my brother did come to the house as a guest but never lived at home again. He now lives in Maryland. The rest of us learned quickly from his mistake and made sure to keep our butts in school, reinforcing the family expectation that we would finish high school, and if possible, go to college. The idea of dropping out of school was akin to a mortal sin.

As for my cousins, their parents were even stricter than my mother, if you can imagine that. Those kids would go on to become very successful entrepreneurs and professionals. My cousin, Debbie Brown Bryant, went to the University of Michigan and was one of the first Black women electrical engineer graduates, near the top of her class. She went to work for Ford, where she faced a lot of discrimination. Many of the employees resented a Black woman telling them what to do. After nearly ten years in the field, she decided to quit and raise her three children.

I asked her why she would give up a good career and education to stay at home. That was presumptuous on my part because she understood the importance of investing in her children and having the financial luxury to do it. Despite the societal challenges for Blacks growing up in the Midwest, our family did well, largely because of those strict family expectations rooted in our religious upbringing.

This strong support for education from the community of Albion found a contrast in my mother, who did not have a high school diploma at the time. I believe it also made her stricter on us. Her lack of higher education did not stop her from regularly critiquing my papers when I read them to her. She would often say, "Bob, that doesn't sound right. This paragraph is not right. You need to do that better."

Mama did get her high school diploma in 1976. A proud moment for all of us.

I didn't realize it at the time, but she was trying to teach me to speak and write English based on what sounded proper rather than employing slang. Her influence helped my writing and speech. I was on the debate team and twice qualified for the state original oratory contest. In my senior year, I placed fourth in the state sweepstakes contest. The sweepstakes required you to compete in four areas. I did oratory, humorous, impromptu, and prose. In my junior and senior years, I wrote editorials and sports articles for the school newspaper. In the summer of 1969, I attended a journalism camp at Michigan State University (MSU) and was later offered a $500 college scholarship.

At the camp, I met a girl named Sherle. She was fun and wild. Whenever I hear the song "Young Girl" by Gary Puckett and the Union Gap, I'm reminded of her. I wanted to attend college at MSU so I could see her again. But in 1970, the tuition was $1,800 per year. Even with the scholarship, I had to refuse because I couldn't fund the balance.

All my work was paying off. Several of my teachers took notice. During my senior year, our class trip was to Paris, France. My family could not afford it, so I never entertained the idea of going. Then, the principal called me into his office.

"Your trip to Paris has been paid for," he told me.

Pleasantly surprised, I asked by whom.

He said the person wanted to remain anonymous.

After discussing it with my mother, we decided we couldn't accept such a generous gift. Plus, my out-of-pocket expenses in Paris were our responsibility. We couldn't even afford to cover that.

Later, I found out that Mrs. Hart, my English teacher, was the person who offered to pay for my trip. I only learned this after her death, about a year after graduating. She had been impressed with my writing, and more importantly, saw my good nature and hardworking character. She was dying from cancer during my senior year. I had my suspicions when she wore wigs or had substitute teachers for her classes. Mrs. Hart knew she didn't have much time. Instead of spending her hard-earned money on herself, she generously wanted to help me with a once-in-a-lifetime experience. Her selflessness remains forever etched in my heart.

Every time I help one of my wrestlers participate in opportunities they would otherwise lose out on because of money, transportation, or other challenges, I think of Mrs. Hart. I think of my coaches. I think of the community members who supported me. She and many other people taught me the value of reaching back and pulling others forward with you. When everyone succeeds together, the community does better.

·_·· ——— ···_·

CHAPTER 2

First Taste of Wrestling

Growing up, we followed a simple routine: church, school, and then home to do chores. That was, until I had a memorable and life-changing physical education class in sixth grade. Coach Kruse pulled double duty as our P.E. teacher and high school wrestling coach. One day he conducted a unit on wrestling for my class. It was so much fun, and I absorbed everything Coach Kruse showed us like a sponge.

After the demonstration, Coach Kruse encouraged a few students to continue with wrestling and visit the high school team practice. He must have noticed that I had talent because I was one of those chosen. I felt important and wanted. So I continued wrestling through junior high. I excelled in the sport and dreamed about being on the high school team.

༈

At the end of each P.E. class, students reported to the gym bleachers and waited for the release bell to ring. One day, an older bully was moving through the bleachers harassing students. When he tried it with me, I beat him in the face with my tennis shoes, holding them by the tied-together laces. Before he could recover, the teachers on duty separated us and warned us they'd send us to the office if we continued. The bully promised to kick my ass after school. I was nervous and thought that maybe I shouldn't have stood up to him. Perhaps I should have acted like my usual, passive self.

When the final bell rang that day, I dragged my feet about leaving, hoping the bully was gone. Believing I was in the clear, I finally exited the building, only to bump into him and his friends near the bike rack. He grabbed me.

Without thinking, I tapped into my wrestling skills. To my surprise I was winning, until one of the Wilson brothers hoisted me off the bully and into the air (the Wilsons, Woody and Karl, were upperclassmen who would also later attend Olivet College).

The senior students scolded us and sent us on our way home. We listened to them because they were like gods to us puny underclassmen. That was the first time I noticed that my wrestling skills were a huge benefit. I decided to stop being passive and, if necessary, defend myself. Wrestling was giving me more confidence in life, further ingraining my interest in the sport.

I could not wait for wrestling season to start in my freshman year of high school. The team had a new coach named Floyd Marshall. Our previous coach, Bart Kruse, transferred to the more reputable Sturgis High. There were three wrestlers in my weight class, two of them upperclassmen. Upperclassmen athletes were royalty, strutting around in their varsity jackets adorned with awards and medals.

Before each season, the school hosted a sports assembly. In the winter sports assembly, Coach Marshall introduced me as the starting varsity wrestler for the 133-lb. weight class. I was in total shock and didn't understand why. I was only a freshman. I knew I was getting better but good enough to beat upperclassmen? To earn a varsity roster spot, one must challenge and beat everyone in their weight class. I worked hard in practice but never formally challenged anyone. Coach Marshall believed in me, continued to call my name during the wrestle-offs, and after some time, I made the varsity team. I had moments of greatness in some matches, but all in all, it was an average season that was, unfortunately, cut short after I suffered a hernia.

Coach Marshall was young, in his twenties, a slightly shorter than average figure, nearly one-hundred-fifty pounds with light brown, early-balding hair. His walk was bowlegged, yet he was strong as an ox. When he wrestled some of our heavier guys, I was reminded of cartoons where a small character easily lifts larger characters and smacks the ground with them, back and forth. His sincerity and immense knowledge of the sport matched his bravado, making him the perfect coach for our team.

I wish he hadn't had to leave our program after one season. He had gotten into a fight with four students who jumped him in the locker room. The story is a little hazy, but apparently, he whupped them good, at the cost of his job. A few of the other wrestlers and I wrote him often. We had so much respect for him that we would bite the bark off a tree had he ordered.

During his short time at Albion High, Floyd Marshall created a booster club that raised money from local businesses. He also encouraged us to do off-season wrestling. He often called my mom to say he'd like to take me to a freestyle tournament and that he had the costs covered. My mom called him my other daddy. "Get ready. Your daddy's coming," she would say when he was on his way to pick me up for a tournament. In Coach Marshall's mind, if it was possible to make a tournament, we had to go. Neither money nor transportation was a reason to abstain. My teammates and I had a special bond with him. We know he felt the same because he returned to Albion and pleaded for his job, only to be denied (he eventually got hired at a neighboring high school, Jackson County Western). He really was like a dad in many ways, and over the years of my career, I fostered similar principles with my teams.

At Coach Marshall's suggestion, Paul Holdren, Steve Wheeler, and I attended freestyle wrestling tournaments the summer before our sophomore year. Freestyle is a form of wrestling with different rules from the collegiate style at the high school level. It's the style done in the off-season. Thanks to our participation in these matches, we were in shape and ready for the new high school season.

Despite my excitement, my mother was not keen on wrestling after my hernia repair. She refused to sign my parental permission paperwork. What was I going to do? I wanted this so badly but wouldn't dare go against Mama. Then I found a loophole. She said she wouldn't sign the papers but never actually said I couldn't wrestle. I decided to send all the paperwork to my dad in Buffalo, New York. I give him credit for sending them back signed. When my mother found out, I was surprised she didn't fight me on it. Her only comment was, "Don't expect me to take you to and from practice." Even with the cold and snow, that was an arrangement I could accept. Ultimately, I caught rides with many of my teammates' parents. If they saw me walking, they picked me up, making it a non-issue.

I was doing very well in my matches, and the small-town word got back to Mama. The other parents pressured her to attend my meets, telling her how good I was. They said she could work the concession stand with the other parents until it was my turn to step onto the mat. She came once but got very worried watching me, her baby, wrestle. When my opponent got me in an armbar, it frightened her into exclaiming, "He twisted my baby's arm!" Then she made her way right back to her comfort spot at the concession stand. It was too nerve-wracking for her to see me in that aggressive mindset. She never saw me wrestle again in high school or even in college. That didn't stop me from playfully and gently grabbing her arm or putting her in a slow wrestling move while messing around in the kitchen.

My mother was very protective of me, always introducing me as her "baby boy," no matter how old or big I was. I asked her to introduce me as Bob, but she ignored my plea. I wish she could have watched me wrestle more. But I appreciate that she supported me in her own way.

Mama eased up on her driving ban when she noticed how often the other parents drove me to wrestling events. It wasn't like her to burden others, so she made herself available to contribute to our rides, despite often working the previous night and almost falling asleep at the wheel. My mother was tough about most things, yet sensitive and nervous about my wrestling. It made me wonder how that could be. Before she died, I asked why she was so hard on me.

She answered, "Because I knew that you could do better."

I have done better, thanks to her and the many other positive influences I would have in my life.

We began my sophomore season with a new coach named Andrew Mawheny. Coach Mawheny was a nice guy, a gymnast, but didn't have any background in wrestling. Because I, and many other wrestlers, thirsted for more wrestling skills and technique, we took it upon ourselves to seek out Coach Marshall at Jackson County Western. After our daily practice at Albion High, we drove to neighboring

Jackson and snuck onto campus for a second practice with Coach Marshall. Also, there were many tournaments where both our schools met in competition. I frequently asked Coach Marshall to be in my corner. Coach Mawheny didn't protest. As a coach myself, I now realize how immature I was and how demeaning that must have been for Coach Mawheny. Looking back, I regret that behavior.

My skills improved so much that I made it into the Jackson County Western High School wrestling tournament finals. They held one of the bigger wrestling tournaments in our area, with eighteen to twenty teams competing. My confidence was soaring, that is, until one of my teammates presented me with a recent *Sports Illustrated* issue. There, in the "Faces in the Crowd" column, was a picture of my next opponent, Dan Overkamp from Galesburg-Augusta High. He was recognized for having the longest pin streak in the U.S. at the time, twenty-seven in a row, I believe.

My brain slowed as I thought, *Oh my God*. I immediately felt some of the worst butterflies I had ever experienced. As the anticipation built, I found myself on the toilet, anxious about my match. Eventually, I gathered myself as much as possible and decided to fall back on my conditioning and quickness. After all, I reasoned, you can't pin what you can't catch.

As I warmed up, I sought out Coach Marshall. That day was one of the few times I had him in my corner during an event. The ref blew the whistle. The match was on.

Dan and I started vigorous hand fighting. Circling in and out, I attempted shots, grabbing his leg. But I didn't fully commit to the takedown. He countered and shot in on my legs. I knew the guy was good, which made me slightly gun-shy. But I was fast as I darted in for feeble takedown attempts and my standup move exploded as I escaped holds. I wasn't wrestling to win. Instead, I fought to not lose, to not get pinned. In the end, unable to pin me, Dan won 10-6, but his streak was broken.

Soon after, I found myself in the locker room sitting on the wooden bench with sweat still pouring from my brow. My heart rate and breaths were slowing. I was exhausted but not so defeated that I couldn't keep my head up. *Dammit!* I thought. *He was good but not as good as I initially feared. If I had focused and really wrestled, I could have won. I psyched myself out too much.*

Moments later, two older White men approached me.

"You showed a lot of resilience, son! What's your grade point average? What did you score on the SATs?"

The questions, the entire situation, confused me. I looked up at the men and tried to make sense of what was happening. Before I could say anything, Coach Mawheny entered the locker room.

"What are you doing? You can't talk to this young man. He is only a sophomore. Even talking to him this early is against NCAA regulations! Try again in a few years. Come on, Bobby, let's go," he beckoned me.

When I rejoined my teammates on the bus, fresh ideas about my future emerged. I began to realize that even though I lost, this match put my name into the consciousness of the Michigan wrestling community. A light came on in my brain. A wrestling scholarship might be a way I could afford college.

For the next few weeks, I mentally obsessed about the possibility of a college scholarship. I was passionate about wrestling and intrigued by its career possibilities. Coupled with my childhood dream of being a teacher, I knew I would coach wrestling one day. The sport I had fallen in love with had now become a passion. To this day, I have never wavered from that feeling. I was now on a mission to make the dream a reality.

First, I had to ensure that I had a good grade point average. This led me to exercise extreme measures regarding my education. Starting after sophomore year, I took textbooks home over the summer and wrote term papers I anticipated my junior year teachers would assign. I stored them carefully, keeping the papers clean and fresh. Then during the academic year, if I needed to boost my grade, I asked if I could write a term paper. My teachers loved my commitment and had no idea I was submitting papers written the previous summer. It was kind of cheating but also ingenious. I've always been a planner. This strategy helped my grades and allowed me more time for wrestling or other activities.

When selecting classes, I sought out the easier teachers so I could attain at least a C grade. If I did poorly on a test, I asked to do another term paper. This plan worked out so well that I continued it into college. I had so many term papers lying around that I shared a few later in college.

At lunch, I started sitting with the smart students because they always talked about class assignments. Skipping lunch was routine to make my wrestling weight, so I used that time to do homework in the library. I also chose more academic extracurricular activities. That's how I ended up on the debate team. Debate came in handy for acquiring magazine citations for future term papers.

I was educationally competitive, graduating in the top thirty percent of my high school class. I ranked seventy-eighth out of two hundred eighty students. My future looked very bright. I could see my dreams coming closer to fruition.

Now, I had to ensure I succeeded in wrestling if I intended to earn a college scholarship. Wrestlers in larger cities have early opportunities to compete and learn the sport. In a small town like Albion, I had to work harder to close the gap in my wrestling knowledge. To do this, I wrestled as often as possible and made sure I was in top physical condition. I entered freestyle wrestling tournaments on weekends and during the summers while continuing extra practices with Coach Marshall at Jackson. In the off-season, I joined both the cross-country and track teams to stay in optimal physical condition year-round.

As my wrestling experience grew, I became formidable on the mat. There were some setbacks, though. I stuck out like a sore thumb on Jackson's all-White campus. Our practice sessions at Jackson with Coach Marshall ended when that school found out a Black student was on-campus. Coach Marshall received an official warning. They banned us from the property. You'd think that would have stopped us, but where there is a will, there is also a way. Coach Marshall loaded Jackson wrestling mats into his truck and moved our twice-a-day practices to his basement.

We got caught returning the mats at the end of the season. This time, unfortunately, Coach Marshall was fired. He moved back to his hometown in Pennsylvania.

It was devastating. Through it all, Coach Marshall never blamed me. He was so passionate, valuing both his former students and the sport of wrestling so much that his focus superseded many arbitrary school rules. Moments like this shaped me to the core. He risked his career to help us become better wrestlers, better people, and put me on a path of selflessness. James K. Houston replaced Coach Marshall at Jackson County Western. I respected Coach Marshall so much it led me to avoid Houston initially. That was hard to do because we were often at the same events. Besides, Jeff Sabin and Dave Tash, wrestlers for Jackson, were my friends. It was hard to interact with my friends while avoiding Houston.

Sabin was a passionate wrestler. He weighed ninety-six pounds and wrestled in the 103-lb. weight class. Sometimes he lost, not because his opponent was better but just bigger. His temper frequently got the best of him, and he punched the lockers or threw chairs. Houston often asked me to talk to Jeff. Somehow, I was able to calm him down. Eventually, Jeff learned to channel his emotions, earned a state championship, and got an appointment to the U.S. Military Academy at West Point. Whenever he was back in town, we always hung out. I was even the best man at his wedding.

After my initial pattern of avoiding the new coach, Jim Houston and I became friends. Years later he was my supervisor, and during my student teaching days, he arranged summer jobs for me. Houston also worked as a wrestling referee when I managed tournaments, and he provided transportation for wrestlers when needed. He's a good man and we've had a lasting friendship since 1969.

The summer following my junior year, I attended a wrestling camp at Michigan State University. It cost $175 for the week. I didn't have enough money to attend. But with the help of Matt Spears, a local Albion businessman, the cost was covered. Matt frequently supported my wrestling pursuits and later, when I organized a tournament, he even let me borrow his truck to transport wrestling mats.

During my senior year, we got a new coach, Ken Kannegieter. He was good and looked out for our best interests. My teammate Paul Holdren wrestled at the 132-lb. weight class, I was in the 138-lb. class, and we pushed each other a lot. The team practiced on the upper deck of the concrete gym with wrestling mats. One day before practice, Paul and I went up there to wrestle. Our egos got the best of us as we both refused to give up any position. Before we knew it, our intensity forced us off the mats and onto the concrete floor. We only stopped when Coach Kannegieter yelled at us.

"What are you doing? You want to crack your skulls on the concrete?"

We ceased and proceeded to regular practice.

Later that day, during drills, he moved me to the 145, 152, and 165-lb. group. It was no big deal because I got used to wrestling Chris Tanner at 152-lbs. and Chuck Walker at 165-lbs the previous year, before they graduated. This became my new routine. I got used to competing against opponents who weighed more than me. During competitions, when I wrestled back at my normal 138-lb. class, those heavier-weight practice bouts made me more competitive.

Paul and I were friends despite the concrete incident. We continued to attend freestyle tournaments together. One evening, coming home from one such tournament, we decided to visit our old coach, Bart Kruse. He was the new head coach at Sturgis High, which happened to be near a freestyle wrestling tournament we had attended. His wife was happy to see us but said Coach Kruse wasn't home. He was at the high school. So we drove there, found him, and updated him on how our wrestling was going.

Coach Kruse began talking about Tom King, his varsity wrestler at Sturgis. Tom was at my weight class and had won the league championship the prior year. Immediately, Coach Kruse had one of his other wrestlers seek out Tom. He pulled Tom from his date at the bowling alley so he could wrestle me.

I'm there thinking, *We just wanted to say hi to our old coach.* I was exhausted after having wrestled all day. The last thing I wanted was another match.

Before we knew it, Tom and I were wrestling on the Sturgis mats. It was an impromptu and informal match, yet it foreshadowed the upcoming league championships at my weight, 138-lbs. It was close, but I beat him for the first time in two years. He had obviously not been putting in the same time and dedication to wrestling that my teammates and I had.

Coach Kruse yelled, "This is why you will not be a two-time league champion! Bobby is working his ass off to beat YOU!"

Tom and I did meet again in the league championships our senior year. It wasn't even close. I won convincingly, and people were taking notice.

By the end of my senior year, I was the talk of the town. A published article spotlighted area wrestlers. The author put me on the list of people to "keep an eye on" during the Michigan State Wrestling Tournament. I had been to the state tournament before, but my inexperience prevented me from making my mark. Now, with a league championship under my belt and the older, skilled wrestlers having graduated, I was expected to do well.

I'll be honest. I loved the attention, and it was nice getting recognition for my hard work. The vanity, however, would come back to haunt me.

I began the 1970 state tournament well, winning my early matches and making it to the semi-finals. To my pleasant surprise, my next opponent would be none other than John Rulick. I placed ahead of him at numerous tournaments earlier that year and thought, *This will be a breeze, an easy walk into the finals.*

When the match began, John surprised me with an immediate takedown. The entire year leading up to state, I had controlled the neutral position in all of my matches, usually getting the first takedown. I thought, *All right. John came ready to wrestle.*

I turned my hips, getting ready for a Peterson roll, and a mild scramble ensued. Instead of grabbing the near leg, I grabbed his far leg. All John had to do to get my back on the mat was to sprawl. He did, and moments later, still in the first period, pinned me. He immediately raced into the stands in excitement, hugging, high-fiving, and yelling with joy at his accomplishment.

Meanwhile, I stood in the center of the mat, ashamed, embarrassed, angry, feeling unfulfilled. I couldn't leave the mat until John came back to shake my hand. It felt like an eternity. Finally, he returned. We shook. I removed the ankle strap that helped the scorekeepers distinguish me from my opponent and stepped off the mat with sorrow.

I was still processing what had happened and couldn't focus on my next match. I lost it. I don't even remember the score because I mentally checked out. I replayed the semi-final match in my mind every day for quite some time after.

What a cheap way to lose what was "supposed to be" mine. What I was entitled to for all my hard work. I didn't realize it then, but that attitude is exactly why I didn't win. I was so presumptuous and full of pride—Shegog this and Shegog that. By the time of the state tournament, my head was so big pileated woodpeckers could have nested in it. I had gone against my earlier upbringing about being prideful. A lesson I try to fall back on, even when writing this book, and one I try to teach as a coach. And even now, more than fifty years later, the name John Rulick still makes the hairs on the back of my neck stand up.

Rulick went on to lose in the finals to senior James Scholton. To make matters more difficult for me, I became uncertain about my college future. My grades were good, and my wrestling looked good until I failed to produce at the state tournament. My scholarship prospects suddenly appeared slim. How could I go to college if I couldn't afford it?

I started looking at colleges. The local option, Albion College, had a wrestling team, but they didn't pay much attention to me. They recruited just one wrestler, my teammate Paul Holdren. It was only prior to Paul's third visit to Albion that Coach Kannegieter stepped in. He told Albion that Paul could only visit if they agreed to let me come as well. On paper, Paul and I were similar academically and athletically. It didn't make sense that he was heavily recruited while I was just a pity afterthought.

When you remove all other explanations for why something is the way it is, that leaves only one reason. Albion College had a reputation for being less diverse. Paul is White. I am Black. In my view, it seemed racism was the reason they weren't recruiting me. It left a bad taste in my mouth, so I turned to my other option, Olivet College.

Coach Klein had been the head wrestling coach at Olivet for three years. While coaching, he worked concurrently as a high school referee. He had formed a good impression of me as a wrestler and actively recruited me my entire senior year. Klein mentioned that I was one of the few Black kids wrestling. I stood out because I was so dark, but also because I was gracious and respectful.

"If you come to Olivet, I'll take care of you," he told me.

Klein hoped to recruit a large freshman class to turn the losing Olivet program around. Even though Coach Klein couldn't guarantee me financial assistance, it felt good to be genuinely wanted. I decided to accept his offer.

Many of my other teammates were also planning on college. As you recall, Albion High excelled at academics. Steve Wheeler, for example, had stopped wrestling after fracturing his collarbone. But he didn't need wrestling to get into college since he was one of Albion's brightest. He went on to become a neurosurgeon.

As the summer approached, I got my bags ready for Olivet, not knowing how to pay the tuition. I just knew that if I wanted to fulfill my dream of teaching and coaching wrestling, I had to make it happen. Just a few days before I was to leave, the Lord answered my prayers. I got a call from Coach Klein saying that I would be attending Olivet College with a monetary grant and room and board covered. I was ecstatic. A huge weight lifted from my shoulders.

Looking back, if I had done better at the state wrestling tournament and gotten a scholarship to a larger institution, I likely would have been met with more temptations and opportunities to get into trouble. I would have been at a college farther from home. Olivet was only twenty miles from Albion, a quick hitchhike away, should I need to see my mother or return for any other unforeseen reason.

Some of my high school classmates who attended universities could not handle the social life. These students were smarter than me, yet they dropped out. Olivet was a safety net for me with rules that would not let an ambitious student fall through the cracks.

For example, the dorm front doors locked at ten-thirty every night. If someone planned to be out later than curfew, they had to complete a form before receiving a key. To get around this, students became friends with residents on the first floor so they could re-enter the building through their windows.

The student-teacher ratio was fifteen to two. With just over eight hundred students, the college was more like a large family, unlike Michigan State, where with eight hundred students in one dorm, I likely would have gone unnoticed. Attending Olivet was truly a blessing in disguise.

•_•• ——— •••_•

CHAPTER 3

The Olivet Years

Coach Klein recruited me for Olivet. It was the right fit for me and for my family. The town of Olivet and its small United Church of Christ (UCC) has a significant underground railroad abolitionist history, going back to its founding in 1844. It was the first college to admit Blacks and women in the United States. Since its inception, the college asserted that education should be available to everyone regardless of gender or race. This view went against societal norms. It was the reason why the state of Michigan withheld the college's charter until 1859.

During that era, women didn't go to college. Instead, they attended finishing school, where they learned how to do their hair, organize and run a household, adhere to the standards of etiquette, and tend to their husbands, among other things. Academic classes were an afterthought at these institutions.

I strongly advocate for women's rights, especially since a single mother raised me. Women, and especially single Black women with children, have not received fair treatment in our society. My mother successfully raised four children. She brought up three Black males, none of whom ever went to prison at a time when seven out of ten Black males were imprisoned.

In 1976, Pulitzer Prize-winning historian Laurel Thatcher Ulrich lamented, "Well behaved women seldom make history." But Olivet College had already put a big crack in that mold back in 1863, when Mary Barber, Sara Benedict, and Sophia A. Keys were the first women to graduate from Olivet. They were among the earliest women college graduates in the USA. Familiarizing myself with this history made me that much more excited to attend Olivet College.

My first wrestling season at Olivet, in 1970, got off to a good start. But it was a big jump going from high school to college wrestling. I was challenged physically in about one in five high school matches. In college, everyone I wrestled was one of the best from their high school. Our team had a lot of these tough guys, and because of that, my freshman season would help propel Coach Klein's legendary coaching status.

We battled and learned from each other daily in the wrestling room. Most of those wrestlers had huge egos and were not used to losing on the mat. When these egos clashed in the room, many boys left practice with black eyes, wounds that would scar, sore muscles, and bloody clothes. Sometimes these practices were fiercer than our actual meets.

Klein had many trademark phrases and techniques that I eventually used as a coach. Immediately after the matches, Coach Klein put an orange slice in our mouths, shutting us up, so he could give a quick recap of what we did well and what we could have done better. When teaching the standup, he would yell, "Teacher! Teacher!" That meant we had to stand up from the bottom position and raise our arm. Once we gained our feet, he yelled, "Pee on the ceiling!" That meant we had to back pressure our opponent and push our hips out. "Plug the hole" was a move from the top position that involved kneeing your opponent's butt forward while chopping his arm to the side. Klein also had his distinctive "Klein pushups" where we stayed in the down position for thirty seconds to a minute before pushing up. I hated "Klein pushups" but respected their value enough that I later adopted them as part of my coaching toolbox, calling them "Shegog pushups."

In the fall of 1970, I was one of twenty-one freshman recruits on the team. There was so much competition in the wrestling room that it often felt like a pressure chamber. Who would survive to make the starting lineup and wrestle in the "pit" beneath MacKay Gymnasium? We called it that because the gym floor was lower than the spectator seats. The place filled beyond capacity during dual meets, exploding with high energy, and roaring cheers when we won. We won often. Every victory reinforced the town's support for us and fueled Coach Klein's ability to recruit and create a prospering program.

It wasn't long into this first season when we had a dual meet against Grand Valley State College. Normally, it wouldn't be anything too special. Except my opponent was none other than James Scholton. As a point of reference, Scholton was the prior year's Michigan State Champion, beating John Rulick in the finals. I had wondered how I would have done had it been me in the finals with Scholton. Now I had my chance.

Scholton was strong as an ox, but I was quick as a cheetah. It was a hard-fought match, back and forth, neither of us able to gain the upper hand. Ironically, that's how things ended. There was no overtime and we tied. My team earned two points. I could live with the tie, but that still didn't stop me from regretting my match with Rulick.

Nevertheless, I bought into everything that Klein coached and did what I could to prepare myself not just to compete, but to thrive at the Division III level. I ran all the time. I didn't drink or smoke. No crude talking, playing cards, or dancing. Even the game Old Maid was taboo when I was growing up. All were too sinful for this church boy.

Because of this, it was easy for the school to select me as the dorm's Resident Advisor (RA) for Shipherd Hall. My clean living made me perfect for the RA job, plus I couldn't pass up the free room and board. I earned a reputation for being too by the book, quick to write people up. Some kids even protested when they learned they were on the same floor as me. I'll admit I was definitely a "square," carrying my Bible everywhere, joining the Christian Fellowship Group, and occasionally preaching to my classmates. As a devout Pentecostal Christian, I wouldn't dare betray my early upbringing, the college authority helping me financially, or worse yet, upset my mother for fear that she might sit in my classes again at Olivet. Ok, that was probably a stretch, but I was definitely risk-averse and routinely played it safe.

Even though I didn't drink or smoke, I still hung out with teammates who occasionally did. When they stayed out late, I left early for the dorm, a habit my mother ingrained in me. While in high school, I was supposed to be home no later than ten-thirty p.m., even if that meant I had to leave football games or whatever event before it was over. My high school friends once tackled me to the ground, trying to force beer into my mouth. It turned out it was only water. They teased, "You think we're gonna waste good beer on your ass?" (They had a point. For underage kids, beer was hard to acquire.) But I carried that attitude of obedience to authority into college.

One surprise when I arrived at college was that my friend Miles Vieau, whom I had met and conversed with over the years at various

Michigan high school tournaments, was also a freshman recruit. During those high school tournaments, Miles and I shared intel on other wrestlers before matches. Often, I'd be in his corner giving pointers. Other times, he'd be in mine. Miles was tough, a middle school Michigan state champ in eighth grade, and a two-time Michigan high school state placer. He was an asset to our team, but more importantly, his presence meant I had at least one friend right off the bat.

Most of the other recruits were from Michigan towns, generally small, White-populated towns. In my first year at Olivet, I was one of four Black recruits and the only one to start. The following year, Coach Klein recruited another Black wrestler, Ron Bates. He was excellent and would become the first Olivet wrestler to place at nationals.

⚛

By 1970, a multitude of civil rights laws had passed. Coupled with the Vietnam War, the nation had a lot in its consciousness. I tried not to draw attention to myself and took a passive stance on controversial topics. Despite that approach, I often found myself in awkward situations where I couldn't avoid hearing disinformation or "fake news," as we call it today. For the most part, our entire team came together like a family despite the politics of the time.

I remember hanging out with the other freshmen when one of the White guys asked me, "Do you still have a nub where your tail used to be?"

It was like the moment when something terrible or embarrassing happens at a party, and the music screeches to a stop. I felt everyone's eyes on me. I thought, *What did you say to me?* My fists clenched as my rage built. I looked him square in the eyes, ready to punch his lights out, and saw that he wasn't joking.

He was serious. Rage turned to sadness and then to pity. I realized someone had fed him these lies his whole life. It's like the final scene in the Ed Norton movie *American History X* when viewers discover that the White supremacist character learned all his bigotry from his father during childhood. It wasn't necessarily my teammate's fault that his parents and family members hadn't ventured out of their bubble to see the truth about other races and cultures. I couldn't imagine what other misconceptions might be filling my teammate's brain. I told him he received false information growing up, that Black people don't have tails.

I didn't realize it at the time, but that was probably the first social teaching moment of many that I would be doing throughout my life. I initially hated that teammate. But over the years, he became my friend, and I applaud him for seeking the truth. I'm not sure where he is now, but I'm hopeful his experiences shaped a more understanding and tolerant future for him, his family and kids, and subsequent generations.

Because we won a lot of matches during my first year, our program's reputation grew. Klein held preseason and postseason meetings about how to work out and train in the off-season. I learned the art of recruiting from him, too. As wrestlers, we were allowed to talk to younger high school wrestlers who were off-limits to a college head coach. In return, we got some meal money or entry fees to high school tournaments. I also used that money to enter off-season tournaments.

My wrestling was improving by leaps and bounds, so I thought I'd challenge myself at one of the off-season tournaments. I entered the Olympic regional qualifier in Indianapolis at 142-lbs. What a big-headed mistake. There were more than forty wrestlers in my weight class, including the legendary Dan Gable. As if that wasn't enough, we only had five minutes between matches. It was a true endurance test. I won my first match, lost my next two, and got eliminated.

Tired and humbled, I began the long drive back to Michigan. I realized that the Olympics were out of my skill set. It was better to be a big fish in a small pond at Olivet and the best Division III wrestler I could be. So, I wrestled in as many summer freestyle tournaments as possible.

While driving home from another tournament in Flint, Michigan, I started to fall asleep at the wheel. Heading south on US-23, I remembered that Miles lived in Brighton. It was on the way to Albion, so I thought that maybe I could rest for a while at their house.

At Miles' house, I was greeted with open arms. His mother, Hazel, and dad, Manning, encouraged me to spend the night. They had an open-door policy for me. I called my mother to let her know where I was and when to expect me home. Hazel set me up in Miles' bed. When he came home, he had to sleep on the couch.

There was a state recreational area near Miles' house called Island Lake where we would take the boat and inner tube. I remember sitting on the tube while Miles drove the boat. He took a quick turn around a small island, hence the name, and I skidded across the water like a stone. The only injury was to my ego, but it did make for a good story that we relive every time we see each other.

Several times I brought Mama to visit with the Vieaus. Miles and I explored the town while our mothers sat by the lake talking about their boys. They had a pact giving each other permission to discipline us kids as they saw fit. According to my mother, since I did not have a father in my life, I was especially in need of good role models, which was another reason the Vieaus and we were all close friends, as close as family.

⚬

During my second year at Olivet, I roomed with Paul Kreiner. He was a member of the Adelphic Fraternity I later joined as a senior, and we were practice partners in the wrestling room. He was a tough-as-nails farm boy. I remember having the upper hand on him when he was cutting, losing weight. But he gained the upper hand on me anytime he didn't have to cut weight. In practice, he used to chin my sternum when he had me on my back. It hurt like a drill carving into my chest. Years later, as a coach, I demonstrated this move and used it when wrestling kids who challenged my authority.

Paul grew up in the Columbiaville area, where very few people of color lived. We decided early on that we needed a car on campus. Each of us took this as a personal mission. I purchased a white 1963 Chevy during spring break thinking I'd be a hero, showing up Paul once school started. Ironically, he arrived in a black 1963 Chevy. We had a big laugh, and it felt good knowing I had a reliable friend.

Over our next break, Christmas, I spent a lot of time at the Kreiner home. The nine-member family lived on a working farm. I helped with their daily chores, even though my presence meant they took longer to complete. It was a struggle feeding the pigs and milking the cows. When squeezing the udders, I got maybe twenty milliliters over twenty minutes. Then Paul would come and fill the pan in just minutes. The pigs were so hungry they ran at me. Frightened, I quickly jumped out of the pen. Paul's family had a good laugh. I learned to pour some feed on one end of the pen to distract the pigs before filling their food troughs. It was a fun experience once I got the hang of things.

While at the farm, Paul and I repaired their old Fiat. When it was finally in working order, we took it on the back roads. Paul taught me how to drive a stick shift, and to this day, when I drive a standard vehicle, I think of him.

Paul's parents and siblings treated me like a regular family member, including me in family and group photos. Even today, the grandchildren ask, "Who is the Black guy, or is that a dark spot in that old photo?" All anyone could see were my eyes and teeth. It's still funny.

I admired them for taking such a strong stance on race relations. The national position on race was very raw. I wonder if they ever faced any backlash for hosting a Black in their home? Years later, when I abandoned Michigan for Los Angeles and shared the reason with Paul's mother, Pauline, she was concerned enough to reassure me, "You did not need to go to LA. You're always welcome here."

My loneliest times with the Kreiner family was when we attended Catholic Mass. The family took up an entire pew. When they went forward for communion I was left alone. In my mind, I yelled, "*Come back!*" and "*Please hurry up!*"

I love the Kreiner family and always remember to send Paul a card for his birthday.

This was also the year I met Ed Jamison. Ed was a year younger and in the Adelphic Fraternity with Paul, through whom we met. He was interested in playing football, but that all changed when he sustained injuries early in his freshman season. He grew up in a small, predominantly White town like many of my Olivet classmates. But that didn't seem to matter. We hit it off right away. Our friendship helped quell some of Ed's preconceived notions about Blacks. It was easy to talk to him about anything—relationship advice, religion, you name it. Over the years, we hung out often, partied together, and took trips together.

Jim Wencel was another friend I hung out with regularly during this time. He was also a year younger, wrestled, lived in my dorm, was an Adelphic, and a real hell-raiser. He saw through my tough exterior right away.

One night he came to the dorm drunk and decided that if he flipped all the circuit breakers, it would stop everyone's alarms from going off. Nobody would go to class on time and he could sleep in. I appreciated the Dennis the Menace logic of it all, but his plan was not getting past me. I caught him in the act and ran after him in nothing but my white boxer shorts. It was dark enough that all anyone could see were my shorts and the whites of my eyes. Once I caught him, I mentioned that his idea would stop alarm clocks, but also refrigerators, some of which held insulin. He apologized and toned down future antics slightly.

I chose not to write him up. Instead, I just wrestled harder against him during practice, like a pseudo punishment. That was no easy task since Jim was very competitive and able to get the best of me a few times. That amazing combination of energy and competition in the room is why our team went on to win sixty-five straight dual meets.

As my second year came to an end, I was responsible, as the RA, to make sure the rest of the students left after their exams. On the last school day, I made the rounds as usual. Outside one door, I smelled something funny. *That smells like dope*, I thought. I opened the door using my universal key and a fog of smoke enveloped me. That was when I threatened the residents with expulsion. Immediately, the four students tackled me to the floor, poured Boone's Farm into my mouth, and pinched my nose until I had no choice but to swallow it down. A few minutes later, my alcohol-naive body was sound asleep.

When I came to, I noticed something in my hand. My eyes lit up, no pun intended. It was a joint. I slurred my speech and pointed my fingers, threatening the students yet again as we sat in a circle.

"Hell, Shegog, you've already had three tokes," they said.

I was just as guilty as them. What had I done? I made it to my feet and stumbled back to my room. I immediately opened my Bible and began praying. I was weak under God for letting alcohol and marijuana enter my body.

The entire summer, I repented and prayed multiple times a day. I often found myself in my car, yelling, asking God to forgive me. Then sometime in August, as the school year approached, I heard a voice say to me, "It's okay."

God had spoken to me.

It is okay, I thought. A huge weight lifted from my shoulders. I entered my junior year a different person, loosened up, happier, and friendlier. When I showed up as the RA, many of the students again tried to switch out of my hall.

I told them, "Guys, I'm not the same asshole I was last year."

It eased their minds and they cozied up to me. A little too much, maybe.

Students used to avoid me. Now they were comfortable coming to me with all sorts of issues. One student in particular, named Mark, told me he had a falling out with his father, was cut off from funds, and selling dope to help pay for college. Had he told me that the previous year, I would have had him removed from school without hesitation. Instead, I ended up turning a blind eye, empathizing with him because of my own financial hardships, knowing that without my RA job I would have had a difficult time paying for college.

Word got out that someone in the dorm was selling weed. As an RA, I attended all the administrative meetings where the topic came up. I didn't have to lie. I just went with the crowd. They narrowed the search for the culprit to our floor. Mark was a nice guy who was really trying to better himself, even if his tactics were questionable. That's why I told him to give me his bag of dope so I could hide it in my room. The next day, the administration and all the RAs were in Mark's room searching for his stash. I even turned over a dresser to make it look like I was on the administration's side. Nothing was found. Mark was off the hook. I gave him back his weed, and he did tone down his dealing. Unfortunately, despite our efforts, Mark withdrew from college the following March.

I didn't write up very many people during my junior year. It was a night and day difference compared to my sophomore year, when if a kid sneezed, they got written up. There was no smoking, drinking, or girls allowed on our floor. So when I smelled smoke, saw drinking, or heard girls yelling in the heat of the moment, I now addressed it from an amicable perspective. Most people understood and were reasonable when I had to talk to them about the rules. After all, they were learning about themselves and becoming adults in college. I even had the occasional beer, most of the time to help me sleep on an empty stomach after losing weight for wrestling.

The team had a four-way meet in Indiana. A wrestler from Defiance College named Clint Dixs, who ranked fifth in the nation at 150-lbs., was there. Coach Klein had me wrestle the other two schools. Larry Boyer wrestled Dixs. I think Klein might have been trying to protect my 8-0 record. Boyer soundly beat Dixs. Because Boyer did well at 150-lbs., Klein began pressuring me to drop to 142-lbs. I pushed back. It was too much weight-cutting. And I wanted to eat.

Eventually, I caved to his wishes and hesitantly dropped to 142-lbs. I had to fast for twenty-four hours before each meet to make weight. Those were the occasions when I drank half a beer the night before a wrestling meet, just to get some sleep, otherwise I'd have been up all night suffering hunger pangs.

Boyer went on to win the Michigan Intercollegiate Athletics Association (MIAA), the oldest conference east of the Mississippi, at 150-lbs. After all my work to cut my weight, I placed second at 142-lbs. Olivet took six out of ten weight-classes in the finals, taking the league. I had been undefeated at 150-lbs and felt confident I could have been a champ at that weight.

At the end-of-season banquet, I thought I was a contender for the team MVP award. My record was excellent. I had busted my butt to move down a weight class to help the team win the league championship. Instead, David Elliot won. After the banquet, several of my teammates told me they had voted for me. A few days later,

I confronted Coach Klein. He revealed that the vote was a tie and that he decided to award the MVP to David because he needed it more. I was hurt but kept my mouth shut. I felt my extra efforts were unnoticed or unappreciated.

The next year, 1972-73, my junior year, Coach Klein wanted me to move down to 142-lbs. again. I didn't want to go through all the weight challenges again just to fail to have my work recognized, so I refused. Klein persisted and I began avoiding him. When we did talk, it was very heated. I often just walked away, using the excuse that I had to get to class.

In December, the pressure boiled over. I quit the team, even though I was undefeated at 150-lbs. I was so angry that I went to the local military recruiting office in Battle Creek, Michigan, to change my draft status from 2-S, a student deferment, to 1-A, available for active duty.

The Vietnam War had been raging for nearly ten years at this point. Deferments were given for a few reasons. These included being the only male in the family, the last male in the family in which other family members lost their lives (like in the movie *Saving Private Ryan*), or for the first person in a family to go to college. That's how I got the 2-S deferment. My oldest brother enlisted and was stationed in Germany. My other brother was eligible for the draft, but his number wasn't drawn.

Coach Klein saw me days after I changed my status and asked, "What did you do?"

Someone from the recruiter's office had called and told him about my change. I walked away without answering. I was so upset with Klein that I would rather have gone to Vietnam than hear him mention "142-lbs." again. It was an immature and hasty decision on my part.

I went home on winter break, worked out with the high school team, but said nothing to them about quitting wrestling at Olivet. By mid-January, I missed the team immensely. I couldn't separate myself from wrestling. I missed the grind, the camaraderie, the competition, even, to an extent, the ritual of making weight.

I contacted Klein about returning.

He said, "You didn't just let me down. You let the team down, and whether you're back on the team depends on them."

The team easily voted me back. It turned out that many of the wrestlers had issues with Klein.

The pestering that Klein gave me continued, but at a lesser level, and he no longer mentioned dropping to 142-lbs. Decades later, in 2000, when one of my wrestlers, Nick Kehagias, went to the University of Chicago, Olivet's rival, Coach Klein still nagged me. It was just his nature, and I learned to wrestle with it. Pun intended.

Upon my return, I also discovered, to my surprise, that Klein or someone else had blocked my military status change. I was back on a 2-S deferment without my consent. Even though I hadn't received notification of the change, I was ultimately grateful someone took care of it. These days, I don't think anyone would be allowed to make a change without consent. That was a different time.

My draft number was twenty-one. With a number that low, I was almost guaranteed to go to Vietnam. During my junior and senior high school years, our school held moments of silence during the morning announcements when the speaker listed names of drafted

Albion alumni who were missing in action (MIA) or killed in action (KIA). I sincerely believe wrestling saved my life by giving me the means to go to college instead of to war.

I took full advantage of this renewed wrestling opportunity and decided to work extra hard to regain the team's trust. I ran every morning and played racquetball before practice. I came to practice so dripping wet that teammates told me to stay in one corner of the room. They complained that they were slipping on my sweat. I was working extremely hard. My thought process was that if I could get in better shape, I would win every match. I finished the year 19-0-1 at 150-lbs. and won the MIAA championship. I did not talk to Klein again about dropping to 142-lbs. Olivet College also won the MIAA that year with ten wrestlers in the finals.

Academically, I did well and even helped my classmates with their papers and other assignments. During my junior year, I wrote a paper on gay acceptance for Professor Parr's class. I was not nervous about it because I took a scholarly approach. Plus, I wanted to learn more about the topic for myself. I had questions about my own sexuality. In the paper, I referenced an article from a Chicago newspaper where I first read the term "gay." The reporter used the word in reference to a gentleman kicked out of the military for being openly "gay." The article mentioned that the gentleman did his job well and that the only reason he received discharge papers was because of his sexual orientation. Gay acceptance was not the norm in the 1970s. That made me, like many others, tread carefully between homo and hetero engagements.

The summer before my senior year of college, I decided Albion High needed a junior high wrestling program. The best way to make it happen was to organize a freestyle wrestling tournament for junior high and high school kids at the high school. I sent out flyers announcing that housing would be provided for non-local competitors. Before I knew it, coaches from all over Michigan, Indiana, and even Ontario, Canada, were booking attendance. Courtesy of Tom Taylor, head wrestling coach at Albion College, we secured a dorm for the more than three hundred visiting wrestlers.

Tom was the coach who paid very little attention to me when I was a high school senior. I think his help was a way of offering an olive branch. It worked. The tournament went off without a hitch and impacted Albion for years to come. One of the junior high kids, Stevie Hill, would go 35-0 and become state champion his senior year in high school. The following year, he attended Olivet and became an MIAA champion as a freshman. Organizing events like the tournament further solidified my interest in teaching and coaching wrestling one day.

When I returned for senior year, I didn't live in the dorms. I worked a few odd jobs to supplement the lost RA income. I was no longer the same straight and narrow freshman who had asked people if Jesus Christ was their personal savior.

"Shegog, you really are a changed man," my wrestling teammates told me when they rushed me into their frat.

I was finally "cool" enough to be initiated. The Adelphic fraternity was one of two frats on campus that accepted Blacks and Jews at the time. Finally, I'd be able to join my friends Paul, Ed, and Jim.

During the rush, the brothers put a sack over my head and kidnapped me from campus. It was scary and exhilarating at the same time. They drove some of the other pledges to places like Kentucky, threw them out of the van with two quarters to call or hitchhike their way back. When I got tossed out, I knew exactly where I was—just outside Albion. I think Coach Klein threatened the frat brothers, so they took fewer risks with me. I viewed my rush as a vacation, hitchhiked into Albion, saved the two quarters, and had a nice visit with my mom. When I made it back to the Olivet campus, I officially became an Adelphic.

As in high school, I participated in speech club forensics at college. When I was a senior, the college let me use a van for our speech tournaments. After one tournament, I joined my frat brothers for beers. After a few drinks, some of us started wrestling. Our college season hadn't started yet, but one of my brothers mentioned a freestyle wrestling tournament taking place the next morning in Dowagiac, Michigan.

"I got a van!" I yelled.

The next thing we knew, we were driving to Dowagiac, cheerfully buzzed and lucky we didn't get into an accident.

I weighed nearly 180-lbs., up from my normal 150-lb. weight class, and I too was a little inebriated. The other guys were definitely drunk, puked occasionally, but still had fun wrestling. Some of our guys even won matches, and Jim Wencel placed. I resisted the temptation to tell some of the guys he beat that they had just lost to a drunken master of the sport. Imagine how well he would have done had he been sober.

I remember wrestling Tom Bradley that day. He was a true 180-pounder, and starter for the University of Michigan. When we shook hands, he smelled the alcohol on my breath and laughed. I shot in on him early and got the first takedown with a single leg sweep move. Then his size difference prevailed. He lifted me off him with one hand on my chest and flung me across the mat like a pebble. We laughed throughout the rest of the match as I ran around the mat while he tried to catch me. When he did get hold of me, I joked, "Oh, I'm gonna puke."

The fun we had that day made the hangover afterward worth it. I worried that the Olivet administration would be upset with me for not returning the van earlier, but Coach Klein smoothed it over. After all, we did go to a wrestling tournament.

It was also during my senior year that I met the most graceful and beautiful woman I have ever known, Charla Batsell. The first time I saw Char, I was like WOW! . . . WOW! She was a freshman and one of forty Blacks out of eight hundred students at Olivet. Her father was the city manager of Saginaw, the third-largest city in Michigan. She grew up well-to-do, even had a formal debutante ball when she turned sixteen. She was always well-groomed, choosing dressy outfits over casual, played the piano, and ranked in the top two or three of her class. We hung out together and eventually started dating. I bought Char her first pair of jeans and took her to her first parties.

Her prim and proper parents were none too happy when they learned I was dating Char. I was a little rough around the edges, from a poor, single mother household in a small town. But I was always polite, respectful to Char and her parents, and had a bright future ahead of me. I could have been Prince Charles for all they cared. That didn't matter because Char's parents wanted her to focus on her education.

To make matters worse, her father suffered a bad car accident seven weeks after she started at Olivet, putting him in a temporary coma and rendering him paraplegic. Char's attention shifted to her family, and she almost left Olivet. But her mother stressed the importance of her education, and as her friend, I was a steady hand. She took comfort from my help, making it easy for our relationship to grow.

Looking back, Char's interest in me made sense. Previously, she had only dated White guys. I was a bridge for her. I had many White friends myself, but unlike Char, I grew up in a lower-income Black community. During my senior year of high school, my girlfriend was White. So was Char's previous boyfriend. I wasn't as conventional as Char, but my mother did teach me to speak proper English, unlike other Black kids in my community. With me, Char felt an ease she probably hadn't experienced before. She could be herself while exploring different sides of her character that might have otherwise been off-limits.

With others, Char was an exceptional friend. She always had time to help them prepare for their recitals and brainstorm solutions to any problem. The more she helped, the more her friends requested and relied on her support. She could easily have said she was too busy but always made the time for her friends.

My fraternity brothers also thought she was great—so great, in fact, that they voted her fraternity sweetheart. That meant when my frat brothers ran into her on the quads, they stopped what they were doing, escorted her to class, and carried her belongings. This practice continued into her sophomore year, even after I left Olivet to teach at Hartland. It made me feel happy and respected that my brothers protected her. Char did express annoyance when they frequently caught her by surprise and wrestled her books away. But I think deep down, she felt honored.

⚡

Wrestling got under way in October. We had just come off a 20-0 season and were ready to repeat as MIAA champions. Coach Klein started an assessment project, having Dave Elliot, Dale Traister, and me complete daily logs. In them, we expressed our thoughts and feelings throughout the season. Klein hoped our notes would give insight into advancing coaching tools and techniques. Later, our logs resulted in a book entitled *The Why – Wrestling at Olivet College*. It was a great reference that tracked our senior wrestling season, social experiences, and mental state.

Still wrestling in the 150-lb. class, Larry Boyer transferred to Western Michigan University. But Brian Jousma was still at my weight and vying for the varsity spot. Ultimately, I secured the weight class, and Brian cut down to 142-lbs. I knew all too well from my sophomore year experience how difficult it would be, so I tried to encourage him.

But my focus was divided. If Char wasn't at a meet, I didn't wrestle as well. Balancing wrestling, time with Char, the fraternity, and interviews for potential teaching jobs, some as far away as Connecticut, was challenging. Something had to give.

At our conference championships my senior year, I finished second in the MIAA, losing to a wrestler from Calvin College. Adding insult to injury, a story in the Grand Rapids Press touted the rise of Calvin College wrestling. It featured a photo of me getting turned on my back in the finals. I was embarrassed. I may not have been a champion, but our team was extraordinary.

In 1974, we ended the season 21-0 and completed back-to-back undefeated seasons. Our entire team qualified to compete in the first-ever NCAA Division III Wrestling Championships in Wilkes-Barre, Pennsylvania.

However, at the national tournament, our team was the victim of sabotage. Suspicion was that the MIAA director, head coach of Adrian College, our rival who finished behind us, failed to submit our individual match records to the national seeding committee. When our team showed up at Wilkes-Barre, the officials had none of our guys ranked, even though a few were undefeated or had only one loss. They even knew we were coming because a local paper in Wilkes-Barre printed a story about how Olivet and Coe colleges qualified their entire teams. Klein met with the seeding committee to straighten it out.

He returned from the meeting with good and bad news. The good news was that we were all in the tournament. The bad news was that none of our guys were ranked. We were placed into random positions in the bracket. It would be a dog fight for any of us to make the All-American rounds. We already had a rivalry with Adrian College, but this trick made it worse. To this day, when someone mentions Adrian College or even says the name Adrian in another context, even hearing Sylvester Stallone say his wife's name in the *Rocky* movies, I immediately cringe.

My performance that day was lackluster at best. I lost my first two matches and was eliminated from the tournament. Ronnie Bates was the only guy on our team who placed. Even though we didn't place that many wrestlers at nationals, our dual-win streak made Olivet a name to be reckoned with. In subsequent years, Olivet would continue its success. Over his thirty-three-year tenure at Olivet,

Klein notched a dual record of 569-116-3 and was inducted into the Olivet, Michigan, and NCAA Wrestling halls of fame. He holds the record in NCAA Division III for winning percentage at 0.813.

I was grateful to have been a part of such a hard-working program. Wrestling at Olivet taught me so much. I learned how to set goals and work hard toward them, to physically and mentally push myself further than I thought possible. Everything that came later in life was easier as a result of my college experiences.

My entire time at Olivet was amazing. Of the twenty-one freshmen wrestlers from 1970, only four were still on the team when we graduated in 1974. One of those was David Elliott. We were rivals for Coach Klein's attention, but we respected each other and became the team's co-captains.

Later in my career, I wrote a paper on Klein's communication style as a coach. I realized that much of my wrestling success resulted from the day in and day out competition with David. David also became a teacher, working only about ninety minutes from Hartland. I wanted to visit and talk about our time at Olivet and how much I appreciated the challenges we shared. However, before I could contact him, he died in a tragic car accident, just a few months after graduation in November of 1974.

The following summer, I hosted a freestyle tournament at Olivet and named it The David Elliot Wrestling Invitational Tournament. Olivet College gave every participant a sweat towel printed with a photo of David. The finalist also received a plaque with an image of David in a wrestling stance. Proverbs 27:17 (NIV) says, "As iron sharpens iron, so one person sharpens another." That's exactly how he and I pushed and bettered each other.

As my senior year neared its end, I focused on finding the school where I wanted to teach and coach wrestling. I hoped to stay close to home and close to Char. I was still a mama's boy and cared very deeply for Char. My two options were returning to my hometown, Albion High, or moving to Hartland High. Hartland, Michigan, was relatively close to my family in Albion, about seventy-nine miles away, and even closer to my best friend Miles' family house. He still lived in Brighton, Michigan, only about ten miles south of Hartland, convenient should I need anything.

I interviewed with the Albion High superintendent first. He seemed happy to have me, although I didn't get the best feeling when he commented, "If we have problems, we know you'll do the right thing."

I knew Albion High had racial issues in the past because I was only four years removed from being a student there. What did "do the right thing" mean? What if I disagreed with the faculty and instead sided with the students? I had no desire to be the answer to the town's racial problems with my first job out of college. I wanted to focus on teaching and coaching wrestling. I didn't want to get bogged down in mediating between a closed-minded administration and students with feelings of injustice. Before saying no, I decided to talk with Hartland's administrators.

My interview with the Hartland principal, Marine veteran Jack Poly, and the assistant principal, Jack McMannis, went well. They were interested in hiring a Black teacher because they were progressive enough to see the importance of diversity within their school. Hartland was an all-White town with only two Black students, who were siblings. I heard about an incident that happened during a field trip the previous year, when a few of the kids were making jokes about Blacks and calling people "niggers." The Hartland administration realized the significance inherent in hiring me as an authority figure in their community. We discussed multiple scenarios to demonstrate how I would handle potentially racially-charged situations. It was similar to, yet I'm sure a fraction of, what Jackie Robinson might have experienced in 1945 before being hired as the first Black player in Major League Baseball. Because I felt supported by the Hartland administration and the bonus of Miles living so near, I accepted the job at Hartland High.

·_·· ____ ···_·

CHAPTER 4

Michigan Coaching Years

Before starting my first teaching job at Hartland High, Miles' family in Brighton let me use their home as a base to search for an apartment. After all, I had an open invitation with the Vieau household. Miles left Olivet after his freshman year because he didn't want his dad to pay a hefty tuition bill. Despite his absence from Olivet, we remained close. I visited his house frequently, often after finishing nearby wrestling tournaments. His parents were special people and very welcoming. His mother, Hazel, always made food for me and had me sleep in Miles' bed when he wasn't home. She picked me up once when my car broke down. Manning and Hazel always introduced me as their son when they had guests. Is it any wonder I claim Miles is my brother from another mother? And I am Uncle Bob to his kids. He is my oldest friend—we bonded back in 1968.

I made calls from Miles' place to Hartland, scheduling appointments to view apartments. Despite setting up twenty visits with managers or landlords in the space of a week, not a single apartment was available, even after meeting them in person.

I told some of them, "I talked to you forty-five minutes ago. You said the apartment was available."

They mostly blew me off, claiming the landlord had rented the apartment within that time. Or, more bluntly, I was informed, "If you had told me you were Black, I could have saved you the time."

It was blatant racism by the manager, the landlord, or the community. I wish I could say these were isolated incidents, but they occurred across the entire United States. It is an ignorant cultural phenomenon that I'm happy to say has improved, but unfortunately, lingers in many neighborhoods across the country.

So with the start of the 1974-1975 school year quickly approaching, I hadn't secured an apartment in the all-White town of Hartland. I discussed my lack of progress with Miles and his parents at the dinner table. Manning rose from the table and stormed off in furious disgust. He returned to say he'd found a lawyer to sue the Hartland school district.

"Now, wait a minute," I said. During my interview I had assured the administration I could handle a situation like this.

The next day, I talked with the principal, Jack Poly. I showed him the list of apartments where I'd received rejections and filled him in on my difficulty securing a rental. He told me to worry about my prep work and lesson plans. He would take care of it.

A few days before school started, I got a call from Jack saying I could stay with a local family. Ruth Anne and Richard Kline invited me to use a room in their home. Their daughter had just graduated from Hartland and was off to college.

I was blessed to have the support of the Hartland administration from the beginning. They were one hundred percent behind me even though the town wasn't quite ready to receive me. Later that first year, I secured housing with one of our music teachers and remained there through my second year.

Despite that initial setback, I was energetic, excited, and motivated to finally fulfill my dream of teaching and coaching wrestling. That had been my goal since the fateful day, during my sophomore year in high school, when I lost to Dan Overkamp and caught the eye of college recruiters. My new hope was that my passion and determination would be enough to win the hearts and minds of Hartland.

On the first day of school, I was full speed ahead. I quickly involved myself in many projects, feeling like the proverbial headless chicken but loving every minute of it. In addition to teaching my classes, I was the head coach for cross-country and track, assistant coach behind head wrestling coach James Takacs, and co-sponsor of the sophomore class. Jack Poly had three sons who wrestled, and Jack McMannis had a daughter on the cross-country team. They saw my energy and dedication to the students firsthand. In fact, I put both our principal and assistant to work keeping score or running the tables during wrestling tournaments. A lot of relationship building took place, and those efforts were breeding success in all the school programs.

In cross-country, we started with six runners. By my second year there, we had twenty-four. This included four girls at a time when there were no girls' cross-country teams. As the team grew, transporting everyone in vans became unfeasible. With support from the parents, we pressured the athletic director to give us a bus.

I was a tough coach, holding practice twice a week all summer and twice a day for the first two weeks of the season. I also encouraged group running by tying a string around all the runners, forcing them to stay together. Everyone knew who the Hartland runners were at meets because they always clumped together.

I ran everyone at meets—guys and girls together—and received resistance from referees because it led to too much pushing and shoving. In response, I brought a measuring wheel and made my team start one hundred feet behind everyone else. It was more important that everyone run as much as possible to improve.

The work paid off. We qualified three runners to nationals for the first time in the school's history. Due to the costs and logistics of driving to North Carolina for nationals, only one student, Danny Skinner, went. He didn't place, but his time showed it was possible to attain a higher level. His showing inspired the program for the future.

As mentioned, I had the team practice twice a week during the summer. But as a reward for their hard work, I organized and helped fund a canoe trip. A few of the parents, including Judge Gee, came along. Judge Gee's son, Danny, got the bright idea to bring a steak on the trip, despite my warning to bring only canned meats to avoid tempting the local wildlife. Not long after we arrived, we heard screaming. Danny was fending off raccoons after his steak.

"Danny!" I yelled. "Let them have the steak, don't fight them over the steak." I remembered wildlife encounters during my Boy Scout days and blurted out, "I know raccoons! They'll attack you to get that meat. Let them have it!"

Raccoon bites and scratches carry the risk of rabies. And there was no hospital for miles on these rural back roads.

Danny reluctantly abandoned the meat and backed away. We had a good laugh at his expense and enjoyed the rest of the trip without attracting more wildlife.

The wrestling team also had success, growing from twelve wrestlers to thirty by my second year. I had learned from Coach Klein that a large team has fewer forfeits and does better due to increased competition in the practice room. Every day I talked about wrestling, even pestering kids in trouble for running in the halls or whatnot to come out for the team if they wanted to avoid the principal's office.

Rich Levitte was one such student who joined the team. He was scrappy on the mat. Rich blossomed in the summer after his freshman year at a wrestling camp run by the legendary Dan Gable. The wrestling champion had just returned from coaching at the 1976 Summer Olympics in Montreal. On day one, he looked right at Rich and picked the boy to be his drill partner. For that entire week, Rich helped demonstrate techniques. Dan Gable's spirit must have rubbed off on him because he came back to Hartland a hellion and began beating kids he had previously lost against. Rich became the first Hartland wrestler to qualify for the Michigan state wrestling tournament.

Rich's parents, Sally and Pete, were always warmly supportive of me as well as the wrestling program. Whenever they saw me eating something from McDonalds, they just sighed and invited me to their house for an authentic home-cooked meal. Between the Levitte and Vieau households, I received an abundance of mental and physical nourishment. Knowing this reassured my mother and gave her peace of mind.

When it was time for Rich to pick a college, he asked my advice. I told him about my experiences at Olivet.

"Good enough for me," he said.

So he went to Olivet, where he became the captain of the wrestling team and president of the Adelphic fraternity.

Rich and I were good friends. I almost told him the truth about me one evening when we went to see the Village People perform in Detroit. But the timing just didn't seem right. I didn't want to risk losing him as a friend. He valued my opinion so much regarding wrestling, college, fraternities, and even relationships. I couldn't risk ruining our friendship. It took nearly six years to work up the courage and disclose to Rich that I am gay.

ᚾᛄᚲ

In the wrestling room, I stoked the mentality that no wrestler, no matter how good they were, was a "Holy Cow." In other words, there was no guarantee a wrestler would start on varsity, even if they were a senior. They had to earn it. Any wrestler could, and was encouraged to, wrestle-off for a spot on the team. This approach kept team members hungry and decreased complacency.

As the team grew, we started having enough kids to make a Junior Varsity (JV) lineup. The JV team actually placed in a tournament and brought home Hartland's first-ever wrestling team trophy. There was a lot to be proud of at Hartland. Unfortunately, that didn't prevent the occasional reminder that I was a Black man in a predominantly White town.

While coaching from the side of the mat, I was animated and vocal. During a match, I couldn't keep my body from mimicking my wrestler's position, arms moving up, legs and torso contorting, while I yelled technique advice. After matches, I was high-spirited with my wrestlers, showing a move that might have helped during their match, putting my hands on their shoulders, or hugging them in joy.

One wrestler, Mike, told me, "Coach, after a match when you talk to me, don't put your hands on my shoulders. My grandpa comes to all my meets, and he gets angry when you touch me."

My cautious reply was, "Okay, Mike. I won't do that."

He reiterated, "You can talk to me from a distance but don't touch me because he gets really angry when you touch me."

I was saddened and upset that I couldn't just be myself. Here we are in the middle of a gym with a few hundred people, and some people still feared me or thought of me as less than human. Did they think that my blackness was going to rub off on the kids? This incident was not the norm. But it did make me more attuned to subtle cues when I interacted with people.

In my status as a new teacher, the students, for the most part, accepted me with no problem. I got the feeling that many were even curious to learn from me, their first Black authority figure. I started with my hard attitude speech so they would know I was the boss, despite only being five years older than the seniors. I made the students take home, review, and sign a three-page conduct contract. Yes, I realize that was extreme, but I had this concept of being an authority and wanted to make it clear I was the teacher, not a friend. Over the years, I shortened the contract. While working at North High, I cut it down to ten rules.

Nevertheless, after the first class on day one, a student called, "Hi, Bob!"

So there it is, I thought. *The first challenge to my authority.*

I turned and said, "It's Mr. Shegog to you."

The girl said, "You don't remember me, do you?"

Then I did. Oh no! It was Sue Larson, now a senior, but her brother was one of my Olivet classmates. She and I first met at a party the previous year. We had talked at that party and smoked a joint together. I lightened up, no pun intended, and we continued our friendship.

At this party, I also met a pleasant girl named Elise. After I spent some time talking with her, other partiers informed me that she was the daughter of the Michigan KKK Grand Dragon, Robert Miles. In 1971, he, and a few other Klan members, were unhappy with the desegregation of the Pontiac, Michigan, schools. The FBI raided the Miles' home. Robert Miles and four other men were convicted for their involvement in the bombing of ten Pontiac school buses.

I choked on my drink at the news. I was cautious but didn't want to judge Elise based on her family. She treated me with respect, so I returned the favor. I haven't kept in touch, but I wish her well.

Sue Larson's mother often helped with Hartland programs, so I got to know her too. They invited me to their house for dinner many times. The first time I arrived for dinner, they had failed to disclose to Sue's dad that I, a Black man, would be joining them. He was an old Marine, an Archie Bunker type, caught off guard seeing me. It was awkward, but we got through the dinner.

"Sue, why didn't you tell him?" I asked.

"My dad needed to be educated. Best way to do it. Mom was in on it too."

After that dinner, Sue's dad told her, "That's the first time I ever had dinner with a Black person. He's a really nice guy."

I saw her dad many times after that. He slowly changed and became way more accepting before he passed. Sue and her mother were right. He didn't know any Black people and, through me, learned that Black people are no different than anyone else, tearing down his preconceived notions.

The school year progressed, and not surprisingly, there were more racial incidents. One day, at the end of my social studies class, a student came up to me and asked me to change her exam grade. She leaned into me so that her breasts touched my shoulder and said, "If you don't change my grade, I'm going to tell everyone you touched my boobs." Then she left.

I was dumbfounded, caught off guard, and wondering what to do. Barely a few months into my teaching career, I found myself asking, can I handle this situation? It's her word versus mine. A Black man touching a young White girl's breasts is all this small town will hear. The distress on my face had to have been perceptible because the next student to enter the class noticed.

It was Sue Larson. She immediately asked if I was all right. I told her what had happened. Just like Mr. Poly with my housing arrangements, Sue said, "I'll take care of it."

Sue and a few of her imposing basketball friends cornered the girl in the bathroom, called her out for what she had done, and threatened to mop the floor with her if she didn't apologize to me. It worked. The student apologized and never attempted anything like that again.

I couldn't help but ask myself if the same thing would have happened to a White or female teacher? I never told anyone else about the incident. But I truly appreciated what Sue did to resolve a situation that could have spiraled out of control. Sue and I are friends to this day. She is truly one of the guardian angels in my life.

Fall approached and with it, new tasks. Hartland is known for its Halloween haunted house. We teachers often took on roles to help it run smoothly. My job that year was crowd control. Ready to report for my job, I donned a gorilla costume. The night's fun started full of energy, and the weather wasn't too cold for that time of year in Michigan. As guests arrived from Hartland and neighboring towns, I rounded them up and slowly funneled them into the haunted house.

Early in the evening, a small boy, about seven-years-old, started kicking my leg. I ignored him at first, brushed it off, and laughed through my gorilla face a bit. Then he said, "You look like a nigger from downtown Detroit."

My cheerful mood immediately turned to disgust. I picked up the annoying kid and chucked him into the nearby bushes.

"My dad's going to sue you! Nyah, nyah, nyah nyah, nyah nyah!" he said.

I ripped off my gorilla head, revealing my Black face.

His eyes opened as wide as they could, then he took off running. I went back to crowd control and didn't hear anything else about it. The young kid learned this behavior from somewhere, just like my aforementioned Olivet classmate had. I might not have handled the situation righteously, but it sure felt good to put that kid in his place.

Despite these few unpleasant moments, most of my experiences in Hartland were positive and inclusive. Through my Olivet alum friends Don Barnes and Randy Wilson, I joined the Jaycees, also known as the Junior Chamber of Commerce (JCC). Through the group, I networked with interesting members, including those who were on the school board, often while socializing at places like the Bloated Goat bar in Fowlerville. I remember showing up early at the bar once and facing stares of abhorrence from the all-White patrons. When the JCC members arrived, they had my back. Those stares subsided, and we began to socialize normally. It wasn't the first time, nor would it be the last time I was the only Black person in the social circle. With the JCC, I would get the occasional question or joke about being Black, but it was never in a derogatory way. The other guys took as many jokes as they gave, so we had great relationships. They were my friends. They cared for me, supported me, and honestly had my best interest in mind.

After two years at Hartland, life was going great. The students respected me, the administration and I had a supportive relationship, and all my sports teams were becoming more successful. The Hartland paper wrote an article about me saying, "The only thing that Shegog didn't do at Hartland was blow up basketballs." So when I heard the news they were letting me go, I was devastated.

The school district RIFed (Reduction in Force) twenty-three faculty members over the town's discontent with how the board was using funds. When renovating the administration building, the board used a private company without consulting Ron Lepeck, the school's shop teacher and a respected contractor. He routinely taught by using his students on construction projects around town. Ron was an immense resource with a talent for building immaculate businesses and homes at very affordable prices. As a reprimand to the board, the parents and townsfolk voted "No" on every board budget item for the next two years. The school managed to hire back some of the $8,000 a year faculty positions by taking out a bank loan. Many parents rallied to include me in what it covered, but the board could not bypass their teacher contracts that explicitly favor seniority. Unfortunately, I was among the newer, less senior faculty unable to recover their jobs.

It was a privilege to work at Hartland. I never realized how much they spoiled me until much later in my career. The setup with teaching, coaching, administrative support, parent support, and town support went unmatched the rest of my career. I only wish I'd had more time to let everything develop. How good could we have been in wrestling if I were able to stay at Hartland for ten, twenty, or thirty years?

I was back to square one, looking for a job. Coach Klein was well-connected within the Michigan wrestling community. I called to see if he knew of any available coaching positions. Within a week, I had a job at Northwest High in Jackson, Michigan. The high school is in the predominantly White town of Rives Junction, Michigan, just outside of Jackson. Because it was close to Albion, I lived at home and avoided the renting debacle I encountered in Hartland. Also, living at home shielded me from the necessity of going into Jackson for groceries or other errands. Confederate flags littered the town's trucks and houses.

At Jackson NW, it was agreed that for the next year I would teach at the adjacent affiliated middle school and attend every wrestling practice at the high school as a volunteer coach. Then the current head wrestling coach, Jim Fullerton, would retire, and I would become the new head coach. I showed up every day, worked hard, took on their best wrestlers, made them better, and earned their respect. I don't like tooting my own horn, but it was unmistakable that I was the most capable coach, next to the retiring head coach. When the year was up, and Fullerton retired, the athletic director made assistant wrestling coach Larry Angus the new head coach.

I protested to the athletic director, "What about our deal? What's best for the team?"

It didn't matter. On day one, the administration lied to me and had already made their minds up before I started. None of my efforts during the past year did anything to advance my career. Although it wasn't overt, I often wondered if race was a factor in their decision. At least many of the wrestlers improved while I was there. Knowing that eased my mind in the face of the deceit.

I left Jackson and was back to the job search. Once again, I called Klein, and sure enough, he put me in contact with Cassopolis High. My old college teammate, Jim Wencel, also had ties to Cassopolis, and he, too, put in a good word.

⚘

Cassopolis, Michigan, is an interesting town with historical ties to The Underground Railroad. As another fun fact, it's also famous for its pig farmers. Though predominately White, the town had many Black residents, including a few Black teachers at the high school.

I arrived at Sanford Justice's office with my portfolio of accomplishments as a teacher and coach (he was the principal and athletic director). The first two pages of my resumé covered my bio. The last fifty outlined plans for the teaching position. I included lists of my previous teams' accomplishments, programs, and extracurricular activities.

I got the job and became the new head wrestling coach. *Finally*, I thought. *Now I can get to work and build a program.*

Even though I held the reins, I didn't have the necessary administrative support. We started a junior high program only to have custodians regularly turn the lights off while we wrestled. Pulling the curtains back from the windows got us through practice but was less than ideal.

In my first year, it was Cassopolis' turn to host the conference championships. To my dismay, Principal Justice turned it down without consulting me. When I went to his office to discuss the situation, Justice was unavailable. I left dozens of notes for him, but it wasn't until near the end of the school year that I finally met face-to-face with him.

I brought up the junior high team and the conference tournament but only received unapologetic and disinterested answers. Justice even seemed annoyed that an inferior subordinate, a mere teacher, would question his decisions. He said he didn't think we could successfully run the conference tournament so he had made an executive decision.

Knowing I had ample experience running even larger tournaments, I pointed to my portfolio and asked, "Did you even read this?"

"No." His answer was blunt.

"You didn't read my qualifications, didn't look at my portfolio. Why did you hire me?"

He looked at me and said, "I looked at the size of the binder and gave you the job."

I'm sure the principal was very busy, wearing the many hats characteristic of the leader of a small-town school, but I was angry. I felt unappreciated and ultimately resigned from my teaching position. Cassopolis was not Hartland, and it was probably a mistake to compare jobs. But I was still immature at that point. Leaving

Cassopolis and Jackson NW after just one year was impulsive. Who knows what could have happened with another year spent building relationships and working out the communication hurdles?

My mind was still on Hartland, so I decided to visit Jack Poly and see if he had any positions open. Adding insult to injury, it turned out that Jack had messaged Justice at Cassopolis stating that a position was available for me at Hartland. I couldn't believe it. Due to Principal Justice's horrendous communication skills, he never relayed the message to me. Another faculty member had already filled the Hartland spot.

Noooo! I thought. I would have gone back to Hartland in a minute.

It had been four years since I started at Hartland, and some of my first students were now graduating. Rich Leavitt, whom I mentioned earlier, had kept in touch and invited me to the high school graduation. I was out of a job, depressed, and feeling so ashamed that I decided to skip the ceremony. Later that night, I ran into a few graduates at a local restaurant.

"Shegog! Did you hear?" they said.

"Hear what?"

It turns out the valedictorian mentioned me in her speech. She talked about milestone events in each of her high school years and recalled her freshman year as "the time when Shegog showed up." She detailed my involvement in the various programs and demonstrated the impact made by my presence at Hartland. My influence on the students was genuine and meaningful. It felt wonderful knowing they were better off as a result. Looking back, I can only imagine how my small injection of positive influence will resonate through future generations.

Having worked at predominantly White schools so far, I was now fated to work at my first predominantly Black schools, Flint Beecher High, or Beecher as the locals called it, followed by the nearby Mt. Morris High. During this time, I worked as a permanent substitute teacher and head wrestling coach from 1978-1982. It was a great experience, and I felt I was giving back to the Black community. However, being Black in Black schools did not prevent me from hitting bumps in the road.

There is an ongoing national debate about the different types of English spoken in this country. Many scholars argue that Black English Vernacular (BEV), now called African American Vernacular English (AAVE), also known as Ebonics, should be accepted. Some claim that if a person doesn't get a job because they speak a different type of English, it could be discrimination. It's been my experience that speaking "proper" English has led to more open doors for opportunities. It is a complicated subject. I bring it up because something as simple as my manner of speaking affects the way others view me.

In the classroom, my Beecher students immediately noticed that my speech was unlike theirs, and some thought I was from Africa. Later, when I taught at North High, some of the Black kids thought the same thing. My immediate response was to help the students understand that the way they spoke was critical and could make a difference in their future.

I remember coming to the point with a few students of saying, "This is English. If you ever want a job downtown, you need to learn this. I'm not coming down on you because you're Black or poor but because I want you to succeed. You cannot go downtown talking the way you do."

One of the students replied, "If I'm downtown interviewing for a job, I'm not going to talk like that."

"Then you have to practice it now. If you talk like that now, you'll talk like that then."

The kids soon had a chance to see what I was getting at.

While on summer break in Flint, I worked for the Genesee County Consortium helping inner city high school kids find jobs. I encouraged my students to participate if they wanted to make a little extra money. Filling out job applications, doing interviews, and managing responsibility was good practice for them. The students also had to fill out a beneficiary form on the slim chance that something happened during work. It was a good experience, and they did great.

I did, however, receive a call from one of the program directors to tell me they had a student beneficiary form they couldn't understand. It was Leroy's. He was already on the job, so I picked him up and brought him to the office to correct the paperwork.

What was confusing, and quite comical, was that his listed benefactor was "My Lady."

Holding back laughter because I knew Leroy had filled out the form as best as he could, I gently asked, "What is My Lady's name? And we need her social security number too."

After dropping Leroy back at work, I finally let out the laughter I'd bottled inside. I should have better anticipated the greenness of the students and presented an example of how a properly filled-out form should look. Needless to say, everything turned out fine. The program had its funny moments, but more importantly, the students learned essential practical lessons.

As a substitute teacher, I traveled between the different district schools, taught almost any class, and even worked in the library, cafeteria, or wherever there was a need. Each school day ended with me back at Beecher High for wrestling practice. Substituting at the high school was ideal because it made it easier to stay up to date with my wrestlers, ensure they were behaving, and doing the work they needed for class. I had high hopes both on the mat and academically for my wrestlers. That's why I followed up regularly with the students and their teachers, encouraging them to meet expectations.

I don't know if it was just because my mother was hard on me, or maybe it was because of the times. But as a Black man, it was instilled in me that to have the same opportunities, I couldn't just be as good as everyone else. I had to be better.

There's a similar message in the movie *Men of Honor.* Cuba Gooding Jr. plays the Master Chief Petty Officer Carl Brashear, the first Black U.S. Navy Master Diver. In the film, Brashear can't just perform at the same level as his fellow trainees. He must execute every test better than his peers to access the same career paths. There is some debate over whether Chief Brashear or Black Chief Petty Officer John Henry Turpin qualified as the first Black U.S. Navy Diver. Some sources hold that CPO Turpin qualified as a Master Diver in 1915.

Whether or not he's the first Black Master Diver, Chief Carl Brashear does hold the dubious honor of being the first amputee diver recertified by the U.S. Navy. If that wasn't impressive enough, he helped invent the underwater cutting torch.

Without full consciousness of it, I might have projected this toughness onto the Beecher kids. Many responded, evidenced by the growing number of kids who came out for wrestling. But some were turned off by my approach. Was I too hard on them at times? Did they not trust me because I didn't speak English the way they did? Even later, at North, I noticed that many of the Black students shied away from me. Was I too much in their business? To this day, these questions puzzle me. Despite our differences, we still achieved success in wrestling. Our program grew steadily, and each year we had at least one Genesee County all-star.

One of my former wrestlers at Beecher, Johnnie Reed, went on to become the head wrestling coach at the school. He retired in 2020, as the COVID pandemic hit, but said he might return once it subsides. That bodes well for the Beecher wrestling program, for it might not survive without him. Shortly after our conversation, Johnnie learned my truth. He, too, has been nothing but supportive, and I am grateful for his friendship.

Working in Flint was a great experience and I feel like I made a significant impact on my kids and community. This was also the time that I was maturing as an adult and reflecting on my own identity. The next chapter explores that journey with regards to my sexual, racial, and professional identity.

·_·· ——— ···_·

CHAPTER 5:

It's All About Relationships

My Relationship with My Sexual Identity

I shared with you my passion for wrestling and how that drove me to pursue a career in teaching and more specifically, as a coach. During this time, I was also searching for meaning in relationships and where I belonged. I was attracted to women, but more so to men. Should I get married and have kids like my Pentecostal and societal upbringing demanded? Or should I be true to myself? What would ultimately lead to the most happiness? What did God want for me? My mind wrestled with these thoughts as I explored various relationships.

Our traditional society has a specific mold for kids. Boys are supposed to be tough, active, and shouldn't cry. Their preferred colors are blue or green, and they wear shorts or long pants with T-shirts. Girls are more sensitive, graceful, and emotional. They should choose colors like pink or lavender, and wear dresses or blouses with skirts. Growing up in the 1950s, a kid who didn't quite fit into these models was often labeled as "funny." For example, if a boy liked the color pink or enjoyed wearing dresses, people would often say, "There's something funny about him." The word "gay" was not yet mainstream in American culture.

A kid in Albion who went to my church, my sister's friend, was more flamboyant than other boys. He did things only girls and "funny" people did, like make certain hand gestures or walk with a sway. He didn't want to be different and tried extremely hard to conform to societal norms. He married and even had kids. Yet he still had desires that conflicted with societal norms. He was gay. Five years after getting married, in his mid-twenties, he took his own life. He had succumbed to the overwhelming pressures of balancing what he wanted against what everyone expected of him. Sadly, this was not an uncommon ending to the "funny kid" story.

His sad tale also reveals a relatively new stereotype. How society believes a "gay" person should appear. Males who display flamboyant mannerisms, emotional sensitivity, elegance in appearance, and extravagance in expression receive the "gay" label. But this is far from the truth. Many gay men do not fit this stereotype. I, for one, fit none of those characteristics. Nor do my partners.

I was being myself all those years while teaching and coaching. That is why it was easy to conceal my private life from people in my work life. Sexuality and gender identity used to be limited to simple terms like heterosexual or homosexual, male or female, but they are much more complex. The LGBTQ+ acronym helps to differentiate the spectrum. But even these few letters do not fully capture the entirety of human identity. Eventually, we will run out of letters. Hopefully, by then, it won't matter how a person self-identifies because the only matter of importance is that all human beings are unique individuals.

My gender and sexuality are inherent to me. When I heard townsfolk call the Albion kid "funny," I thought, *I am glad I was born a man and that "funny" people are men who want to be women.* That was not me, so I never categorized myself that way. I grew up like most people in a religious household, rarely talking about sex, and going through the conservative motions of society. I didn't think about sexuality much because it was rarely the subject of conversation.

Even though I was oblivious to my sexuality when I was young, I noticed weird things happened. Like when bullies picked on me and grabbed me from behind to get my lunch money, I remember noticing a boner on my back. I didn't realize it at the time but, upon reflection, I wonder if I was an easy target? Or did I just give off a certain vibe? I was soft-spoken, passive, and did what adults told me to do like any good church-going kid.

I went through all the usual adolescent changes as my body figured itself out hormonally. It was not uncommon to need to cover my pants with my book because I sprang a random erection after accidentally rubbing up against something. In seventh grade, I had my first girlfriend, though we never kissed or held hands. Patty, who was Black, said we should hang out together, partly because she thought I had too many White friends and felt she needed to balance it out. We lasted about three months before going our separate ways. It was about this time that I began devoting more time to wrestling at junior high school. The bullying stopped because I'd had a girlfriend, my peers had more respect for me, and I was doing well in wrestling.

Some people might think I wrestled because I was gay. Nothing could be further from the truth. I love wrestling for the same reasons the average person loves it. It was about challenging myself day in and day out, setting and reaching increasingly demanding goals, pushing myself to exhaustion in order to learn what I could do. That grew to include the thrill of competing one-on-one with advanced techniques. And finally, as a coach, it was about passing down my knowledge of the sport. I didn't know I was gay, nor did I have gay thoughts. But there was something about me that drew others to me. This charisma led to my first sexual encounter in ninth grade.

During my freshman year of high school, I worked at a grocery store on the north end of town after wrestling practice. I finished late each evening, about a quarter past nine. Then I walked or ran home in the south end of town. One of the local business owners caught on to my routine and kindly started giving me rides home. Then, one day, instead of taking me home, he drove just out of town. He stopped the car and asked me to pleasure him. I wasn't sure what to think. I know now that it was molestation.

Up to this point in my life, I'd learned to listen to adults, obey them, and to trust everyone in our town. So I did what he wanted. Then he took me home. During four more rides he requested the same intimacy. I was conflicted. I didn't feel victimized. Truthfully, I was curious. Maybe I wanted more. He was a married White man, which also bewildered me. Surprisingly, the idea that I'd been disobedient to the teachings of my religion didn't cross my mind. Ultimately, I decided to do what most perplexed ninth graders would.

The next time I saw the man waiting for me in his car, I avoided him. I walked the other way, then ran home. He never gave me a ride again. I believe I missed our encounters but was too immature to process everything, to communicate or fully understand my feelings. I did see the man in other social settings, but nothing ever happened, nor did we talk about it again.

Men were attracted to me. I thought of myself as "manly" since I liked sports, was tough, and happy to be a man, but I confess my demeanor was gentle. Maybe that's what made men comfortable approaching me? Later, as a junior in high school, I was propositioned by a guy in town.

He asked, "How big is your thing?" He wanted to compare.

By then, I was a little more mature and realized this was a rabbit hole I didn't want to go down. I ended the conversation and walked away.

I believed that nobody in my social circle suspected I had gay curiosities. In fact, at reunions decades later, many of my high school peers were shocked to learn I was gay. Part of their surprise might have been because, in senior year I dated my first serious girlfriend.

About this time, my daily schedule was overfull. My classes met from 7:45 in the morning until 2:35 each afternoon. From 3:00-5:00, I was at wrestling practice. Then I worked in the meat department of a local grocery store from 6:00-9:00 p.m. If I finished my tasks early, I left before 9:00 and ran almost two miles to the Albion Public Library to study before it closed at 10:00 p.m.

I spent a lot of my free time in the library doing research for term papers, for debate, and for forensics. That paid off. I qualified for the Michigan Forensic State Championships the first three years, finally placing third in my senior year.

One of those winter evenings in the public library, I asked the librarian for help finding a book. I was tired, still wet from my run, and totally missed the book right in front of me. The White librarian bent over to get it and strategically placed her butt in my groin area. My eyes widened in astonishment as I lost control and popped an erection into her dress. She turned, handed me the book, and smiled pleasantly. I tried to explain my reaction and apologize. She interrupted me, said to call her if I needed any other books, and she would have them waiting for me on the counter. Shyly and gratefully, I called her and saw her a lot over the next few weeks. For books, only books. I had zero game.

Then one night, just before closing, she asked me to walk her home, telling me a man had been following her. It was true, and I yelled at him, threatening him with bodily harm as we walked to her apartment. *Very manly of me*, I thought.

She invited me inside. The next thing I knew, I was losing my virginity. My Pentecostal upbringing conflicted with my current situation. But I felt good. I was excited and looked forward to visiting the library more than ever now.

I remember having to shop at multiple stores for condoms. Everybody knew everyone else in town, and I feared word of my shopping list would get back to my mother. She knew nothing of my relationship with the librarian. I enjoyed being with her, considering her my girlfriend, though I still thought about being with men. I started understanding my sexuality and began to think of myself as bisexual.

My librarian girlfriend often helped with my homework, and we always ended the evening in bed. That was our routine until late May, when she informed me that she had missed her period and could be pregnant.

She was twenty-five with a college degree. I was eighteen with no scholarship, a failed attempt to place at state, and with no clear path to college. I knew my way of life had to change if I became a father. So, here was the plan I came up with. First, we would get married, and I would select a college. Both of us would get jobs. After the baby arrived, my wife would work part-time. That seemed logical to me. After all, five other students in my high school class were already married. Also, my grandmother had started introducing me to girls for marriage purposes, but each time I respectfully declined, using my plan to attend college as an excuse.

I informed my mother about our plan even though she and my girlfriend hadn't yet met. My mother hosted a dinner to get to know my future wife. Everyone was polite and proper. When we finished eating, Mama suddenly said to me, "You need to leave. And don't come back for two hours. I need to talk with her."

When I returned, everything had changed. My fiancée wasn't interested in our plan anymore. She left my mother's house without saying much, but we were no longer together.

My older brother, John, also felt the need to give me "The Talk" about White women. He invited me into his car, and we drove around town. His basic message was, "Don't date White women. They are dangerous."

I took his advice with a grain of salt. After all, it's not like he was the best authority on the subject. Not long after our talk, he himself married a White woman after impregnating her. Tragically, his daughter was born prematurely with disabilities. My brother often hung out on the streets with friends and didn't win any Father of the Year awards. He ended up divorcing his wife. Sadly, she died of cancer at a young age.

The narrative of not dating outside of our race was strong and consistent within my family. To go against that would be an uphill battle.

I was left with questions. What happened between my mother and girlfriend? What did Mama say to her? My mother wouldn't give me a straight answer. When I saw my ex in public, she only smiled in passing but didn't stop to converse. Her behavior also left me without answers. At a loss to understand what had happened to my happy relationship, I was now back on my original track for college and went to Olivet the following September.

Two years later, I ran into the librarian at an Albion grocery store. We talked for over an hour. She had gotten married since we last saw each other. Regarding our situation, it turned out that she just had a late period and wasn't pregnant.

"What happened when my mother told me to leave?" I asked.

"Your mother told me that I needed to stay away from you."

The "why" question never got answered, but I suspected it had to do with us being from different worlds. Things would have been more difficult for sure, but I accepted that and felt up to the challenge.

Her husband was a local White man whose family was racist and often used the word *nigger* in conversation. She even apologized about them and stated that they could never know she had been with me or any Black man.

"How can you exist in such an environment?" I wanted to know.

She insisted, "It is a secure and safe home."

We left it at that. As she walked away, I couldn't help but watch her go and remember that first night when she so seductively found my book. I grinned and thought, *You always remember your first.*

My Relationships within My Racial Identity

In 1970, when I graduated high school, the United States was still quite divided. Starting with the murder of Emmett Till in August of 1955, followed by Rosa Park's arrest in December of 1955, the chain of events was set in motion for the numerous marches and protests that made up the civil rights movement. The assassination of three national leaders in the mid to late 1960s, Malcolm X, Martin Luther King, and Robert Kennedy, fueled civil unrest. The ongoing Vietnam

War and Kent State shootings in May of 1970 further propagated the national divide.

Being passive by nature and conservative by religion, I never sought trouble or violence. I respected authority and knew it was risky to protest. Those who did protest never knew if they'd be met with a firehose, dogs, or guns in another massacre like Kent State. My mother, as well as other Black and minority parents, feared for their children's safety. The atmosphere of unrest made me and other students reticent about what was happening around us. Many wanted change to happen but didn't want to be a part of the winds of hate sweeping across our land. I saw myself in this light.

My neutral stance during race riots got noticed. That is why I received multiple Martin Luther King awards. Some students resented me for my stance, but most respected me enough to listen to my perspective. I was the first in my family to go to college. I would never have been able to attend without funding from the college. Don't get me wrong, I was upset about the atmosphere of intolerance and knew about the injustices taking place. They still exist today. But patience got me further, gave me a louder voice, and did more to counteract the wrongs than rashness and blind hate ever could.

In an attempt to help me assimilate to college life, Olivet College placed me in a room with a Black freshman from Detroit. Our views on race relations were polar opposites. As a result, I spent most of my time away from the room, hanging out with the twenty-one freshmen wrestlers. I used my room mostly as a super walk-in closet.

Social topics were on everyone's mind, especially in my forensics and speech events. Debate training taught me to see multiple sides of an argument and present them coherently and effectively. Yet I remember constantly losing to Mildred Edwards, from Kalamazoo Central. Her powerful speeches frequently referred to Malcolm X and his points on Afro-American unity.

There were campus protests while I was at Olivet. Two of those events were staged in an effort to get Black teachers hired and to advocate for an African American studies program. A Detroit newspaper overstated by calling them riots.

One evening, during my sophomore year, Olivet had an intramural basketball finals game between the African American Society (AAS or the Black club) and one of the fraternities whose written bylaws forbade accepting Blacks or Jews. The game was physical and intense. The physical aggressiveness boiled over, and a fight broke out before the end of the game. Nearly the entire audience in the gym climbed down into "the pit" to join the battle. Shocked, I remained in the stands. I believed fighting should be the last recourse. Once I start swinging my fists in anger, I've given up thinking of a better way to solve the problem. My decision to stay out of the melée is what MLK would have done. That's why Olivet gave me the MLK award.

Martin Luther King attracted many supporters to his nonviolent approach in the civil rights movement, but most people are unfamiliar with the person who led him toward this path. A man named Bayard Rustin. Rustin was an early civil rights organizer who grew up in Pennsylvania, where he was exposed to Quaker pacifism at a young age. In the mid-1940s, he traveled to India and learned from the leaders of the Gandhian peaceful protest movements. Rustin organized and orchestrated numerous civil rights marches, protests, sit-ins, and other peaceful demonstrations. So why haven't most people heard of him? One simple reason. He was openly gay.

Critics of the civil rights movement used Rustin's lifestyle to argue against their policies and protests. They claimed homosexuals were ruining the country by staging these protests. While national support for desegregation and Black equality had improved, the issue of homosexuality was still taboo. Rustin felt gay rights were also civil rights, but many fellow leaders feared the movement would be less effective in garnering national support if it took the same position. Consequently, Rustin worked behind the scenes, a less-known hero of the civil rights movement. In 1964, Congress passed the Civil Rights Act. A slew of marginalized groups fell under its protection, including gay rights. Yet it took decades for these rights to be more established as Rustin had dreamed.

In my junior year, I was elected president of the African American Society. Olivet had about forty Blacks out of a student body totaling nine hundred. I organized meetings with the governing board, during which I praised Olivet College's past abolitionist, women's suffrage, and progressive school policies. Then I called for a practical approach (no demand protests) and suggested we compromise. Instead of using college funds to hire a new faculty member, we could appoint a current history teacher, a White man named Professor Walker, to teach African American studies. Such courses required at least eleven students to enroll in each class. There were not enough Black students to sustain this plan. We would need White students to participate as well. The board was amenable, but the program never got instituted. Most important to our cause, a conversation we could build on took place. It would take nearly twenty more years, in the mid-1990s, before Olivet finally offered African American studies courses.

I am not a radical Black. Sometimes, when I observe some Blacks, they embarrass me. For example, in the 1960s Detroit riots, many young Blacks burned and looted the city. Even in the 2020s, some Blacks responded in the same manner to George Floyd's death. I understand there's pent-up anger at recurring injustices. Some of the looting was the work of folks who did not support Black Lives Matter (BLM) but wanted the movement to look bad. I feel that too. Punching the situation in the face might feel good in the moment, but only at the expense of shutting down sustained dialogue. There's a way to stand up for your rights without violence.

My Pentecostal upbringing taught me to use my words. When people resort to violence, they have stopped thinking. Martin L. King was on the receiving end of violence but he never returned it in kind. People are defensive when someone questions the foundations of their beliefs. It may take days, weeks, or even years before they process new information they receive. I believe that real change takes time, ten to twenty years, a whole generation. Things still might not be fair, but they have improved over the years.

The Brown v. Board of Education decision in 1954 ruled that segregation of public schools violated the Fourteenth Amendment and was therefore unconstitutional. Though the trend to desegregate schools began then, it wasn't until 2016 that the last segregated school became integrated. Cleveland High School in Cleveland, Mississippi integrated its all-White and all-Black schools that year, becoming Cleveland Central High School.

Indian School Road, in central Phoenix, got its name from the old Phoenix Indian School, where the state brought children from Arizona's Native American reservations to live and be educated. Kids from tribes all over the southwest were taken from their families and bussed to this boarding school, some from as far as four hours away. Prevailing sentiment said Native Americans must assimilate into U.S. society. For a few Native students, it was a positive thing, offering an escape from a harsh family life. But most students, wrenched from their homes and familiar cultures, suffered negative experiences. Abuse of the students was common, both verbal and physical. Children received punishment for speaking Native languages or displaying symbols or items from their Native culture. The state forced compliance by threatening indigenous families with losing their government rations if they didn't send their children to the Phoenix Indian boarding school.

Many of these public schools had religious partnerships with churches that operated the facilities. Part of their intent was to convert the students to Christianity. The Catholic Church was the largest proprietor of these schools and known for its strict control of the children. This is a piece of history the church prefers to ignore. If the national estimate is accurate, that one in every ten individuals are gay, then the gay Native American children in these schools were in a living hell.

My Relationships within My Teaching Identity

To coach a high school team requires building good relationships with the staff, parents, and community. When talking with faculty, I always directed the conversation toward my team. One day, a faculty member stopped me in the middle of a conversation and asked, "When do you breathe?"

I understood that her concern was not with my breathing but with my dedication to wrestling. I learned to talk less, listen more, and take an interest in their daily concerns.

Building a strong wrestling team meant working with the staff to increase wrestling opportunities within the school. To secure coolers and ice, I needed to foster a relationship with the cafeteria staff. I needed the wrestlers to clean up the gym after each meet, thus building a relationship with the custodians. Everyone needed to behave on the bus and clean it when we returned home. Expending that small effort made for a good relationship with the bus driver. (One bus driver shared with me that, when driving assignments were posted, he signed up for all of the wrestling trips.) After every major wrestling event, I sent thank-you notes, personally said thank you, or for female teachers, had a rose delivered to the classroom.

As relationships and routines solidified at North High, teachers, some parents, and community folks started contacting me early in the year about our wrestling schedule so they could request time off work. These are the relationships I valued the most. Folks like Patty Lapadura, the Burdicks, the Levitte Family, the McAllisters, Ted Faz, Doc Eitner, Mr. Nerini, Laura Fisher, sponsor of the wrestlerettes, and Lynell Arnold. These were only a few of our numerous supporters.

Lynell was the school bookstore manager. She completed the paperwork for team travel, using her free time to walk the paperwork around the district to get the proper signatures. English teacher, Christine Reed, talked to new students about getting involved in school sports, stressing wrestling. Like the best recruiter, she handed me names of new students with an interest in wrestling. There were so many advocates who contributed to the success of the team. It is hard to name them all, but I am incredibly grateful for their support.

Doc James Eitner, a remarkable man, devoted nearly half of his life to student-athletes, usually after working his normal day as a family medicine physician. He joined North in 1991 and did everything from conducting physicals, treating athlete injuries and ailments to offering exercise and diet advice. Kenny McAllister kept Doc busy all by himself because at least five broken bones resulted from Kenny's wrestling throws. All legal moves, by the way.

When Antonio dislocated his elbow in Yuma during the last match he ever wrestled for North, Doc was there to help treat him. He traveled with us to various wrestling events, even giving rides to students when needed. Other schools were so used to Doc that if they didn't see him with us, the first thing they asked was, "Did you bring your doctor?"

Later, Doc Eitner provided his services to Maryvale High. John Moraga requested Doc's presence in his corner during Ultimate Fight Championships fights (UFC). This highly-public appearance ballooned into more mixed martial arts (MMA) involvement as Doc expanded his repertoire. Today, my friend continues serving his patients, from students to professional athletes to those in his clinic. I thank him for being a part of the rich community we all fostered together.

My relationship with Ted Faz is unique and has stood the test of time. He arrived at North in 1986, two years before me, and was a security guard. We hit it off right away. He, too, was a relationship builder, though I would say his job was more challenging than mine. Ted built relationships with the student body and gained the trust of some of the most troubled students. He was respectful yet raw. The man cursed more than I did, didn't know how to beat around the bush, and flat-out told it like it was. That may be why he connected so well with the students.

His talent defused situations before they could spiral out of control. For example, he often got tips about things like suspicious bags on campus. These bits of confidential information helped the security team quietly handle any situation and remove the problem. Lots of the city gangs had a presence on the North campus. They included the Doble, the 21st, the 8th, and the 9th Street gangs. Breaking up fights and confiscating drugs, guns, and knives was a typical day for Ted and his team.

Ted defused not only student situations but many of mine as well. He once saved me from hitting one of my wrestlers with a chair. Michael Nerini had a history of obnoxious, high-energy antics. His nickname was Psycho Michael. In retrospect, that moniker probably only encouraged that kind of behavior. His dad, a wrestling referee, had given me full permission to do what I needed to keep his kid in check. I came close to pulling a WWE chair move on the kid, but Ted got to me first.

So it was surprising when Mike Nerini came out for wrestling. He put his energy to good use winning regionals. Ironically, sometime after he graduated, Nerini worked security at North. Proving that, given enough time, most immature kids will mature into contributing adult members of society.

When not occupied with security matters, Ted often covered my PE class so I could make a trip to the office or take care of an errand for the wrestling team. The running joke was that Ted could've issued the kids' grades because he covered for me so much. Eventually, Ted became a part of the wrestling team, often driving vans, barbequing at wrestling banquets, making sure the wrestlers and wrestlerettes got picked up after school, and ensuring they were doing well in general.

Ted's influence extended beyond school. He manned the grill during Coach Wright's wedding, helped me drive to Michigan a few times when my mother had health issues, and helped Ruben Rico move to Olivet for college.

During one of the trips to Michigan, Ted and I got stopped in Oklahoma. I ended up in the back of a highway patrol car while troopers bombarded Ted with drug-related questions. A Black guy with a Mexican guy driving a van across the country triggered law enforcement's suspicions. In their viewpoint, we must be smuggling drugs or committing some kind of crime. They let us off with a warning along with the saddest excuse for pulling us over, claiming my license plate was too hard to read, despite the obvious fact that it had no extra attachments or obstructions.

Not even one hour later, another set of troopers pulled us over. We explained our situation, and the cops let us go. Within the next hour, we got pulled over for the third time. Now I was irate. Very firmly, yet respectfully—with my hands on the steering wheel—I explained the situation to the officer and expressed my displeasure. This time the officers "read the room," apologized, and were respectful in return. They even said a prayer for my mother and wished us a safe drive. These incidents definitely tested my patience, but there are good people in this world. I just wished the previous officers hadn't profiled us.

I remember when I told Ted I was gay and had HIV. It was during one of our Payson trips. Because we were both responsible for the kids, I needed him to know I was on medication should something happen. A dizzy spell with the shakes during the tournament prompted me to share my truth.

He looked me straight in the eye and said, "I don't give a fuck. I like pussy. You like dick. That's it."

Crude, yet effective, we had a good laugh. After that, Ted was even more supportive, always asking how I was doing and making sure I was taking my medications. To this day, I will be there for him and know that he will be there for me.

Ted was with the team from the beginning and experienced our early loss after loss streak. Then we started winning, got more wrestlers out for the team—sixty wrestlers at one point—and success began to breed more success. We used to be the whupping boys of Arizona high school wrestling. Now we were a feared entourage of wrestlers, wrestlerettes, parents, and committed faculty who, year after year, contributed to the team's success.

🤼

Many parents rarely received recognition for sacrificing for their kids who wrestled. When Kenny and Karl were making weight, it was Debbie McAllister who sought healthy food options and soup recipes to help optimize her kids' nutritional success. In Payson, I remember the McAllister parents bringing in a stationary bike so the wrestlers could lose weight. I tried to thank them between matches, tournaments, and at the year-end banquets.

The parents invested emotionally in their kids and the program, so they deserve immense credit for our successes. It was an honor, a privilege to be trusted with their kids, and I feel they understood that I treated them all as if they were my own.

My relationship with the wrestlers and wrestlerettes was different. I called them my kids. In social groups, I had to clarify that they were not my biological children. After my relationship with Char, I realized I did not want to have and raise my own kids. I felt it would be complicated to raise kids in a gay home while keeping that part of my life a secret. In the 1970s and 1980s, gays could not adopt, and surrogacy was the only way to be a parent. Also, my home was a respite. I gave so much of myself to my teaching and wrestling programs that I needed my personal space as a recharging station.

The goal I held for my non-biological kids was for them to be happy, be the best person they could be, and to learn to be of service to others. I followed up with each wrestler, randomly checked grades, and visited their classes to make sure they were behaving. If it seemed necessary, I talked with their academic counselor. I strolled around campus at lunchtime to see where they ate and with whom they socialized. If a wrestler missed school or practice, I often called or visited their home. As an educator and coach, it was my duty to ensure they were first academically successful and then successful in wrestling. As a result of my dedication, our team had one of the lowest dropout rates of all school programs and even won scholar-athlete team awards. Wrestling showed the students another way of belonging and sometimes made the difference between life and death.

I genuinely believe wrestling saved Moises Sandoval's life. He wrestled for me in the early 2000s and was one of the kids I recruited from my lunchtime strolls. When Moises came out for the team, I helped him cover his school insurance costs and got him a pair of wrestling shoes from our equipment box. It didn't take long for him to get in shape, win some matches, and start enjoying the sport.

Moises' friends were gang members, identifiable by their signature brown pants. It is impossible to lie down with dogs and not get fleas. The more Moises wrestled, the more his gang felt threatened. They became passive-aggressive when he honored his practice and schoolwork commitments. They called him "schoolboy" when his grades improved. Their resentment culminated one night when his gang threw a party. Moises didn't know it, but the gang intended to harm him. Sensing their intent during the party, Moises left. His so-called friends followed and ran him down with their car. Under the vehicle, Moises' brown pants got stuck in the wheel. He got dragged far enough to sustain significant road rash and burns over nearly eighty percent of his body. The emergency crew took him to St. Joseph's Hospital, where doctors determined he would require numerous surgeries and skin grafts.

I tried to visit him, but the hospital didn't allow me to enter. I couldn't help but wonder if wrestling got him into this mess. Since his injuries were gang-related, the hospital admitted Moises under a false name. Rightfully so, as some gang members tried to get to him to finish the job. The only person allowed to visit him was Ted Faz because he was with North High security, so he delivered my best wishes for Moises' recovery.

Years later, in a Fry's grocery store parking lot, I ran into Moises.

"Shegog!" he yelled, looking happy and excited. He told me he worked for Wells Fargo, was studying for his business degree, was married with two kids, and doing very well. We talked about wrestling and how grateful he was to have had the opportunity. He only wrestled for one season, but that was enough to change the trajectory of his life. Moises went from a gang-banging, future high school dropout to a successful business and family man. Our chance meeting brought me great joy and reaffirmed my passion for the sport. The sport not only saved my life many times over, but I was learning how many of my kids' lives as well.

Our wrestling practices were hard and fair. Sometimes the best technical wrestler didn't make the varsity team if they didn't follow our standards. If they didn't attend practice the night before a meet, they shouldn't expect to wrestle. In addition, wrestlers needed to be academically up to speed and exhibit good behavior on campus and at home. Failure in any one of these areas endangered mat time. We believed that if we worked hard and stayed in top condition, we could beat anyone regardless of their ability or wrestling experience. If our opponent was better but couldn't pin us before the third period, then we were most likely going to win. I did everything possible to convey this belief to my kids by talking to each wrestler immediately after their match about how they could improve.

To that end, I spoke to their parents, posted inspirational statements in the wrestling room, and updated the student body with the results of matches and wrestling events during morning announcements. I also posted wrestling images around the school and placed news releases in the local paper. Setting these standards and expectations made it just a matter of time before my kids met and exceeded them.

I wanted my Black children, of which, sadly, there were fewer than I hoped, to have the same opportunities. As a coach, I could have done a better job of reaching more Black student-athletes. The Black wrestlers who stayed with the program became outstanding citizens. Michael Seay, Troy Mckown, Johnnie Reed (at the time I'm writing this, a wrestling coach in Michigan), Adam Scott, Brian Manley, Shawn Turner, and Ashliegh May-Hall are only a few that I celebrate.

I am proud of the boys and girls who chose to be part of our programs. They are good citizens who make an impact in their chosen careers. The relationships established during those high school coaching years are the forever kind. I'm never more than a call, card, or visit away.

·_·· ____ ···_·

CHAPTER 6

Spreading My Wings

Los Angeles Dreams

Rupert Holmes released his hit, "Escape (The Pina Colada Song)," nearly three years before I answered a personal ad and abruptly left everything in Mt. Morris, Michigan behind for Los Angeles, CA. It was the summer of 1982. The man from the ad sent me cash and a credit card to facilitate my travel. I informed my landlord I was moving out and immediately hit the road. When I got to St. Louis, Missouri, I finally mustered enough courage to call Mt. Morris and tell them I would not be returning. It was just three weeks before the school year started. I felt horrible moving without much explanation, but I had to leave. My life was in danger. But that's a story I'll share in chapter eleven.

Within two weeks of arriving in L.A., I learned that their grass was not greener. The man I went west to join was controlling. He demanded that I walk around in short shorts, leave my car keys with him at all times, and constantly update him about where I was and where I planned to go. He owned a computer store and was involved on some level with what appeared to be the mob.

One afternoon, I drove so he could pay someone a visit at their home. While I waiting in the car, I saw him take the guy's car keys and heard him loudly lambast the man, threatening his life. The violence of my boyfriend's voice and actions was overwhelming. I was still a small-towner at heart, unused to such harsh interpersonal interactions. Soon after, I stole back my car keys, left his place with my one bag of clothes, and never talked with him again.

I accessed what little money I had from my retirement account, barely enough for one month's worth of rent. To make it last longer, I decided to sleep in my car over the next month. For safety reasons, I parked at new locations daily, hoping it would decrease the chances of getting robbed. I did frequent the occasional gay bar, not sure what I would find, and hoped for something better than my current rock bottom state.

Gay bars seldom displayed signs and hid their entrances, ironically, in the back. I found their locations via word of mouth or magazine ads. From these sources, I also learned the gay community had its own version of everything from bars, restaurants, chambers of commerce, and even an world sports competitions. Gays were constantly at risk of violence wherever they went, even from the police, so it was essential to establish safe places.

Then one night, while at one of the bars, my prayers were answered. Dan, an old friend from Michigan, bumped into me and gave me the boost I needed. He let me live with him until I was back on my feet, gave me a job at the Sizzler he managed, and even introduced me to the L.A. Metropolitan Community Church (MCC) branch. Troy Perry founded the all-inclusive MCC in California in 1969. As you would expect, the MCC dealt with numerous acts of discrimination, vandalism, and uprooting in its early history. With hundreds of locations worldwide, it has become a haven for the LGBTQ+ community. Flint, Michigan, had a branch. That is where I received my first introduction to this church. I left the Pentecostal church because they took a stance of condemnation against gays, especially during the HIV epidemic.

Now that I was back on my feet, I began preparing for the necessary California State classes and the teaching exam so I could teach again. During this time, I also applied for a non-teaching job in the L.A. public school system just to get my foot in the door. I needed three letters of recommendation. Dan wrote one, and despite my having left Flint so abruptly, I was able to get fantastic letters from both Beecher and Mt. Morris High. They helped me land an L.A. public school system job as a bus supervisor.

My main assignment was riding the school bus with the students and monitoring their arrival to class. Wrestling was still my priority, even though I wasn't yet teaching in the classroom. So I volunteered at a private high school eloquently named Harvard High. I was there for one and a half years with Coach Roberts. He was an honorable man and a good coach. He even tried to secure funds to pay me, but I turned him down. I told him that wrestling had given so much to me that I felt like I had to give back.

By 1984, my life was as busy as ever. I was practicing wrestling at the high school, had joined the L.A. gay wrestling team, worked for the L.A. public schools, and still worked with Dan at Sizzler. When I frequented gay bars, I danced a lot, sweated a lot, and thought of it as a workout. I was in great shape and had the body to flaunt. I didn't squander the results of all that work. If I ever had to buy myself a second drink, it was time to go to another bar. And yes, in my mid-thirties, I was still making weight. Instead of wrestling at my college weight of 150-lbs., I was now at 180-lbs., so it wasn't as much of a struggle to maintain.

While I was on the L.A. team, we hosted wrestling meets or traveled to San Francisco, Houston, or other locations to attend them. That's where I met Kevin Elzia, my younger brother from another mother. He was on the San Francisco gay wrestling team. No phone conversation with Kevin has ever lasted less than an hour. He's a truly larger-than-life figure who tells it like it is and always has my back. Like I do for him.

My life was a lot of working hard as well as playing hard. After our wrestling meets, we would then go out to a bar or party that same night. I was living my free spirit, L.A.-adventure dream to the fullest. Some relationships were born, and I had a few flings. That all changed when I met my life partner.

It all began one night in a bar, at the pinball machine. Yes, another fortuitous night. While playing in what friends called my "charismatic" style, I hit the side of the machine with my left hip. I was eye candy, sporting tight leather pants, lining up dozens of gifted liquor shots as I played and bumped the machine. The drinks started to catch up to me, so I took a bathroom break, leaving the seven or so full shot glasses on the pinball machine to save my place.

When I returned, I saw this burly, really built man playing pinball on my machine.

"Excuse me, don't you see all these drinks and unplayed games?" I asked.

The man smiled and introduced himself. Russell was in L.A. representing the Phoenix MCC branch at their annual conference. He and a few other members had come to the bar afterward to unwind.

We continued to play pinball while the crowd in the bar grew, forcing us to squeeze closer together against the machine. When I rubbed against Russ, I felt an electric current traverse my entire body. My hair stood on end. I wanted to know more about this man. We ended up spending that evening and the next two days together, getting to know each other.

Russell was special. He was attractive, comfortable to talk to, thoughtful and caring, nonjudgmental, established in his career, and had a great smile. Oh, and did I mention attractive?

I opened up to him, wanting him to know I wasn't a barfly twinkie and that I had plans. It sounds desperate, but I actually showed him my pay stubs, the diploma for my BA in education from Olivet. Even my $2,500 bank account that I was saving to get my own place.

Being the mortgage banker he was, he commented, "You could get a house in Phoenix for that much and have money left over."

I didn't quite understand what he meant until later. I just wanted him to know that I was a good person.

The night after Russell left, he called me. For the next twenty days, we talked daily. We were infatuated with each other and decided that he would fly to L.A. We would then drive my truck to Phoenix together.

Before they would let me leave, my friends from the gay wrestling team wanted to throw me a going-away party at the pizza parlor owned by one of the team's couples. Russell and I were immediately separated by the adoring mob when we arrived. They grilled him to get an idea of his character, making sure I wasn't at risk of harm.

My teammate, John Buse, was there. He took me aside to say, "I've got you a ticket. If you get there and anything is funny, just get to the airport and give them your name."

I truly appreciated my friends but didn't share the same worry.

At the end of the evening, Russell and I drifted back together.

"Your friends are kind of possessive, aren't they?" he teased.

"What happened?"

"I thought I was gonna have to pull out my bank book to get you out of here," he said. We laughed about my friends interrogating him, said our goodbyes, and set out for the Valley of the Sun.

At Last

It was the summer of 1984 when I took that leap of faith, moving to Phoenix, Arizona, with Russell. I had no use for John Buse's backup plane ticket because every day with Russell honestly felt like a holiday. We loved each other so much that we quickly became in tune with one another's needs and wants. We were intimate and often spent the entire day in bed together.

We traveled all over the country. It was nothing for us to go to New Mexico for one night, just to eat dinner at Russell's favorite restaurant on top of the Sandia Crest Mountains. The romantic experience began before we reached the restaurant. We parked at the base of the mountain. Then, holding hands, we watched the sunset while a cable tram lifted us over a mile to the top of the peak.

I met a whole new group of friends in Arizona and felt accepted into Russell's community. When socializing, we often finished each other's sentences as if we were an old married couple. At bars, we danced and talked with other patrons without worry or fear of censure.

It was clear we were monogamous. We may not have been together long, but we had spent significant quality time with each other. We didn't argue for the first eighteen months.

That didn't stop people from hitting on me.

They'd ask, "What are you doing with Russell? He's kind of chubby."

To which I'd reply, "I love him." End of story.

⚘

Russell was the top mortgage banker at his bank. He was charming, always going above and beyond. He employed two strategies that worked for him. First, he routinely went to the DMV, introduced himself to new Arizona residents, gave them his card, and even installed their new Arizona license plates. Russell knew that, in a year or so, these new residents would be ready to buy a home. He input their information into his computer with a reminder to follow up in a year. Secondly, Russell would negotiate directly with the seller if the buyer backed out of a mortgage deal and figure out another way to make it work, often buying the house himself. He made great money, about $300,000 a year, and owned multiple properties.

We wanted the properties to look well-maintained, so we often worked on the yards together. Each of us would start at an end of the yard. When we met in the middle, Russell would often brush up against me. Immediately, that contact would cause full-body piloerection. Our reward for finishing the yard labor was spending hours in bed together as we relaxed and found elation in each other's arms.

But it wasn't all peaches and cream with regards to properties. Once, Russell and I were prevented from purchasing a house even after the sellers accepted our offer. We learned that the seller's parents were also her neighbors. When they noticed that Russell and I were a couple, they went into damage control mode, somehow got our offer overturned, and purchased the property themselves. We didn't want to create any problems for Russell's bank job, so we left it alone.

Gays, transgenders, all kinds of people buy houses. Yet narrow-minded people still push their values on anyone different. In Phoenix, through the mid-1980s, some communities still refused to show houses to Blacks or Jews. Some Homeowners' Association (HOA) bylaws included remnants of "Caucasians only" rules. Such discriminatory policies, and even state laws, known as legal anachronisms, are no longer enforced but still on the books. Despite this history, things have improved as more diverse groups moved into Mesa, Scottsdale, and other parts of the Phoenix metropolitan area.

It was different with early immigrant communities. They elected to live in neighborhoods separated by religion or nationality. Shared languages and customs made these areas comfortable, familiar, and safe. But as time went on, racial policies forced segregation of these neighborhoods. Discriminatory regulations led to increased disparities in wealth, education, and employment. These events create a complex history that deserves its own story.

⚘

I didn't have a job, which made me feel I wasn't contributing to our household. I confessed to Russell that I felt guilty about that.

He asked, "Why do you want to get a job? Why don't you work on your master's degree?"

I said, "Because my mama taught me to work."

We saw a counselor, and our sessions made me realize I could contribute in other ways. I started doing more things around the house like the laundry, waking up early with Russell so I could starch and iron his clothes, and shine his shoes before work. I know what you're thinking, a Black man shining shoes. But it wasn't like that. I did it out of love and because we were partners. My man was going to look pristine.

His colleagues noticed. One of his office coworkers asked, "Where do you get your shirts laundered?"

To which he replied, "If you marry right, you don't have to worry about laundry."

We were also more playful after counseling. One of our houses was large—three-thousand square feet—so we fooled around using the intercoms.

"Russell, honey bear, where are you?"

"Oh, I'm on the back patio." he'd say.

Being with Russell taught me so much about what makes a good relationship. I made sure to pay those lessons forward over the years.

After living an active life since youth, it was hard for me to quit work and wrestling. So despite Russell's mild and loving objection, I got two jobs. One at Pizza Hut, and the other at a group home. I also began working on my Arizona teaching certification. I remember coming home from work one day and being happy to see Russell doing barbell curls.

I smirked. "Put that barbell down. I got a barbell for you."

We laughed and embraced each other.

I ventured out more and saw there weren't many Blacks in north Phoenix. When I walked into stores, I frequently noticed customers and employees watching me. It got old fast. Sometimes I even played to their fears by hiding an item in my jacket, only to place it on a different shelf before leaving. Then when, predictably, I was stopped and searched, security didn't find the item on me.

At restaurants, waitstaff always gave Russell the check. The assumptions people made annoyed me. Even some of the gay bars Russell and I frequented didn't understand when they were racist. It was not uncommon for a bar to host a night when patrons would wear all white in the role of "innocent angels." The next night they would wear all black as "dirty devils." I confronted the owners of that bar about it.

They brushed me off. "If you don't like what we're doing here, go to another bar."

Dismayed, I quietly left. Over time, I became more vocal when I saw racism or injustice. Being more financially secure allowed my pocketbook to do the talking, or I just left the situation, a luxury I hadn't had in California or Michigan.

ॐ

I thought about my family and friends in Michigan and realized I'd been out of touch since abruptly leaving Los Angeles nearly four years ago. Aside from my mother, I talked to nobody from my past, and no one had any clue that I was gay. I really didn't know how to discuss my life with my other family or older straight friends. Russell insisted that he and I take a trip to Michigan to see them. I hesitated, but soon realized it was an important life milestone. So we made the trip nearly a month later.

We got antsy during our drive across the country and felt a stop at a gay bar would refresh us. So we stopped in Oklahoma City. Unsure where to go, we pulled up next to a local cop at a stoplight.

Russell rolled down the window in his usual flamboyant manner, and asked, "Sweetheart, can you tell us where the gay bars are?"

I was embarrassed and slightly fearful. I'd seen the movie *An Officer and a Gentleman*. There's a drill instructor's taunt in the film. "Oklahoma! Only two things come outta Oklahoma. Steers and queers. Which one are you, boy? I don't see no horns, so that narrows it down!"

The officer surprised me by giving us directions without giving us a hard time.

At the gay bar we were safe. Had we patronized a straight bar, there's a greater chance the locals would have had an issue with us.

Once we got to Michigan, we saw my mother first. She already knew I was gay. I introduced Russell as my friend.

He immediately interrupted, "No, I'm his husband."

Oh, Lord! I thought.

Big-eyed, Mama pulled out her Bible and started reading.

Over the next few days, Russell and my mother warmed up to each other. He had a solid knowledge of the Bible because, before becoming a banker, he studied it thinking he'd be a minister. The two of them discussed the Bible each evening over dinner and bonded over their shared interest.

That didn't stop her from making us sleep in separate beds.

Months after our trip east, Russell flew my mother to Arizona. He even spent time alone with her and drove her to the Grand Canyon.

When Russell planned our Michigan road trip, we added a visit with Jeff Sabin to our itinerary. I knew I had to tell Jeff and his wife early in our visit that I was gay. Otherwise, Russell was likely to grab my butt and shock them. I did not know how they would take the news. Russell was notorious for being openly gay. Trying to keep him in the closet was like trying to stuff an elephant into a picnic basket.

It was nice to see Jeff, and I was happy his family was doing well. We kept it cordial, but I could tell things were a little different now that he knew about me. When we left, I didn't know it would be a while before I talked with him again.

Jeff broke off communication with me. It saddened me to lose the connection we had. We were very close friends once, but sadly, that wasn't enough to supersede his negative feelings about my truth.

Decades later, we ran into each other at our mutual friend Jim Houston's wedding.

He put his arm around my shoulder. "Oh, come on over here. I'm gonna let you off the hook."

I thought, *Off the hook for what? For being gay?*

We didn't talk much after that because I wanted to keep things friendly. We focused on our friend's wedding. I wish Jeff and I were still friends, but he hasn't reached out since.

After that stop, I began to visit and come out to my old friends. Russell, the social butterfly, had a great time talking and interacting with everyone.

First, we visited Al and Peggy Minert. They were as loving as ever. We saw Miles as well. Miles was the exception because he knew I was gay back when I was teaching in Michigan. It was enjoyable rehashing old stories and watching him and Russell banter while we sat beside the lake.

I saw Sue Larson, now Sue Hutchings, along with a few other friends. Nervously, I choked out my truth to them, fearing how they would respond. They answered my revelation with nothing but love and relief that my prolonged absence made sense. Now they understood why I was MIA for so many years after moving to L.A. It was an emotional yet uplifting trip. I even expressed the wish to have some of my ashes spread around Olivet when I die. It was dramatic but also true. Life was going so well. I finally felt free and comfortable being myself.

The last piece of the puzzle needed to complete my life was to satisfy my burning desire for wrestling. I volunteered at schools near our home. The first was Moon Valley, with sixteen-hundred students but only five Blacks. Two of those Black students were twins and happened to be on the wrestling team. Brian Smith was the head wrestling coach. After a brief interview, he warmly welcomed me in the practice room. Brian had an entertaining habit of obsessively whistling during matches.

I also met Ed Kunect, a volunteer who had been a finalist in the Pan American Games in the early 1970s. Ed was about 130-lbs., while I now weighed around 165-lbs. He worked with the lightweight wrestlers, and I focused on the heavier-weight team members.

Not long after I returned to work, Russell purchased a house on the west side of town. When we moved, I left Moon Valley to volunteer at Apollo High School with head coach Carrol Tolleson. At practice, Tolleson would call out four or five wrestlers to work out with me in round robin matches. Occasionally I threw in some tips and taught special moves, including one that leads to a pin from the down position. It was a Midwest move I hadn't seen in Arizona. At Apollo, there were no Blacks and few Hispanics. The boys called the move "the Oreo." It was a reference to me being Black but acting White. I probably should have been offended by the name, but I appreciated their creativity. Besides, I had moves like "pee on the ceiling" and "plug the hole." Coach Tolleson was very kind to me and, at the end of the season, gave me credit for two of the boys qualifying at state.

In the 1985-86 school year, I became a volunteer coach at South Mountain High after getting wind they might soon have an open teaching spot. I soon secured the position and became an official member of the Phoenix Union High School District (PUHSD).

The original Phoenix Union High School opened in 1895 and was, at one point, the largest high school west of the Mississippi River. At that time, it was segregated and associated with its all-Black counterpart, Carver High School. Soon after the SCOTUS Brown v. The Board of Education decision in 1951, Carver closed and the district integrated.

A biology teacher turned counselor named Betty Fairfax started teaching at Carver High School in 1951. She had a fifty-seven-year career with the PUHSD before retiring in 2006, at the age of eighty-nine. In 2007, a new PUHSD school was built and named after her, an effort spearheaded by Nancy Kloss. It was quite an honor for Betty, going from teaching at the segregated Carver High to having a new high school named after her. Betty Fairfax exemplified selflessness and gave her own time and money so her students could maximize their opportunities and potential.

A quote from John Wooden, the NCAA's winningest coach, resonates with me. "You can't live a perfect day until you do something for someone who will never be able to repay you."

Also worth noting is that South Mountain High School's mascot used to be the Rebels, named after Southern soldiers during the American Civil War. Until 1985, the school displayed a Confederate flag in the gymnasium as a prop for their mascot. Regardless of how the mascot came to be, it was a very offensive sight in the gym. As assistant principal, Nancy Kloss spearheaded changing the mascot. Her efforts were not accomplished without resistance, as many of the faculty and students had grown accustomed to being the Rebels, despite not fully understanding its meaning. The demographics of South Mountain HS had shifted from predominantly White in the 1950s, to mostly Black, in the 1980s. Eventually, there was a vote. The jaguar, native to southern Arizona, became the new mascot.

The South Mountain wrestling team had a few good wrestlers, but they needed a lot of work if they were going to improve as a team. Former Olympian, Charlie Tribble, was the South Mountain head wrestling coach. Jerry McCarty coached JV. Jerry also taught history and economics and later worked with me at North after being driven out of South Mountain. To make a long story short, let's just say that Jerry was kind of like the coach Samuel L. Jackson played in the 2005 movie, *Coach Carter*. Like the legendary Carter, Jerry put his students' education above their sports participation. If their grades were inadequate, they couldn't play. That premise I deeply supported and emulated. Unfortunately, Jerry received no support from the school district or teacher's union, so he ended up leaving South.

⚭

I was still in pretty good shape from wrestling with the high school kids, so I decided to go back to L.A. to represent the L.A. gay wrestling team at the 1986 San Francisco Gay Games.

Russell and I made the trip together. While walking around the pavilions, we noticed a vendor selling designer leather pants and chaps. Russell saw me eyeing the chaps.

"Do you want a pair of those?" he said.

"I don't totally mind having them," I said sheepishly.

Before I knew it, I was on the vendor's podium, measured, and fitted for the chaps. I stayed there for a few minutes, modeling them and a few other garments. My turn on the platform was an immediate enticement for three other patrons to purchase pairs.

I did well in my wrestling matches, making it to the finals. I earned a silver medal at the 180.5-lb. class for my age group. It was competitive but, more importantly, great fun. So much so that we got Russell entered into the Heavyweight (HWT) Division for the over-thirty-five age category.

He and I practiced some moves leading up to the tournament. Despite his lack of wrestling experience, Russell won a few matches and received a gold medal. That was an impressive feat, and his name remains forever etched in the Gay Games record books.

When I returned to school, something must have been in the air because the kids were acting extremely unruly. They threw things, blew spit wads, spoke over me, fought with each other, and disobeyed instructions. I stopped teaching. The assistant principal, Mr. Jenkins, called all the parents to inform them the kids would be staying after school to finish the class.

I told the kids, "I'm a volunteer coach, and we will have class after school."

They protested, but I continued. "I will make time to speak with each of your parents."

One of the kids shouted, "My parents won't show up."

"Then I'm coming to your house!" I quickly countered.

They replied, "I have a dog!"

"Well, I have a stick!" I said, continuing to one-up them.

Afterward, many of the kids wrote me an apology letter. And students in my classes were more respectful. "Don't mess with Shegog" became a thing at South Mountain.

⁂

Art Lebowitz was another assistant principal at South Mountain. He later became the principal at Trevor Browne High School. Impressed with my after-school extracurricular activities, Lebowitz requested that I transfer to Browne, where I would teach two health classes and supervise the in-school suspension (ISS) room. I accepted and brought my brand of discipline to the ISS room. The students at Browne learned early to avoid getting sent to the ISS room at all costs.

I made any student sentenced to my room handwrite the class expectations, a five-page typed document. While they wrote, I notified their teachers and got their homework assignments. Every student had to finish their homework assignments in class so that I could check them. Students reworked any wrong answers before I approved their papers. I even made calls to parents, read ahead about incoming students, and set up new assignments for long-time ISS detainees.

One student came in on a three-day suspension and stayed with me the entire semester. His mother called and wanted him permanently assigned to ISS because she noticed his grades had improved, from Fs to all Bs and Cs. The program worked, and students improved both academically and behaviorally. It was very rewarding.

My reputation carried over into wrestling where the kids and coaches appreciated the level of my involvement. At South Mountain, and then at Trevor Browne, I continued encouraging kids and taking them to freestyle tournaments. If they couldn't pay the fee, I took care of it. If they needed transportation, I drove. Like Coach Marshall taught me, lack of money or transportation should not deter kids from participating in wrestling or any sport.

·_·· ____ ···_·

CHAPTER 7

Champions at North High School

In my second year at Trevor Browne, 1987-88, all fourteen weight classes qualified for state. We even had one state champion. Unfortunately, after two years there, I was surplused, a common and sad theme in the teaching world. I subsequently transferred to North High. I wanted to continue coaching at Browne, so at the end of each school day, I rushed to make the thirty-minute drive to their wrestling practice.

On three occasions after finishing class at North, I sped to Trevor Browne only to learn the coaches had canceled practice. I felt angry and unappreciated. A simple phone call would have been considerate of my time and energy. Why couldn't they just call me? Were the coaches trying to tell me something?

I learned from one of the Trevor Browne security guards, Barbara Peniston, that the head coach and assistant felt threatened by me. They thought I was encroaching on the head coaching job. I didn't want a repeat of what happened at Jackson NW. There, the administration bilked me out of the head coach position. I had no interest in the head coaching job at Browne, yet the staff shunned my help. I just wanted to coach the kids I had run, wrestled, and sweated with over the past two years. Sadly, I severed ties to Trevor Browne wrestling.

Where one story ends, another begins. I transitioned to North wrestling and coached there from 1988-2006. Nancy Kloss became the principal at North during this time. She probably suspected I was gay because we saw each other at a party hosted by our mutual gay friends, Glen and Charlie. Our friends both died from complications related to AIDS nearly a year later. Kloss and I never talked about it.

Nobody else at North knew my situation. I made every effort to keep it that way, with few exceptions. Outside of school, I attended pride parades to support the gay community. But at these, I kept a low profile. One of the math teachers at Alhambra High school was gay. I tried to avoid him. I had nothing against him personally, but I worried someone or something could blow my cover at any time. I feared losing my job, not for being a bad coach but solely for being gay.

There was a law in Arizona banning instruction on HIV/AIDS that portrayed homosexuality as a "positive alternative life-style" or suggested that some methods of homosexual sex are safe (that law, ARS 15-716, in effect since 1991, was repealed in 2019).

I'm not telling anyone to be homosexual. I'm telling everyone to live life the way they feel it in their heart. And if telling people "love is love" portrays an alternative lifestyle in a positive light, then I'm guilty. Unfortunately, most people in the US, in Arizona, in the PUHSD, weren't ready to accept me as I was during my time at North. The other LGBTQ+ teachers in the PUHSD were in the same boat.

I didn't want some administrator telling me I couldn't coach wrestling because the students needed protection from me. I heard rumors of faculty being denied department chair roles after word got out that they were gay. Faculty and administrators with whom I worked in committees openly spoke negatively about homosexuals, not knowing I was gay.

Did my long and committed hours in the classroom and on the wrestling mat mean nothing? I did these things because I love to educate and love the sport. Do girls need protection from their straight male soccer coach? I am not like those coaches or doctors who have made headlines for abusing their athletes. The whole idea of people needing protection from me is a fallacy. Gay and straight people alike can choose to behave decently or dishonorably. Yet those who fear anyone different seldom make that distinction. With those questions in mind, I preferred to stay under the radar and avoid any potential issues.

On many occasions, during a meet, the fathers of my wrestlers came up to me. They wanted to talk about their sons and how proud they were of the program. Sometimes they'd put their hand on my shoulder in a brotherly way. If the man was my type, a husky, older White man, it caught me off guard. Yet I always behaved appropriately and with respect. I thanked them for their kind words and moved on, explaining that I had to tend to another wrestling match. If I were a straight man, I might have had similar feelings had an attractive mother put her hand on my shoulder. The point is, a person's sexuality doesn't matter. Proper behavior IS what matters.

In the 1988-89 season, the wrestling program was woefully underdeveloped. One coach got fired for sleeping with a student. The other, Bob Perz, frequently showed up late to practice because he drove all over the valley for his T-shirt business. The program had only seven or eight kids, and we didn't achieve much success. When Perz left, I became the head coach in 1991-92. I was excited and nervous, unsure what would happen if I were to get sick from my HIV during the season.

One of the first things I did was comb through the old North yearbooks looking for wrestling alums. Klein taught me that alumni support was a huge bonus for any program. I hoped that a few alums would assist in the wrestling room, run concessions at meets, or get involved with the program in some way. At a minimum, we could take a group photo and, just maybe, they might write a check to the program. One alumni wrestler responded.

Anthony Zozaya (Coach Z) was the first to come back and assist. Coach Z wrestled and graduated from North in the spring of 1988 before serving in the Marines. With his assistance, we slowly created a bond with and within the team, bringing stability.

Even though I wasn't Coach Z's high school coach, he told another wrestler, "I wish I had had Shegog as my coach."

It was an honor to hear that sentiment.

I was the head coach but still searching for a replacement should I get sick. That's when I cornered one of our new teachers, David Smithers. I twisted his arm and begged him to take the head wrestling coaching job for the 1992-1993 season. He didn't know much about wrestling, but I assured him all he had to do was be there for the kids, and I would take care of the technique and handle the logistics for tournaments and meets. He agreed. Now it was time to build the program.

I demonstrated techniques I learned in Michigan and even adopted some of coach Klein's workouts, such as what I now called "the dreaded Shegog pushups." When I showed technique, I noticed some of the wrestlers shy away, hoping that I wouldn't call on them. I'll admit that at times, I was a little rough when showing a move. But that's only because of my passion and excitement. I wasn't sadistic or purposefully trying to inflict discomfort. And honestly, if done right, some moves do hurt a little. Nevertheless, the team was on its way to long-term stability and grounded technique.

Before I knew it, in addition to wrestling, I was involved with all kinds of programs and events. I was on committees for the North Family of Leaders (NFL), our annual Renaissance Festival, the dance department with Ms. Altemas, and the Arizona Public Schools (APS) scholarship board. Nancy Kloss saw my value as a good listener and a hard-working and thoughtful faculty member. Being a teacher and authority figure who happened to be Black allowed me to offer a perspective different from that of White teachers. She requested my involvement in many school events. I felt support similar to what I experienced at Hartland. Kloss even got me off jury duty to attend these programs.

The faculty members did a lot for the students and even took part in school performances. During intermission at one of the student dances, I organized a show with the PE faculty and Willy, our large and in charge head of security guard. We drew faces on our bellies with special ink that lit up under a black light. While applying the ink, one of the other PE teachers noticed my large nipples.

"Wow!" he yelled.

"That's my wife's favorite playground." I joked like I always did to conceal the truth about my sexuality. He had no idea I was gay. We laughed and headed for the show. The students cheered when we used our hands to move our belly flesh, creating weird expressions on the inked-on faces. And we dancers had a great time making the students laugh.

But my dancing wasn't always on-par with the Nicholas Brothers. The following year, I partnered with Coach Laura Fisher, one of my PE colleagues, for a *Saturday Night Fever*-themed duet. Part of our routine called for me to lift her immediately after she slid into the splits. I accidentally stepped on Fisher's wrap skirt and lifted her out of it. I instinctively pushed her back down as soon as I realized she wore just a leotard. The audience laughed and then cheered as I apologized to Fisher profusely. Despite my inelegance, or maybe because of it, the audience cheered. The number was a success.

I had owned the dance floors as a young adult in the gay bars, but maybe that was more liquid courage than anything else. When faculty and students approached me afterward, I told them, "Most people think all Black people can dance. Well, I can't. And I also can't play basketball."

We had fun and that's what mattered.

At North, I taught and coached at the same facility, so following up with my wrestlers was easy. Tuesdays and Thursdays, I had prep periods, allowing me time to eyeball wrestlers in their classrooms. My unscheduled visits came as a surprise to many of the kids at first. But they quickly learned that my academic and character expectations of them were serious.

I remember paying Jonathan Sarager a visit in Ms. Brahs' English class. I walked into the classroom just in time to see him bully and slap a kid. John was shamefaced as soon as he saw me standing there.

I looked at him and promised, "We'll take care of this at practice."

When he finally got to practice, I pointed at the ground. "Shegog pushups."

John shaped up after that incident as much as any energetic adolescent could. He reminded me of my old teammate, Jim Wencel. Both loved to teeter on the edge of appropriateness.

The other teachers started telling each other, "If John Sarager or any wrestler acts out, just tell Shegog, and you'll have a new kid the following day." I appreciated teachers coming to me with any issues. It saved having to do write-ups and decreased all-around behavioral and academic problems.

When I got reports about my misbehaving students, I tried to address the entire team without calling out individuals. For example, when Roger Long got caught cheating in class, I didn't discuss it with him. I addressed the entire team. Roger was very mature as a freshman and looked like a grown man. That made him very popular with the ladies, and they often did his homework for him.

After my team talk, he started doing his own homework. As expected, his grades went from As to Cs. His parents were upset and made him sleep in the garage as punishment. When I finally sat down with Roger and his parents, I expressed that his falling grades were a good sign. It meant Roger was taking responsibility for his actions and making things right. Before long, he got back on track. He remembers me telling him, "The sweetest rewards are just beyond the greatest temptation to quit."

Roger succeeded in bringing his grades up and became one of the few students to graduate from North as a four-year, three-sport athlete. He told me something very wise. "Follow your heart. If you're passionate about something, do it, and no one can stop you." He is now saving lives in New Mexico as a paramedic.

Building Acceptance for Diversity

At North High, we held a yearly North Family of Leaders (NFL) camp. This unique retreat embraced different perspectives and backgrounds. Support for diversity and inclusion was at the forefront. Students and faculty often returned from the retreat with better empathy and understanding toward their fellow students and community members. It was during my first NFL retreat, in 1991, that I opened up to Monique Mendel, Jerry McCarty, and Zita Robinson about my sexuality and that I was living with HIV. They were all loving, supportive, and empathized with me because they, too, had lived through very challenging experiences.

I even felt inspired to open up to the rest of the NFL camp but was advised against it by Jerry and Monique. They told me the people at North, and most of Arizona, weren't ready yet. Jerry, a Black man, had experienced numerous racial injustices over the years, including betrayals from people he thought were friends. Monique Mendel's parents were Holocaust survivors. She knew numerous stories of family members turned in to the Nazis by friends they believed they could trust. Jerry and Monique both told me that coming out was too big a risk. They didn't want the false sense of security fostered by the retreat to fool me.

After learning each other's stories, we shared nothing but love. It was a huge relief to have other teachers I could trust and confide in. For many years, they were the only PUHSD faculty, aside from Linda Goins, who knew my entire truth. Upon meeting my close-knit NFL group, my mother remarked, "I'm glad Robert has good friends like you."

Later, influenced by the retreat, we flew kids to L.A. to visit the Simon Wiesenthal Museum of Tolerance. We hoped that by educating them about the Holocaust and other atrocities, we could extinguish intolerance. We taught them to be upstanders instead of bystanders. Meeting people with a nonjudgmental mindset makes stereotypes insignificant and puts a person's character at the forefront.

I had come out to those few teachers at NFL but still worried about telling anyone at North. There were even a few students I suspected were gay. I wanted to talk with them and answer any questions. I understood the depth of their struggles because I was once in their shoes. The atmosphere at North felt more tolerant about sexuality and race due to the NFL retreat. But was that enough?

One student named Robbie, who wrestled for two years, was criticized for wearing a dress to school. In the old days, he'd have been considered "funny." In the 1990s, people defined him as gay. He was a natural on the wrestling mat, exhibiting great awareness and top-notch agility. I assumed that all came from his avid rollerblading background. I wanted to open up, be honest with him, console him, and tell him that certain feelings are okay. But I just couldn't let my guard down for fear I'd lose my career.

Nevertheless, Roberto, as he's now known, managed to excel. Decades after the dress incident, he mentioned that he wore it simply to see how others would react. He is very supportive of the LGBTQ+ community though not gay himself. He has a Ph.D. and is an assistant professor of learning sciences at UC Santa Cruz. Roberto told me he would have appreciated me reaching out to him that day but now understands my position.

Becky Ingram was one of the first wrestlerettes to cheer for our team. She knew I had HIV through her dad, a nurse who frequented wrestling events. During one meet, I sustained a cut to my hand. Her dad approached to treat it.

"Back off, I'll take care of the cut." I was blunt about not wanting his help.

Puzzled yet persistent, Becky's dad put on gloves and insisted it was his duty to take care of it with gauze, cleaning solution, and tape. I calmed down and let him.

Later that night, Becky and her dad had a long discussion about my reaction. He told her that he suspected I had HIV or some other blood-borne illness. So Becky knew but never told anyone. She still respected me, treated me with dignity, and understood that only hysteria would come from other people knowing. I'm still thankful for her excellent judgment and character.

Katie Curiel was another former wrestlerette who became squad captain. She was one of the first students to whom I told my truth. There was something about Katie that made it easy for me to talk about things. She is very approachable, nonjudgmental, and highly supportive. The year after she graduated high school, I told her that I was gay and had HIV. Her first response was to worry that I might be dying. But I reassured her that though I had been sick in the past, I was currently stable on my medication. It turns out she was exploring her own sexuality at the time. She later joined the LGBTQ+ community at ASU. That may explain why I felt comfortable talking to her about the truth.

Up until that time, whenever I was sick enough for people to notice, I lied or diverted their attention. I blamed my scrawniness on a non-existent diet and said I couldn't eat red meat. Or I suggested I was skinny because I ran a lot.

Then I spoke with Dr. Ken Fisher, my family doctor. He suggested that when questioned, I should ask myself four questions before answering. First, why does this person need to know? Second, what are they going to do with that information? Third, can I handle whatever they do with that information? And finally, if I couldn't answer those questions with certainty, I shouldn't share.

He and I discussed many possible social scenarios. Then he suggested that I tell curious people that I had Epstein-Barr virus.

"What's that? I asked.

"It's one of the viruses that can cause mononucleosis (mono)."

Telling people I had the Epstein-Barr virus was brilliant. Few people knew anything about it, and most didn't know how to respond. It became the conversation-ender I needed to get anyone off my HIV trail.

To treat my HIV symptoms, Dr. Fisher often put me on significant doses of steroids. I needed help with the administration of intramuscular injections. I turned to my friend Zita Robinson. Before teaching biology and the previously discussed HIV-education classes, Zita worked as a microbiologist. That gave her a better understanding of HIV than most people. Zita told me she was honored that I confided in her but concerned because she also knew that my life expectancy at the time was only one to one-and-a-half years.

We would show up to school early when it was time for the injections. To ease both our minds, right before giving me the gluteal shot, she would enthuse, "What a beautiful black butt you have." We could laugh about it, and I appreciated her dearly. After receiving my shot, I would go to the PE department as if just arriving.

The other coaches were unaware, except for one person. Before beginning the series of steroid injections, Dr. Fisher warned of possible "'roid rage," explaining that it was imperative to let someone in the PE department know what I was going through. The only person in the department I was even halfway comfortable telling was Coach Richard Curran.

Coach Curran was a deacon at his Catholic Church, accustomed to counseling couples and individuals. Knowing this, I hesitantly told him about my health and the treatment. He was receptive, true to his word, and metaphorically donned his deacon's biretta. As time went on, we shared more personal information and met each other's families. Robert Orlick, my then partner, and I went to Coach Curran's house for social events. Exchanging Christmas ornaments with his wife, Gayle, became a treasured tradition.

Curran suggested that we come up with a safe word in case the steroids sent me into a rage. We chose MICHIGAN. If necessary, he could use it in a sentence like, "Shegog! How's your mom doing in MICHIGAN?"

Curran was even more honorable than I had hoped. Sadly, in 2006, he passed from lung cancer. I am grateful for everything he did. I would not have gotten through some of my most difficult teaching times without him. We never had to use the safe word, and thank God, because I had numerous, almost routine, encounters with defiant students.

᪲

In addition to issues around sexuality, North High also dealt with racial challenges. On March 3, 1991, police officers beat Rodney King. School administrators got a tip that many students planned to take part in a walkout. Nancy Kloss made a preemptive decision to get ahead of it with a school announcement. She empathized with the students saying that she too was upset. To avoid truancy, Kloss gave the students two options. One, they could stay in class, or two, they could meet her in the auditorium to discuss the issue. Before long, the auditorium was packed. Teachers passed around a microphone to anyone who had something to say. For three hours, the students expressed their thoughts and feelings. It was extremely cathartic for both students and faculty. Then everyone went back to class. Nobody left campus. No riots or violence ensued. It was a proud day for faculty members and one of self-respect for the students.

From 1988-2006, while at North, I only had maybe two handfuls of Black kids who wrestled for me. Was there a lack of interest in wrestling amongst the Black students compared to other sports like football and basketball? Was it me?

One Black student once told me, "You get into my business."

Was I too much into their business in making sure the students were doing well in class? Was I too rigid? I felt untrustworthy because I spoke without slang and had certain expectations of them.

Another student initially thought I was a symbolic gesture to diversity. You know, a token Black teacher-coach who knew nothing about wrestling, hired only to make the school look good. That idea left the students quickly once I demonstrated my abilities not just in practice but in PE.

At North, like in Flint before, most of the Black students were unreceptive to my approach, but a few kids joined the team. Brian Manly and Adam Scott were some of the first Black students who wrestled for me at North in the early 1990s. Brian in particular was a talented wrestler and gifted student. He got a lot of crap from his friends whenever I was around.

One incident occurred when Brian and a group of friends got in trouble for causing a ruckus in the bleachers during an assembly. I walked over to his row and waved for him to come down and talk with me.

His friends teased, "Your daddy called you, better get down there."

Embarrassed, Brian stepped down.

I pulled him aside. "Not one of these friends is going to pay for you to go to college. They're not going to give you a single dime. So why are you giving them your time? You need to find someplace else to sit."

Brian protested, "But they're my friends."

"I don't care. They can be your friends. But when your friends act out, you need to separate yourself from them," I told him.

Brian had been selected as an NFL advisor his senior year but lost that role after the bleacher incident. When I didn't plead his case hard enough to Ms. Kloss, he suggested that he wouldn't be at wrestling once the season started. Eventually, he realized wrestling's importance and how short a time we all had to participate in the sport. Plus, he had unfinished business.

Brian did wrestle and got even with many opponents who had beat him in the past. He ended up being one of two North kids to qualify for state that year (Gilbert Lopez being the other). More importantly, Brian graduated from the International Baccalaureate (IB) program and attended Arizona State University (ASU). Today, he runs a successful multi-state real estate business. I am very proud of him and know how hard it must have been for him to navigate social pressures in high school.

No matter the reasons for it not happening, I still wish I had connected with more Black students, especially for wrestling. The other major ethnic groups represented the North team proportionately throughout the years. You better believe I was in their business, too, but I was probably a little harder on the Black students. My philosophy derives from the *Men of Honor* mentality that tells us that as Blacks, we can't just be as good as other people. We had better be exceptional to gain similar opportunities. Every student who wrestled knew I meant well and was there for them.

"Because Coach Shegog could, I knew I could," said one of my Black North wrestlers, Shawn Turner, after reflecting on what inspired him during his wrestling years.

I am humbled to have had such a positive impact on my wrestlers, and I continue to search for the right balance of toughness and support in my mentorship.

⚏

Even though I carefully separated my home life from my work life, I did go out and socialize with faculty from time to time. I had many friends in the English department, such as Marilyn Buehler, Suellen Brahs, Diane Escalante, and Christine Reed.

As friendships with my colleagues grew, I slowly opened up and revealed my truth. I learned that many faculty members had a devotion like mine to their students.

Marilyn had a beautiful home in north-central Phoenix. If we weren't at a bar, she often hosted parties. At one event, I learned that early in her career, she'd spent years following up with absentee children at their homes, encouraging them to improve their attendance. She saw poverty and neglect like you couldn't imagine. It was her mission to get these kids to graduation. A large number did get their diplomas as a result of her hard work, and inevitably broke their family cycle of learned helplessness, discovering a better way in the process.

I was especially close to Christine Reed. Christine was one of the most compassionate and empathetic people I met. She was the type of person who would walk into an animal shelter, ask which dog had been there the longest, and take it home. I often relied on her help with recruiting, or for transporting my wrestlers to events. She and I even encouraged her adopted son to wrestle, thinking it would help him stay out of trouble. He tried for a week but wasn't passionate about it. I applaud him for giving the sport a chance—I know it's not for everyone.

Building a Winning Team

At North, faculty members stressed that education was the critical priority. Wrestling was also important, but a privilege, the reward for good academic work. If a student became ineligible to wrestle because of poor grades, I made them do their homework during practice, in the wrestling room, adjacent to the mats in a designated desk area equipped with textbooks. This way, they could absorb some technique by proxy, regret not being on the mat, and hopefully think twice about slacking on homework in the future. I was preemptive about enforcing educational priorities and never had an administrator pull a wrestler off a bus or away from a meet like they had to do in other sports. It was my responsibility to make sure the students were not just eligible to wrestle but thriving academically.

My relationship with faculty was so good that I routinely received invitations to promote wrestling at freshman orientation. I discussed our athletic and academic success stories. These speaking opportunities led to record turnouts, and the team continued to improve. Support from the entire North community was truly the recipe for our success.

Christine Reed helped take a group of our first-year wrestlers to the Freshmen State tournament in Cottonwood, Arizona. I needed to take my partner to some healthcare appointments, so was unable to attend. The Freshmen State tournament was one of the greatest confidence-building experiences for my wrestlers. One of our wrestlers, Danny Barrera, went to Freshmen State twice. First as an eighth-grader, under the pseudonym Bam Bam Barrera, and then when he was a freshman. An extreme talent, he succeeded at Freshmen State both years, placing third and then first place.

In 1994, John Brigham came to North High to teach English. Brigham was a fit, larger-than-life figure. A Division III (DIII) college All-American at heavyweight, he finished in second place for Norwich University. David Smithers was happy to relinquish the head wrestling coach title to Brigham. That allowed Smithers to begin his tenure as head swimming/diving coach. I should note that as the swim coach, Smithers fostered numerous academic and athletic All-Americans over his more than twenty-year career. An amazing accomplishment.

I promised Brigham, as I had the coaches before him, that all he had to do was coach wrestling while I managed the logistics. Surprised, Brigham asked why I didn't want to be the head coach. I couldn't tell him the truth about my HIV diagnosis, so I lied and turned it into a joke. I told him my wife lived in California, had jungle fever, and

I needed to be there more than wrestling allowed so I could satisfy her needs. He was amused. My reputation grew in a male bravado kind of way, and more importantly, the story thwarted any suspicion about my real life.

We weren't a large team at the time Brigham joined us. Only four wrestlers came to the first practice. I instilled the work ethic and mindset that if we weren't the most experienced, we could still win if we were in better physical condition. We sure were. The team ran about three miles each day in practice, including the infamous "hospital run."

Banner Good Samaritan Medical Center, now called Banner-University, had a devilish garage stairwell. We ran from the school to the foot of the stairs. Everyone did twenty-five pushups at the bottom, ran up the six flights of stairs, did another twenty-five pushups at the top, and ran back down. We repeated this set five or ten times depending on whether we had a meet the next day. There was no need to cut any kids from wrestling—they cut themselves. We did the opposite of pushing kids off the team, encouraging them to keep going. The hospital run was hard at first. For those wrestlers who pushed through, it became as routine as walking. Years later, referring to this training and the associated mindset, Kelly Barnes coined our team slogan, "We train for overtime."

Also arriving at North in 1994, Mike Garcia taught photography and volunteered with the wrestling team.

Brigham and Garcia were young and tough themselves, Brigham a heavier weight and Garcia a lighter weight. We even used their talents to recruit wrestlers and raise money for the team. Together we had a significant influence on the program and helped foster some of North's earliest high-caliber wrestlers.

At assemblies, the team demonstrated exciting throws and other wrestling techniques. During the school's annual Shakespeare Renaissance Festival, we set up a booth with mats. Students paid a dollar to challenge either Brigham or Garcia to a takedown. If the student won, they kept the contents of the jar. We noticed some of the kids getting burned by the mats, so we discontinued the event. Phoenix isn't known for its "blistering heat" for nothing. By that time, we'd raised a few hundred dollars because not a single student won their match.

The team continued to grow to about seventeen athletes by the end of the season. More of our wrestlers qualified for state. Andrew Valenzuela, Anthony "Chief" Myhalov, and Nelson Curley were a few of the wrestlers competing at that time.

In practice, Nelson Curly always wrestled and lost to a kid named William. Before the next school year, William transferred to South Mountain, where he continued to wrestle. When we had our season meet against South, William and Nelson were matched up, yet again. This time, Nelson pulled out the victory. It felt good seeing the progressive improvement our guys had made. One of the best experiences a wrestler can have is beating someone who has beaten them in the past. This became a familiar occurrence over my years at North as our wrestlers grinded through practices, improved, persisted, and eventually succeeded.

I used to tell the kids, "Excuses are like assholes. Everyone's got one, and they all stink." Andrew "Mighty Mouse" Valenzuela had many reasons to make excuses, but he refused to give in. Andrew had fathered a son in eighth grade. His son's name is Anthony. It was not unusual to see the boy running around during our wrestling practice. To support his child, Andrew worked on construction projects and even cut palm trees at the age of sixteen. Had people known he was a minor, it might not have gone over well. Andrew also played football for two years, rocked the guitar in band class, and did freestyle wrestling during the off-season.

The team held car washes and other fundraisers so Andrew could raise money and go to freestyle nationals in Fargo, North Dakota. Ms. Kloss wrote him a check from her personal finances. Kloss and I shared a similar view about helping students get past small financial hurdles. In fact, many of the faculty at North did, making it a uniquely student-centered school. Extremely appreciative of everyone's help, Andrew went to Fargo. He didn't place at the tournament but gained experience that led him to qualify for the next Arizona State tournament. Nobody balanced life and wrestling better than he did.

Andrew wasn't the type of person who made homophobic jokes like his peers did. It wasn't unusual to hear kids say, "That's gay" or "What are you, a fag?" I overheard him shut people down when they made jokes about me in the locker room. That led me to wonder why he was so different. It all made sense when he invited me to his high school graduation party. It turned out Andrew's mother was gay. We laughed when I first found out because they had suspected that I was gay too. Apparently, they picked up on some small mannerisms I didn't even pay attention to. Andrew went on to graduate from ASU and now works in construction project management in New York City.

Andrew's wrestling room partner, Chief, had a match that made me proud. I remember his vigor during our Trevor Browne meet. He threw a headlock, took the guy straight to his back, and pinned him. It felt good, almost like vengeance for the way the school treated me nearly six years earlier.

This is why I'm here, I thought. *Let's keep taking North to higher levels.*

Brigham, Garcia, and I expanded the wrestling program to include a cheer squad called the wrestlerettes. Coach Laura Fisher agreed to sponsor the girls. Fisher was the girls' track coach. She knew nothing about wrestling but agreed to be a part of the wrestlerettes because she was inspired by my passion for the sport.

"I had never seen such passion from a coach in my thirty-two years of teaching and coaching," she said.

Teresa, daughter of Ted Faz, was one of the first wrestlerettes. She and the other girls had autonomy regarding organizing uniforms, cheers, and practices. It was a great lesson in responsibility. The wrestlerettes grew from eight girls in 1994 to over twenty by the early 2000s. In its early years, North wrestling wasn't a winning program. Our girls often took heat from the wrestlerettes of other schools like Trevor Browne. However, in the late '90s and early 2000s, our team was successful, and our girls got the upper hand in the rivalry.

Unlike the North cheer squad, also known as the spirit line, the wrestlerettes never turned anyone down based on appearance. So long as they worked hard, conducted themselves with dignity, and fulfilled all of their academic responsibilities (the same way all my wrestlers did), anybody could be a wrestlerette. Some, like Lisa Knight-Mcgrath, did go on to join the spirit line, so the relationship between the two programs was cordial.

At one of our Payson tournaments, I remember seeing an autistic girl so happy interacting with our wrestlerettes. She was there with her mother, supporting her brother who wrestled for Payson High. Our girls were kind to her, taught her our cheers, and even combed and braided her hair like she was a part of the squad. Her mom was grateful. It was a proud moment for me.

The wrestlerettes did more than just cheer for the team. They crafted posters for events, made goodie bags, and, more importantly, organized many of our fundraisers. They were the backbone of the wrestling club. Like I did with my wrestlers, I instilled the same qualities of structure, motivation, and integrity into the wrestlerettes.

🤼

Early in my career at North, kids used to challenge my authority during PE class. A few times a year, I was compelled to wrestle kids to the ground after they laid their hands on me.

One day, after class, Coach Bejarano, the department chair, commented on my appearance. "Coach Shegog, what have you been doing? Do you always grow grass in your hair?"

I said something to the effect of, "I warned them" or "I told them not to mess with me."

He replied, "I believe you can defend yourself, but if you hurt one of those kids, or one of them goes home and says, 'Coach Shegog beat me up,' you could lose your job."

I had similar discussions with Nancy Kloss. I knew losing my job was a possibility, but each time I wrestled a kid, I immediately called their parents and described how they were out of line. I conveniently omitted the wrestling part. Then when the kid arrived home, often, their parents chewed them out before they got a chance to tell their side of the story.

There was one student in particular that I fought and wrestled with almost every year, Richard Cachola. Richard was a tough kid who

144

grew up in the gang-infested central Phoenix projects. He had to be unwavering, never back down, and show no weakness just to survive. You can imagine the problem this presented toward authority. Each year he defied my PE instructions. And each year, I put him on the grass. I asked him to join the wrestling team multiple times, but he refused.

When his senior year began, he was enrolled in Coach Curran's class. Unhappy and wanting to transfer into my class, Richard asked my permission.

Knowing he had a problem with my authority, I had to know. "Richard, why do you want to be in my class? We always end up fighting."

He simply said he liked my class better.

The kid was a great athlete who wasn't afraid to bust his ass. He was tenacious in PE and ran a 6:21 mile. I told him I'd sign his transfer only if he became my captain during PE. He agreed. Then I asked him again about coming out for wrestling. This time he opened up about why he hadn't come out for the team the previous years.

Richard was one of four kids raised by a single mom, and they simply couldn't afford the wrestling shoes and other equipment. It was an all-too-common scenario for the kids on the team, and I stayed prepared.

"Not a problem," I told him. I had a bin of shoes and knee pads for circumstances like this.

I also knew Richard was taking mechanic classes at Metrotech, the PUHSD trade school affiliate. So I made him a deal. If he fixed my red Mazda B2000 truck and was able to sell it, he could keep half the proceeds. He fixed it, sold it for $1,200, and used part of his share to buy new wrestling shoes.

In his single year of wrestling, Richard did very well. He placed in a few tournaments, took second at regionals, and qualified for state, where he went 2-2.

"Coach, why didn't you make me come out for wrestling earlier?"

I just looked at him, smiled, and was proud of what he had accomplished.

After high school, Richard served in the Marines for thirteen years. When he returned from deployment, he had custody battles with his ex-wife. I wrote a letter on his behalf, vouched for his character, and strongly stated that he served his country and deserved to be with his kids. Currently, he has full custody of them. And he continues serving veterans, working at the Arizona Department of Veterans' Services (VA) in Phoenix.

He continues to defy my expectations. Now in his early forties, Richard has completed multiple marathons and is training for the Ironman triathlon, hoping to qualify for the championships in Hawaii. It's incredibly humbling and rewarding to hear Richard say that he has no doubt I changed the trajectory of his life. He commented that usually, people only help when they want something in return, yet I had never asked for anything. The only thing I ever asked from Richard, or any of my kids, is that they set goals, work hard to reach them, and continue bettering themselves. Wrestling molds your mind in a way that helps you persevere through any situation. To paraphrase sports commentator Heywood Hale Broun, it [sports] doesn't just build character, it reveals it.

Not all PE wrestling encounters with students ended favorably. I remember one student refused to leave the PE coach's office, instead, stepping up to challenge my authority. He, too, ended up face-planting on the floor.

Later that day, I spoke to his dad, telling the same story I'd told multiple times—that his kid was out of line. His other two sons wrestled for me so I assumed he would be on my side.

He said, "I understand, Coach. But don't put your hands on any of my children again."

Taken aback, I said okay, and we left it at that.

I realized I was lucky. My approach to discipline could have cost me my job. Needed a new, less aggressive plan.

From then on, at the beginning of each semester, I announced, "You may have heard rumors that if you mess with me, I will attack. It's true. Is it not true?" I pointed to a student I had whupped before to confirm.

He did.

I continued, "I'm going to ask once, maybe twice, then put my hands behind my back and take a step back. This is the sign that you're about to get your ass kicked. DON'T test me on this."

It worked. I don't know if it was because the kids feared me, respected me, or just saw that the wrestling team was winning. Maybe that made me cooler. Whatever the reason, having to wrestle kids in class became a non-issue.

Unfortunately, as was often the case, Brigham was surplused and left North early in 1995 for Chandler High. He and I saw each other at the 2000 state finals when my senior, Nick Kehagias, wrestled his senior, Robert Araiza.

It was a back and forth match. Araiza led 9-6 in the third period. Nick escaped a hold and took Araiza down in the last few seconds to tie the match, sending it to overtime. Nobody scored in the first minute, so the match went to double overtime. Finally, Nick managed to escape for the win.

My emotions were off the scales as I grabbed Nick and lifted him in the air. We both shed triumphant tears. He was the first and only North wrestler to that day to win state. Nick didn't start wrestling until his freshman year of high school. It's almost unheard of to have that kind of success after only four years of wrestling. He busted his butt in daily practice. No cutting corners during the hospital runs or mat sessions. When we demonstrated different techniques, Nick analyzed the moves and asked questions. He was always mentally playing out different match scenarios, thriving in our program.

Like many of my wrestlers, Nick grew up in a single mother household. He is the oldest of four kids, Tino being the second oldest. Their mother, Christina Garvin, worked three jobs at one point in order to provide. There's no doubt in my mind that being the oldest child, coupled with witnessing Christina's tough work ethic, translated into Nick's poised, yet relentless, performance on the mat. He wrestled with baseline anger and a chip on his shoulder. I related because I, too, come from a household run by a tough, single mother. Off the mat, Nick was a different person, very respectful, kind, and a quick wit.

The state championship was a life-changing achievement. The work we put in, four years for Nick, twelve years at North for me, was all worthwhile. Nick now knew that everything else in life would be attainable with reasonable ease. The knowledge and focus required to set and pursue challenging goals were his for life. He would go on to attend the University of Chicago before being accepted to medical school at the University of Arizona College of Medicine. Now he is a practicing anesthesiologist in Chandler, Arizona.

What we were doing in our program at North was practical and functional. We were giving our wrestlers opportunities not just to succeed but to attain high levels of achievement. Giving kids chances for new possibilities is the reason I wake up every day. Teaching them how to set a goal and bust their butt to reach it gives my work meaning. Wrestling provides an extraordinary rubric for this type of goal setting. That is why I believe it is the best sport in the world.

After the match between our wrestlers, I kept in contact with John Brigham. A few years after that tournament, he had some trouble with the law and spent several years in prison. I continued writing to him while he was incarcerated, until his release around 2019.

"Don't sweat the small stuff . . . and it's all small stuff," he would quote. He saw that I had found my purpose in wrestling. But within wrestling, he noticed my other objective, which was to help others find their own sense of relevance, their own passion.

With North now in need of a head coach, I turned to Mike Garcia and told him he had to take the head coaching job. Coach Garcia's situation was similar to mine. He was a minority authority figure, talented, and compassionate. North High, with its sixty-percent Hispanic student body, needed more role models like him.

I recited the mantra I used with the previous coaches. "All you have to do is coach. I'll take care of everything else,"

He, too, asked why I didn't want the job. Once more, I used the same wife in California jungle fever story I told Brigham. Garcia found it funny, my excuse worked again, and he became the head coach in 1995-1996. His brother Jerry assisted too. The Garcia brothers wrestled for ASU and were on the university's national championship team. Together, we further developed the skills of our wrestlers.

North High was privileged to be the location for filming a movie during the 1995-1996 season. You may have heard of it—*No One Would Tell.* Actor Fred Savage plays a high school wrestler. Fred Savage did a good job picking up some wrestling techniques with just a few practices. To bring authenticity to the film, our team members played wrestlers in numerous scenes. Some of our guys appeared as extras. In one scene, a young-looking Coach Garcia is cheering from the opposing team's bench. Gideon Richards dances during the prom scene. "Chief" and Andrew Valenzuela each wrestled Fred Savage in the film's matches. I even made it into the movie in a wrestling match scene. At least the back of my head did, as seen from the opposing coaches' corner. The whole experience was full of excitement and fun. Plus, the wrestling booster club received about $3,000 from the film company. The money went to tournament entry fees, new uniforms, and traveling expenses.

ᐧᕗᐧ

In the summer of 1996, I got horribly sick. My husband, Robert Orlick, and I didn't know if I would survive. My CD4 count was low, AIDS had set in, and I was battling Pneumocystis Jirovecii Pneumonia (PJP). I was so weak I couldn't get out of bed. Robert bathed me, fed me, helped me to the bathroom, and rolled me daily to change my sweat-soaked bed sheets. I knew exactly what he felt because I had done the same nearly eight years earlier for Russell.

As August approached, I was still in bed, with no recovery in sight. Robert suggested, "Don't you think we should call the school and tell them you won't be there? School starts in two weeks."

I had been sick twice before and rebounded, but this was the closest I had ever come to my deathbed. I started thinking about my kids, my wrestlers. They needed me. Instinct told me I needed to get better so I could make it back to wrestling practice. I was not yet broken. Faith motivated me to say to him, "No, I'll be there. I have to get back to wrestling."

To my mind, it was no accident that I was sick during the summer and not during the school year. God helped me get through this tough time in a way that protected my school responsibilities. With His help, I found a fierce resolve not just to live but to return to wrestling. I fell back on my mother's influence, picked myself up, and literally put one foot in front of the other to get back to school.

I also made a change to my HIV medication regimen. I had been on AZT since it first received approval in 1987. I switched to highly active antiretroviral therapy (HAART) medications. This triple-therapy medication, first available in 1995, was revolutionary in treating HIV, leading to reliably undetectable viral loads. Somehow, despite my improvement, I still felt I was living on borrowed time.

When school started, I was still very weak. Coach Garcia observed my emaciated condition and commented, "Coach, you look skinny. You need to eat more."

I wanted to tell him everything. That I had been sick nearly the entire summer, so weak I couldn't get out of bed on my own. Mike Garcia is a good man, but I just couldn't take the risk of losing my teaching or wrestling positions. So I just laughed a bit, like I always did to ease concerns, and told him I had been running a lot.

We picked up where we left off the previous season. Garcia took care of most of the practices while I handled team management. That included making sure my wrestlers were staying out of trouble. And there were occasional fires to put out.

One flared up when Gary Barnes got into a fight at a Wendy's restaurant drive-thru. Gary, a sixteen-year-old high school kid, beat up a twenty-seven-year-old man. When I discussed de-escalation techniques with him, all Gary could say was, "But I made him bleed, Coach."

I'll be honest. I took pride in knowing that wrestling helped Gary hold his own, but I also needed to express to him that with great wrestling ability comes great responsibility. A message similar to that iterated by Marvel's Spiderman.

Gary and I have always had a respectful relationship, even talking about such topics as religion. Gary had his introduction to wrestling through his friend Mark Lewis. Then, with far more influence than he knew he carried, Gary convinced a lot of friends, and even his brothers, to come out for the team. As an older brother, he was a leader and a strong influencer.

ㅅॢ٪

Gary is Mormon, as were many of the other kids on the team at North. I studied world religions in college and knew that Mormon doctrine banned Blacks from the priesthood until 1978.

While I admire the steadfastness and purpose in how Mormons live their beliefs, at the time I coached Gary, the church still held centuries-old racist and sexist views. It wasn't until 2013 that the

Mormon Church published significant retractions of their old religious restrictions on Black members and interracial marriages. Today, the church has locations in many African countries and has ordained many Black priests.

In addition, before 2019, Mormons prohibited children of same-sex couples from the sacrament of baptism unless, once they turned eighteen, they denounced their parents. As church sentiment shifted in recent years, church leaders revoked that stance. Change does happen, and I applaud that. Martin Luther King echoed nineteenth-century abolitionist and Unitarian minister Theodore Parker to remind us, "The arc of the moral universe is long, but it bends toward justice."

This early racist history of the Mormon Church left a bad taste in my mouth. So what does God do to test my faith? He gave me a team full of Mormons.

Thankfully, the old church views were not evident amongst my wrestlers. In fact, many of them went out of their way to prove the opposite, that they weren't racist. I like to think my mentorship helped them question some of the stereotypes created in their upbringing by setting a caring, hard-working example. For many of my wrestlers, I was one of only a handful of Black authority figures that they had.

In the 1996-1997 season, North won its first dual meet in over twenty years. I needed to get the team into tougher tournaments with more competitors to maximize their experience and improvement. We started going to more team tournaments like Deer Valley and the Rim Country Duals in Payson, Arizona. During those events, it was not uncommon for the kids to wrestle ten times in a two-day weekend. You'd think the North administration would have supported us. But in the case of competing in Payson, that was not true.

The athletic director denied approval for us to participate because the tournament was located more than fifty miles from North.

I protested, "Why did you deny the wrestling team, when the volleyball team at Central High gets to go to California and Las Vegas? We don't even need funding. The wrestling club has the funds. We just need approval."

After the third denial, I became confrontational. "If you don't approve our trip, I'm going to go to *3 On Your Side.*"

That local news show aired various citizen grievances. The threat worked, we got approval, and we were on course for more competitive matches.

Tricks of the Trade

Austin Kleon published a book titled *Steal Like an Artist*. He states that great artists will look at the work of other artists for ideas to expand their own. "Everything is built on what came before and every new idea is just a mashup or a remix of one or two previous ideas. Nothing is completely original." All success is a shared endeavor as mentors pass skills and tricks of the trade down to their protégés.

One of my most valuable tricks is that prior planning prevents poor performance. I call this the "5 Ps." Before the wrestling season started, I looked ahead in the schedule and ordered large vans in advance. Basketball coaches who hadn't planned accordingly requested that I switch for their small vans that didn't comfortably accommodate their tall players. I told them their poor planning was not my emergency.

This problem did not exist for long because my teams grew, and the vans became impractical. We started using buses.

Having a large team allowed us to weigh in two or three wrestlers per weight class. If one wrestler did not make weight, there was always a second wrestler to take their place, so we didn't have to forfeit and give six points to the other team. Gone were the days when my wrestlers won most of the individual matches only to lose the meet because of forfeits.

Another trick is that "appreciation is the cement that binds us together." I made sure to give thank you cards or gifts to supporters who went the extra mile for the team. We hosted parents and gave them booster awards at the end-of-year banquet. Involved parents or boosters received team T-shirts during the season. Parents routinely asked how they could purchase a T-shirt. My reply was that they could only earn one. They started planning their schedules around our wrestling meets and made sure to request time off work.

Each wrestling season kicked off with a family banquet where we reviewed my expectations of both students and parents. The parents received an outline of the varsity requirements, a tour of the wrestling room, and directions on where to pick up their child at the end of each practice. Good communication between the coaches and parents made it easy for them to support the team. Still, there were children whose parents never attended any of our events. When adults I didn't know arrived to pick up these wrestlers, I questioned their relationship to the child and asked to see a driver's license. My kids had to be safe.

Next to safety, academics was my primary concern for all kids involved with the team. I checked their grades not only on paper but in person. Then and now, all schools enforced a No Pass No Play policy. But some students needed encouragement to meet their responsibilities. The parents of honor students often had separate meetings with the school administrators at the start of the year. I attended these meetings and outlined my academic follow-up during the season. If their child elected to join the team, I would be an extra pair of eyes watching them.

The state of Arizona selects the team with the highest GPA in each sport to receive an academic award. North won this two years in a row. We won because I made sure all the teachers had a list of my wrestlers and asked them to contact me if there were any problems. By becoming aware of issues early, I addressed them quickly before the principal got involved. Any wrestler with no academic issues had priority for wrestling varsity, regardless of talent.

I kept copies of textbooks in the wrestling office. If a wrestler needed help, they could study during practice and receive assistance from teammates. Classmates were encouraged to help each other with the schoolwork.

At the end of practice, I would remain at school until someone had picked up every wrestler. If parents couldn't pick up their children, I delivered them. This was actually against school policy, but to me, it was more important that every wrestler return home safely. In my first meeting with parents, I made sure my driving their children was okay. If the parents were on my side, school policy was secondary. When dropping kids off, if it was dark outside or inside the home, I honked the horn until the lights came on or someone opened the door. The neighborhoods varied from extreme poverty to extreme wealth. Seeing where these kids lived helped me understand them better.

Sometimes I went into homes and saw difficult family lives. I remember giving Alfredo "Freddy" Jimenez a ride home during his sophomore year. It was late, after a wrestling meet. As we got to his house, Freddy was worried his dad was going to beat him for arriving late. Concerned, I walked into the house with him. A man started yelling from the other room.

"Is that Alfredo! Why are you home so late? I'm gonna kick your ass!"

Freddy's dad had just come back into his life after being gone for the last three years. He entered the room yelling and was moving to hit Freddy as he had often done before. Once the man saw me, he stopped.

Sternly, I explained that Freddy did nothing wrong. "We were at a wrestling meet. I'm his coach. Nobody was at the school to pick him up so, I gave him a ride home." Then I looked the man straight in the eye and threatened that if he touched Freddy again, I would be back to kick his ass and call child protective services.

Freddy's dad blurted something in Spanish that I didn't understand and went into the other room. That was the closest I ever came to fighting a parent. I'm glad cooler heads prevailed.

Freddy was an excellent wrestler. He was one match away from placing in state his senior year. After high school, he joined the Marines in the reserves, and concurrently attended ASU on a scholarship. After graduating, he became an officer in the Marines. Freddy is still a reservist in the Marines and a police officer with the Tempe Police Department.

At away meets, our team sat together in the stands. If a wrestler needed to leave that area, they had to take a buddy. If they left an away event, I expected them to sign out with a parent or family member. These rules appear extreme but are based on harsh lessons.

I once had a wrestler who stopped coming to practice. I talked to him at school but didn't contact his parents. When the season was over, we learned the wrestler's girlfriend was pregnant. He had been spending time with his girlfriend instead of wrestling practice, and no one had been aware. Now this young man had to face the responsibility of being a teen father. The only thing I could do was resolve that something like this would never happen again under my watch.

So I stayed in touch with all my parents and set rules for safety. If any wrestler needed a ride home under any circumstance, at any time, I expected them to call me. Only two wrestlers have ever used the "safe ride home" rule. I wanted to know in my heart that I had done everything possible to keep my team safe should something unfortunate occur.

During wrestling matches, rules of the sport allow two coaches in the team's corner. They shout out technique and encouragement. The wrestlers frequently picked out my voice from the cheering crowd and responded accordingly. I passed down code words from Coach Klein and even made up a few of my own. These included "Teacher! Teacher!" for the standup. "Chop! Chop!" meant to attack the near arm in top position. "Pee on the ceiling!" told the wrestler to escape using back pressure and rotate the hips toward the ceiling. "Plug the hole!" was to bump his opponent's butt with a knee and drive forward. "Find a friend" was code for discreetly getting out of bounds to restart the match. The "Scramble the eggs!" move forced the opponent's arm between their legs, then rotated the arm upward. "Wildman!" meant keep moving in any direction. Boston Celtics player Kevin McHale inspired the Wildman move with the way he swung his long arms back and forth.

A few other code phrases included, "Act like a cat!" meaning to do a body twist in the air when lifted by the opponent in order to land feet first. "Stay center!" reminded the wrestler to return to the center of the mat. That move was advantageous when opponents wrestled near the edge of the mat. Chandler High made a habit of using this strategy. By wrestling at the edge, wrestlers took shots toward the center and had a higher chance of getting a takedown. Their opponents' shots were less successful, often ending up out of bounds. Wrestling in the center took away this advantage and made the edge wrestlers appear to be stalling.

One of the wrestlers asked how the "plug the hole" move got its name. I told them the old story of how I dated the librarian in the past. I thought it would sound macho to falsely tell them that I accidentally slipped while she and I were getting it on and how she yelled, "You're plugging the wrong hole!"

They laughed with me. Now they understood the joke, and more importantly, they thought I was manly, not gay, with many sexual conquests. It was an inappropriate story to tell high school kids, but it succeeded in getting them off the track.

As wrestlers prepared for their matches, I encouraged them to warm up well, so their bodies were sweaty, loose, and they were in the right state of mind. I sometimes slapped them on the side of the head, on their head gear, to get them focused. A parent once questioned what I was doing. Before I could answer, their son enthusiastically replied that I was getting them ready to wrestle.

We were in great shape, and I wanted our opponents to feel this. I coached my wrestlers to get up quickly and run to the center if they went out of bounds. With our wrestler already waiting back at the center of the mat, it played a mind game with the opponent as they questioned their own conditioning. It also made the other wrestler look like they were stalling.

I taught my team to employ another intense mind game by taking the opponent down before the referee blew his whistle to start the match. It was a false start with no penalty other than a warning, but extremely effective in getting into their opponent's head.

After each match, I mimicked my own coaches, shoving an orange slice in my wrestler's mouth so they could not talk, only listen to my comments. In addition to talking to each one, I kept notes and worked on technique during the next practice. Just to up the head games a notch, I required each wrestler to jump rope one hundred times following their match. I observed our opponents as they watched us jump. They had to wonder how we had the energy. Our high energy and focus only emphasized that "We train for overtime."

·_·· ——— ···_·

CHAPTER 8

We Train for Overtime

My wrestlers continued to gain confidence, self-esteem, and the respect of the entire school.–Our work ethic inside the wrestling room improved.

Mark Lewis absorbed everything we taught. He set the standard for how to wrestle, workout, and run, run, run. He was so infatuated with wrestling that after practice, he ran some more. Partly because Mark didn't want to go home. Both of his parents had drinking problems, and Mark saw wrestling as his escape. As a kid, he once fought someone to protect his mom. The next day, he showed up at school with a black eye. After that, he made up his mind to be an MMA fighter. That would be his way out. Out of being responsible for putting his parents' money aside for rent or utilities. Out of worrying about being homeless. Out of the feeling of helplessness. He'd no longer have to struggle to survive.

I shared my L.A. experiences of homelessness. The conversation helped foster mutual respect.

Mark qualified to state multiple times, won a few matches, but never made it to the podium. Nevertheless, he raised the bar for teams to come.

After a few difficult years, he is doing well, living in New Mexico, producing documentary films. Mark told me he likely would not have graduated high school, let alone made it out of his twenties, had it not been for my consistent support, guidance, and mentorship. When I came out to Mark a few years after he graduated high school, he made it easy by being very supportive.

Over the next few years, Nick Kehagias, Alan Barnes, Dustin Robinson, Gideon Richards, Jared Burdick, Craig Milton, Michael Nerini, Michael Phasely, and Ruben Rico were notable state qualifiers.

Alan joined wrestling through his brother Gary. But that wasn't his only reason. Early in his freshman year, a bully poured orange juice on him. After that, he committed to lifting weights and joined the wrestling team. That freshman incident nearly repeated in his junior year when he spotted two bullies looking for their next victim. One of the kids pointed at Alan. Then Alan heard the other whisper, "No, not him. He's a wrestler."

Ruben Rico was our heavyweight and came the closest to medaling in the state in 1997. He was one match away from placing in his sophomore year, a feat that had eluded North's team throughout its history. He was very supportive when he learned I was gay.

Unlike Ruben, not all my wrestlers were initially receptive when they learned my truth. Michael Phasely and Ruben were close friends who graduated together in 1999. They had similar views except when it came to me. On this subject, it was always difficult for Ruben to have a conversation with Michael.

When Michael's father, Robert, died, I attended his funeral to pay my respects. I spoke about memories of when his sons wrestled, recognizing his moral and financial support for the team. That was the first time in fourteen years that I'd seen the family. I knew Michael and his dad had been very close, so I sent Michael a letter outlining my past experiences with loss.

> "I know what you're going through, and you're going to want to withdraw from everyone. But it's important to stay connected to your family support system."

I didn't realize it at the time, but the letter had life-changing implications.

Michael later told me if it weren't for that letter, he probably would have left Arizona and continued his depressed and reckless path. By staying in Arizona, he managed his grief, found his future wife, and started a loving family. Now he is thriving and has expressed nothing but love and support for me and my truth.

Jared Burdick, nicknamed "Ralphie" by Brigham because he resembled the kid in *A Christmas Story*, was team captain and Mark Lewis' primary practice partner. Jared, like Mark, and other wrestlers in their class, helped recruit new wrestlers.

Jared's home life was quite the opposite of Mark's. His parents, Jim and Twila Burdick, are wonderful people and were very supportive of the team. We held a postseason wrestling banquet at their house, and they continued their yearly donations to the team even after Jared went off to college.

I remember one day after practice when Jared came back into the wrestling room to grab his bag just after I had turned off the light. I wondered if he would see me.

He said, "Hey, Coach!"

I joked, "How did you see me? My eyes were closed, and my mouth shut."

We snickered about Jared's "super" vision as we left the room.

Gideon Richards, good friends with Jared, came out for the team in his sophomore year. Gideon was lean his entire time in high school, but during his junior and senior years, he amped up to lean and mean. During his Alhambra match, his opponent kept trying to flee the mat to force a restart. Gideon grabbed him by the ankle, dragged him all the way to the center of the mat, and finished the takedown. In practice, not long before, I had encouraged our guys to wrestle in the center of the mat to ensure their takedowns. It felt good seeing him take my coaching to heart. But it felt even better seeing Gideon control the match the way he did.

The team also had a manager during this time. Nicole De La Garza, now Nicole Graybill, joined the team after talking about wrestling with Coach Garcia during his photo class. Her dad, Marvin, wrestled in Iowa. Which meant she'd always had an interest in the sport. Her job entailed helping with record keeping, video recording, and other team tasks. Nicole was on point and did amazing work, fully contributing, which made my job a whole lot easier. Marvin also came to the meets and supported the team.

I was very protective of our manager because it was not uncommon for the wrestlers to be inappropriate adolescents.

"If the wrestlers ever give you a hard time, let me know." I let her know I had her back from the first day she showed up.

The team quickly learned I was serious, and it became a non-issue. Nicole was mature and ahead of the curve academically. She graduated high school in three years and is now a VA pharmacist in Phoenix.

Nicole also planned my surprise retirement party in 2006. On that day, I thought I was having dinner with Nick and Tino Kehagias. Nick picked me up and then drove to North, supposedly to pick up his brother Tino. When we arrived at the high school, a large group of old friends, colleagues, and wrestlers shouted, "SURPRISE!"

I had no idea anyone planned to celebrate my retirement. The emotion I felt that so many showed up for the gala event took me aback. All the wrestlers signed and framed a classic red North singlet. Gideon Richards signed it on the crotch, fitting for a future urologist. That cherished piece of fabric currently hangs on my wall. The party was unforgettable, and I am so thankful to Nicole for her love and thoughtfulness.

Nicole eventually passed the manager reins to Siri Ballesteros, now Siri Kirtan Hilke. In eighth grade, Siri wrestled along with Antonio Sandoval and Kelly Barnes at Osborn middle school. Her family members were influential yoga instructors in the community. She felt wrestling would be a fun and natural transition. She enjoyed the sport but didn't wrestle in high school because guy wrestlers confronted her, making negative comments. Mostly kids from other teams. Lots of guys didn't want to wrestle her because of their insecurities—the fear of "losing to a girl."

It's a shame Siri came to wrestling ahead of her time. In the years since, many girls have wrestled at North. Annette Wallace, Ashliegh May-Hall, Marrisa, Toni, and Crissy, to name a few. Now, women's wrestling has its own state tournament in Arizona. It is one of the fastest-growing women's sports in college and in the Olympics.

Annette was one of the first girls to wrestle at North. Her Junior Reserve Officers' Training Corps (JROTC) friend and wrestler, George Fulton, introduced her to our program.

"Why don't you come out?" I suggested.

Never one to shy away from a challenge, Annette joined the team. From the beginning, Annette was all in despite her parents' concern for her safety and health. She did all the hospital runs, worked hard in practice, and earned the team's respect just like anyone else who sweated and bled with us. Annette began to have success, beating many of the guys, and even placed third in the first year of girls state.

During her senior year, she had some disagreements with her mother, moved out of the house, and had to grow up fast. After graduating high school, she did cage fighting for about six months and worked odd jobs, including framing houses. Annette understood that nothing was hard. It just took persistence and pushing through until the job was done. This sounds funny, but when she gave birth to her two children, Annette described her labor in a similar way. She said, "It was uncomfortable, but I just had to literally push through until my babies were born. Kind of like with the hospital run. You just keep pushing through until you finish." Now she's fighting the good fight as a criminal lawyer in Lawrence, Kansas, home of Sam and Dean Winchester on the cult TV show *Supernatural*.

A few years after Annette's time with the team, Ashliegh wrestled for us. She was the most successful girl wrestler to come out of North. She started wrestling in junior high when our high school kids coached the younger students. In high school, she probably amassed a 0.500 record against the boys. As a result, she often had to overcome comments from other wrestlers or parents.

"You lost to that bitch!" or "She must be a dyke, or lesbian."

I recognized and understood the effect those comments could have on Ashliegh's self-esteem. She questioned whether or not it was worth it to wrestle. Eventually, she told me, "Fuck these people. I'm doing what I want."

She became a two-time Arizona state champion in women's wrestling. Today, women's wrestling has grown into a separate college and Olympic sport. Ashliegh, along with other girls at North like Kirste Brooks, Maressa Olmedo, and Toni Miserantino, just missed that boat, but they did pave the way for those who followed. American women like Tamyra Mensah-Stock and Helen Maroulis became Olympic champions. After competing in wrestling, everything else in life is easier.

At the start of the 1997 school year, the athletic director at Tempe High, where Coach Garcia was teaching, sat down with him and asked, "How much money do I have to pay you to leave North?"

It made sense for Garcia to coach at Tempe High since he was already teaching there. So he took the significant pay increase and left North. I appreciated him discussing his reasons and his decision with me.

Soon after, a local newspaper interviewed Garcia and asked why he thought he could be successful at Tempe. He referred to what he had done at North, saying that before he got there, they were nothing. I wished Garcia success but felt sad that he didn't recognize me or Brigham and the hard work we had put into the program. When Coach Garcia joined North, our program was already on the rise. He helped the program immensely. But to claim that North had nothing going for it may not have been the best choice of words.

Once again, faced with a lack of recognition for my efforts, I asked myself, *Why am I doing this?* I quickly refocused and saw that my EGO was getting in the way. EGO, also known as "Edging God Out," went against my upbringing and principles. I realized that it wasn't about me. What I most cared about was the program and the kids.

Later I found out that Coach Garcia's assistant at Tempe got tired of hearing my name in reference to how effortlessly I handled all the wrestling team's behind the scenes needs.

"I'm not Shegog!" he would protest.

That information did bring a sense of appreciation I think I needed to hear. Nevertheless, I set out to find our next Division I caliber coach. That's when Jeff Wright joined our team.

Coach Wright was the North head coach from 1997 to 2002 and fostered numerous successes. He wrestled at Cal Poly as a lighter weight, coached with ASU, and approached wrestling with a simple yet persistent modus operandi.

"Start running!" he'd yell at 2:45 p.m. sharp, the start of practice.

The kids would protest, "But, Coach, . . ."

"Start running!" he would cut them off.

Every time they tried to say anything or failed to follow his direction, he repeated, "Start running!" until they got moving.

His tactic worked. Our teams won dual meet after meet.

At the beginning of the 1998 wrestling season, the freshman football coach, ex-wrestler Greg Aniceto, brought all of his players straight to the wrestling room.

He told them, "This is where you will be now that the football season is over."

Instantly, we had twenty new wrestling recruits. Greg and I, and numerous professionals like Roddy White, wide receiver for the

Atlanta Falcons, shared the belief that the two sports complement each other.

One of the new recruits, Brandon Russ, had a real problem with authority. He challenged me in the wrestling room. Bad idea for him. Even though he probably outweighed me by fifty pounds, I took him down to the mat fast, toyed with him, and made him squeal. He learned a lesson that day and never mouthed off to me again.

Of those twenty recruits, about ten stayed and wrestled all four years. It was not uncommon for sports to support each other. Many of our wrestlers joined the cross-country, swim, or diving teams to help advance those programs.

I remember Gary Barnes, Dustin Robinson, and Alan Barnes joined the swim team to get in shape for wrestling. There was about a two-week overlap between the swimming and wrestling seasons. All three wanted to quit swimming early to start wrestling. I was against it because it wasn't fair to Coach Smithers and the swim team. It also set a bad precedent of failing to honor one's commitments. So they stayed and didn't start wrestling until after the swim season. I was proud of them for their honor and integrity.

With our increase in recruits came added team depth. With that advantage, we started winning more dual meets. I remember beating West View High School with a limited lineup because we benefited from our depth. You see, earlier that day, a bomb threat forced North High to evacuate. The campus locked down, but I grabbed as much equipment as possible on my way out.

Getting locked out of our room threw our weight-making routine for a loop. I remember Thien Nguyen stepping up. He told me he had butterflies in his stomach, but he volunteered to wrestle up a weight class. He was explosive in competition, but often at the cost of running out of steam. Not this time. With a tie match in the third period, both wrestlers were in neutral position. Thien squatted, grabbed his opponent's heels, and ripped the guy's legs out from under him to get the takedown. As a result, we beat West View, champions of their region the year before. Imagine what we could have done had our entire team competed.

From that point on, we won team tournaments, individual tournaments, even regionals. Andy Charlie, Karl McAllister, and Kelly Barnes placed at state. And Nick Kehagias won a state championship.

⚎

With success, however, came pushback and resentment from other schools. North had a reputation as a "ghetto" school, mainly due to its location in central Phoenix. But also because stuff went down on or near campus. Every year, there were school fights, mostly gang-related. There were occasional shootings and even one death. I'm not familiar with the circumstances, but in the late 1990s, a student was shot in the leg while on the city bus, just off-campus. A few years earlier, the body of another student was found, his dead fingers clutching onto the outside of the school fence. He had been shot and tried to reach safety on campus but didn't make it. It was no surprise that when we attended wrestling meets hosted by affluent schools, they often eyed us with unease.

Deer Valley High School was in a wealthy part of town. I remember overhearing a parent threaten Deer Valley wrestlerettes that if they didn't do as they were told they would have to go to North the next year. It was unfortunate that people wouldn't judge us solely on our team's skill and success.

The following year, we chose a different tournament over Deer Valley. So it came as a surprise when our athletic director, Mr. Munoz, got a call from Deer Valley's administration complaining that someone from North had spray-painted "North Rules" in one of their bathrooms.

I told Munoz it couldn't have been us since we weren't even there that year.

He called them back and took care of it. But it goes to show some of the social obstacles we faced. Honestly, it made our success that much sweeter because not only did our opponents learn to respect us, they feared us too.

Munoz used to be the coach at a rival high school, Maryvale. We weren't always allies. In fact, we almost hated each other, stemming from early arguments at seeding meetings. In 1999, I argued for one of my wrestlers, Jonathan Sarager, during the regionals seeding meeting. The criteria clearly stated that the percentage of wins ranked higher than total wins. Sarager had a ninety percent winning record, so he should have been seeded higher than Munoz's Maryvale wrestler.

I said, "I don't even know why we're spending time on this. The record of 9-1 has a higher winning percentage than 25-10. The simplest person can understand that."

Munoz yelled, "Are you calling me stupid?"

I just left the debate at that. Sarager got the higher seed. Later in the tournament, Sarager got to wrestle the Maryvale guy. Right before the match, Sarager wanted me to slap him in the face to pump him up. I was pumped up too but started thinking how it would look to the crowd.

"Hit me, Shegog!" he yelled. Sensing my hesitation, he yelled louder, again, and again, "Hit me, Shegog! Hit me, Shegog!"

So I slapped his headgear. He went out there and won decisively over Munoz's wrestler. It was poetic justice.

Jonathan Sarager is now a successful lawyer working in Washington D.C. He has worked with important political figures like Jeff Flake. The tough, energetic, and headstrong teenager has done pretty well for himself. I like to think that wrestling played at least a small role.

It was the following year, 2000, when Munoz became the athletic director at North High. I feared I'd run into roadblocks from him, but he was extremely supportive. Every year I gave him a box of itemized receipts for purchases I had made for my students or the wrestling team. In fact, my wallet, which I kept in my back pocket, was so thick from these receipts that it started causing me back problems. After some time, Munoz trusted me to the point that he said, "Shegog, just give me the number."

He signed off on all my tax-deductible receipts, on my tournament preferences, wrote letters of recommendations for some of my graduating seniors, and even suggested that other coaches talk to me for advice on growing a successful program. I give him credit for his support and for putting the kids first.

꙳

For the longest time, the North High team was considered the "whupping boy" in the Arizona wrestling world. Now we had kids and coaches asking during tournaments, "Is Ruben here?"

Ruben was our heavyweight. He made a name for himself by being one match away from placing in state. He was the nicest kid, yet his outward appearance as our muscular heavyweight was intimidating.

I often wrestled him in practice to push him so he could improve. Eventually, his size caught up to me, and I ended up breaking one of my ribs. I have calcification on my right rib cage to this day. I didn't want to admit it, but my age was slowly catching up to me. I was nearly fifty years old at the time.

Despite my injury, I got back out there and continued showing technique in a slightly curtailed fashion. I demonstrated one move called the treetop. When a wrestler has an opponent's leg in the air, he can rise onto his tippy toes and pull the leg high and away from the opponent's body. This removes the other wrestler's ability to maintain balance against the momentum, resulting in the opponent falling onto the mat for the takedown. Many of the wrestlers doubted it would actually work. Just one week later, at the Apache Junction Tournament, it proved its effectiveness.

Tino Kehagias, a sophomore at the time, made it to the finals of the Apache Junction tournament. He was scheduled to wrestle a kid from Queen Creek High who had beaten him earlier that tournament and who ranked fifth in the state for the 2A Division. Tino had the guy's leg in the air, lifted it up and away like a natural treetop, and flopped his opponent to the mat for the takedown. It was an awesome moment and a big confidence booster for him. That was the first time he had bested someone ranked in state, and the first time he had defeated someone who had beaten him previously. I looked at the kids and said, "See, it does work."

We were also lucky during the 2000 season to have a young, energetic coach named Richard Fimbres join the team. Richard was working as a security guard at North when he happened to see my wrestling shirt. We started talking about wrestling. I learned he was a two-time Arizona state placer from Marcos De Niza High School in Tempe. I invited him into the practice room. From day one, he brought an extra intensity. Our practices were crisper, harder, and more active. I saw the kids improving their skills on a daily basis.

Unfortunately, Richard was coaching our practices while technically on duty as the evening security guard. The administration told him he had to stop coaching if he wanted to keep his job. School administrators did not understand what a gem he was to our program. In protest, our team ran to the office, expressed their support for Richard, and asked that he continue coaching us. But the team's appeal didn't work out. There was just too much liability should something happen on campus while he practiced with the team.

Richard's time at North was short-lived but still instrumental to the team's growing success. The season ended with North reaching eleventh place, the highest we ever finished in state. Nick Kehagias' state championship and Andy Charlie's state runner-up bolstered the team's successful year.

The following season, Richard went on to coach at Maryvale, where his training efforts came to fruition. Maryvale produced numerous state placers, state champions, world placers, world champions, UFC fighters, UFC champions, and even an Olympic gold medalist.

The Cejudo brothers were among them. Angel Cejudo was a four-time Arizona state champion, undefeated except for an injury default to Antonio Sandoval. You may have heard of Angel's younger brother Henry—he became an Olympic gold medalist and UFC champion at not just one, but two weight classes. Truly unique and impressive.

To this day, Richard thanks me and says he would not have accomplished all he did had I not given him the early opportunity to coach at North. His path to success illustrates how when someone believes in a person, it gives them confidence. He and I have a lot in common in that sense and shared similar goals.

When he learned my story, Richard was nothing but supportive. We have deep respect for each other. I thank him for his kind words and am happy to have had the chance to work with him. Anyone who coaches needs to be a good teacher and student because there's always something new to learn and add to your repertoire. It's not the "my way or the highway" but the "our way" mentality that is most effective.

⚜

In 2001, coaches came up to me asking, "Where's Andy Charlie? I don't see his name on the tournament bracket." A junior the previous year, Andy finished second in state in the 119-lb. weight class.

Without exaggeration, it was one of my proudest coaching moments when I confidently answered, "He didn't make our team."

The look of terror in the coaches' eyes pleased me, making me excited to see exactly how good our team was and what it could do. Andy didn't make the team because, wrestling at 125-lbs., he lost a wrestle-off to Kenny McAllister. Then he lost again in the best of three. Finally, he lost for the third time in a best of five. Kenny, a junior, was busting his butt day in and day out, running every morning before school started, getting in better shape, and sharpening his technique. Andy, on the other hand, was missing practice and not being a good teammate. And still, Coach Wright let Andy wrestle the varsity spot when we had meets. This irked me to the core and went against everything I believed.

When finally given the opportunity to wrestle-off, it was no surprise Kenny beat the previous year's state runner-up convincingly not once, not twice, but three times. After that, Andy quit the team. Sadly, I lost contact with him. I heard a rumor he had gotten into some kind of trouble with the law but can't be certain of that information.

Also during this time, arguably one of the most knowledgeable wrestlers North ever had, Antonio Sandoval, claimed the 119-lbs. weight class. Antonio attended his first North wrestling practice as an eighth-grader, coming with Kelly Barnes after Osborn Middle School's daily wrestling practice. He fell in love with the sport. Even if he lost a match, if Antonio got a good slam on his opponent, it was a win in his mind.

I remember handing Antonio his PE uniform on the first day of his freshman year. He was barely thirteen when I asked if he planned on going out for any sports. When he said wrestling, my eyes lit up, and I gave him all the necessary information. Antonio weighed a mere eighty-eight pounds because he had skipped two grades. His small size concerned his mother and she was against him wrestling in high school. Antonio pleaded with her. I met with her and guaranteed that I would look out for him like I did with all my wrestlers. She agreed, so long as he maintained at least a C average GPA. That was never an issue with Antonio.

His first varsity match was against Trevor Browne. We could tell he was excited and nervous. Freddy told Antonio that his Trevor opponent had lost a match to a guy Antonio already beat while on JV. Now with an extra sense of confidence, Antonio started the match fearlessly. He took the guy down, wrestled well, and only lost by a few points. It turned out that his opponent was not a beginner but ranked in the top ten in the state. Freddy fibbed, but scoring points in his first match made Antonio realize he could compete. He was on his way to mastering the mental component of the sport.

Antonio was one of the few North wrestlers who did freestyle wrestling in the off-season. In the beginning, he went to freestyle events and just watched. Coach Garcia, who wasn't at North anymore but attended the events, noticed Antonio's presence and asked why he wasn't out there wrestling. Antonio didn't have the required USA wrestling card because he couldn't afford it. Realizing the small barrier to entry, Coach Garcia purchased one for him, and immediately Antonio was on the mat competing.

Together with Coach Wright, we showed him technique and drove him to numerous tournaments.

"Do it right, do it slight. Do it wrong, do it long," I told Antonio at practice.

I opened the wrestling room and grabbed two kids from PE class for him to practice with in order to lose weight. One of those students, a freshman, was John Espinoza (now called John Moraga after adopting his presumed biological father's name). John had no wrestling experience, yet he had a spark, and gave Antonio a challenge. I could tell he would be something special. John came out for wrestling for the first time the following year.

The work paid off. Antonio earned a spot on the Arizona National Freestyle team. The following summer, he received invitations to compete in Hawaii and New Zealand. We held a parking lot fundraiser at North for Antonio to raise money for the trip. He was so excited and motivated that he sold his bed, stereo, and other personal belongings. After a few weeks, he had enough money to attend the competitions. Sleeping on the floor was a small price to pay. Antonio became the New Zealand North Island Champion.

During his junior year, Antonio qualified for state but was unable to place. In his senior year, he captained the team and was a man on a mission at the 119-lb. weight class. Early in his senior season, he wrestled a phenom from Maryvale named Angel Cejudo. Despite being a freshman, Angel was one of the top-ranked wrestlers in the state. Antonio led by two points in the final period when Angel had to injury default, giving Antonio the win. This match ended up being the only loss in Angel's four-year high school career, as he went on to be a four-time Arizona state champion.

Regionals, unfortunately, was where Antonio's season ended. He led 10-0 against Yuma before dislocating his elbow. An ambulance was called. The EMTs gave him morphine before Ted Faz followed the ambulance to the hospital with our school van.

Medical staff had to hold Antonio down. Realization of the seriousness of the injury, the physical pain, and the emotional culmination of four years of blood, sweat, and tears grew overwhelming. Reality hit, and Antonio started crying. He wanted to go back, wanted to wrestle, and was heartbroken that he wasn't going to state. He knew his career was over.

Ted cried too. I vividly remember Ted telling me they couldn't get ahold of Antonio's parents. So he called Kloss for permission to sign the consent for elbow surgery.

After the procedure, Antonio and Ted were exhausted. By then, it was ten at night. Neither had eaten all day. They stopped at McDonald's before Ted took Antonio home. McDonald's must have never tasted so good.

Antonio wrestled and placed on the international stage but never quite accomplished what he had hoped here at home. Nevertheless, he was one of North's most technical wrestlers, young in age but mature in mind and soul.

Antonio and Kelly were both products of Osborn Middle School wrestling. To further North's success, I knew we needed to increase our efforts in building more local middle school programs. I took my wrestlers (Kelly, Karl, Kenny, Tino, Rafael, and Zotero, in particular) to hold wrestling practice at Osborn, Longview, Clarendon, and Monticello middle schools two days a week for four weeks. I even recruited and paid middle school teachers to stay on campus and supervise. At the end of the four weeks, we held a middle school tournament at North High. It was a happy success. Some of the middle school kids, like Dominic Palomino, eventually came to North for high school. Others went to Central High or other schools. One kid named Seth, whom Tino had mentored and coached, joined some of our wrestlers, including Said Martinez, at wrestling camps. Both would go on to place at the high school state tournament.

All along, Coach Wright and I had frequently argued about the team's direction. I began to cede a lot of decisions because my partner Robert Orlick was struggling with complications from HIV. Even some of the wrestlers noticed the conflict. One in particular, John Moraga, a junior, asked me as I drove him home, "Coach, are you going to be at North next year?"

I had an honest conversation with him about Coach Wright, omitting what I was going through regarding my partner. I couldn't confirm that I would be at North the following year.

John said, "If you're not at North, then I'm going to go to Maryvale next year."

I told him that I wished he wouldn't do that. Ultimately though, I couldn't control what he did. He did go to Maryvale for his senior year, 2001-2002. It was a big loss for us.

Despite wrestlers leaving, despite my disagreements with Coach Wright, and despite my partner's declining health, the 2001-2002 wrestling season was the best North ever had. We had two returning state placers, Karl McAllister and Kelly Barnes, and most of the starters were four-year seniors. We won every dual meet and tournament that year. And it wasn't just our seniors carrying the weight of the team.

Before the 2002 Payson team tournament, our 171-pounder got injured. I pulled Jeremy Taliman, a freshman, out of class to take his place. Jeremy started wrestling in sixth grade at Osborn Middle School. Jeremy also competed in freestyle and Greco. He was the next most technical wrestler North ever had after Antonio. He'd been around the sport since 1993 when his brother Jeff was on our team.

We made it to the finals where we went up against Payson High. It was a tough dual, and we were down by three points with one match remaining. The 171-lb. match. It all came down to Jeremy. Even though he was a freshman, Jeremy wrestled like a stud and pinned his opponent. We were Rim Country Dual champions for the first time since we started going to Payson nearly six years earlier. It was an amazing feeling. I was overjoyed to see how far we had come. We were a team built from the ground up and our hard work was paying off.

Then came regionals. After eight months of failing health, Robert passed away in February of 2002, right when the regional wrestling tournament was getting underway. Some of the wrestlers noticed that I wasn't at practice and I could not tell them why. I was emotionally unavailable right when they needed me most. The team felt the mental exhaustion of four years of wrestling, grinding, running, and cutting weight. A few of the wrestlers noted that the attitude in the room was different—less intense, less focused, and less fun. I mean, just the year before, the kids were doing things like growing out mullets and having fun together during the season (Kenny had an especially great mullet).

Finally, the pressure became too much. That's when Coach Wright let the wrestlers move up a weight class for regionals. As a team, they didn't want anyone getting bumped out of the lineup. Almost all agreed to move up a weight class. Kelly Barnes was the last holdout. He had cut down from over two hundred pounds before the season to the 145-lb. weight class. He ran before school, during school in a special PE class I helped arrange for him, and again after practice. He had put in the work and felt others needed to do their share for the team too.

I agreed with Kelly. Unfortunately, I couldn't sufficiently defend my position because my partner needed me at home. Someone then pointed out to Kelly that Alex Pavlenko, the 152-pounder from Marcos De Niza High, was the phenom to beat. After much thought, Kelly accepted the challenge and changed his mind to move up to 152-lbs. so he could face Pavlenko. That paved the way for the rest of the team to move up. Even though I disagreed with the policy, I couldn't help but notice that it was this same attitude of team support that made them one of the best teams in the state. They truly cared for each other. The value of that level of connection often gets overlooked in team sports. Winning is important, that's the main goal when we compete, but we cannot lose ourselves or our souls in the process.

Despite having everyone compete in heavier weight classes, North won regionals, beat Maryvale, and qualified most of the team to state. Notable state qualifiers include Justin Makekau, Rafael Amavizca, Kenny McAllister, Tino Kehagias, Karl McAllister, Shawn Turner, Kelly Barnes, Chris Hightower, and Nathan Phasely. Unfortunately, North didn't have the same success at the state tournament. Moving wrestlers up a weight class thinned out the team. They were unable to place anyone. Kelly got injured two days before state. He won a state match but never placed. He never got to face Pavlenko.

In contrast, Maryvale finished fourth in state that year. John Moraga, the ex-North wrestler, was a state champion at 112-lbs. He went on to wrestle for ASU and then fight in the Ultimate Fighting Championships (UFC). While in the UFC, he battled for the title, only to lose to Demetrious Johnson.

In 2002, the North wrestling team was the best we ever had. I couldn't be with my wrestlers like in years past, and that saddened me. At the time, only a handful of people knew that Robert Orlick died. Dr. Fisher called me the Black Widow. It was in good humor, but I was not in good spirits. I yearned for a life-long partner but feared that was not in the cards for me.

The wrestlers thought Robert was my roommate and knew nothing about his passing. Not only could I not share the truth with my athletes, but many of them laid heavy criticism on me for what was happening with the team.

"Why didn't you stop Coach Wright from moving us up in weight? Wasn't that a questionable coaching decision on your part?"

Coach Wright had his own domestic problems during the 2002 season and even apologized to Kelly Barnes years later for seeming disconnected.

Sometimes life pulled me in more directions than I could manage. I'm sorry I couldn't be there for my wrestlers. I did the best I could.

As my wrestlers learned the truth over the years, they comforted me with their supportive responses. They tell me they knew in their hearts that I never gave up on them. That I did support them and did kick them in the butt when they needed it. They often wondered how I managed to spend so much time on them and on everything I needed to attend to in my home with only twenty-four hours in the day. Others asked how I managed to fulfill my dream to coach wrestling under the shadow of my real life. Well, the 2002 season revealed it wasn't without cost. Sometimes having to wrestle with the truth leads to compromising other things in life. Talent doesn't reach its full potential. Opportunities are sometimes lost. I did what I could and hope that others who walk a similar path in the future have more freedom to be open while devoting themselves to their passions.

As the 2002 season ended, the time came for the seniors to transition to college or their next step in life. Some needed more push than others. Rafael Amavizca was undecided about college. Actually, he hadn't thought about it at all. He had excellent grades so I presented him with the Cox Communications scholarship application form. Anyone pursuing study in a health-related field was eligible for $4,000. I knew Rafael was interested in nutrition because he and his brother Zotero studied my food booklet. I distributed it to my wrestlers to help with dieting and losing weight. Rafael lost a lot of weight to make 119-lbs.

The day before it was due, I asked him, "Did you fill out the application?"

"No," he said, seeming somewhat ashamed he may have disappointed me.

"Well, why don't you fill it out tonight, and I'll turn it in for you tomorrow."

He agreed, worked on it all night, handed it to me the next day, and I mailed it for him.

A few weeks later, he discovered he'd been selected for the scholarship. Now Rafael had a scholarship but hadn't even applied to a college yet. So he scrambled, applied to ASU, and was accepted.

Today, Rafael is a nutrition specialist for the healthcare industry. He also coached wrestling at a local San Diego high school for the five years leading up to the COVID-19 pandemic. His brother Zotero is a master farmer in Tucson. Another set of siblings raised by a single mom, Rafael and Zotero were the first in their family to graduate from college. I am so proud of them. Their accomplishments and their dedication to their communities inspire me.

Coach Wright left North after the 2002 season. Coaches came and went over the next few years, but none had a significant wrestling background. Crucial help came from the many young alums who began to pop into practice and devote a significant amount of time back to the team. This growing tradition started in the mid-'90s with Anthony Zozaya (Coach Z). The trend really took off with Kelly Barnes, Tino Kehagias, and Karl McAllister. The three were in college but dedicated time to attend most of our high school practices and keep North competitive.

Kelly Barnes was unique in this regard. Aside from myself, a part of North wrestling from 1988-2006, Kelly would spend the most time with the North program. He first attended a North practice in 1994 as a fifth-grader, accompanying his older brother Gary.

During wrestling in seventh and eighth grade, Kelly ran his middle school wrestling practices at Osborn, then afterward attended our

North practices. When he reached high school, he wrestled for North all four years. He played a huge part in our team's success during his senior year in 2002. After graduating high school, he came back and coached at North from 2003 to 2016. Kelly only missed two years— to go on his Mormon mission to the Philippines. He and I talked often and I advised him about coaching and planning. I thank him for his selfless dedication and service to North even after I retired. Kelly continues to serve our community as a sergeant in the Phoenix Police Department.

One younger wrestler, Ryan Gustafson, was a sophomore during the 2001-2002 North dream team. When he joined the team in his freshman year, he introduced himself as "G-Man." Karl, a junior at the time, turned it around and started calling him "G-Spot." The name stuck. Our wrestlerettes made a big "Go, G-SPOT" banner. When he wrestled, we hollered, "Come on, G-Spot!"

I had to refrain from laughing when I explained that the team couldn't use that nickname or the cheer when spectators packed the gym.

For Ryan and many other White students, I was the first Black adult mentor they encountered. Although my skin color drew their attention at first, as time went on, it was an afterthought. All they saw was the dedication, integrity, and fairness reflected by any role model coach.

I remember telling Ryan that there is a difference between being injured and being hurt. An injury needs time to heal, but you can work through being hurt. That applies mentally as well.

Many would say that I was often hurt as I dealt with my HIV, the death of my partners, and hearing insensitive comments from my friends who were in the dark about my life. If I wanted to work with my passion, I had to push through mental and physical hurt. Wrestling was my bandage, helping me work past the emotional wounds.

By Ryan's senior year, in 2003-2004, he was lean, mean, and qualified for state. He had grown to over six feet tall. That meant he needed to learn different techniques for his lankier body type. I helped teach him leg riding. Unfortunately, at state, he ran into nationally renowned Alex Pavlenko from Marcos De Niza high school. You know, the same guy Kelly had hoped to challenge two years earlier. Only now, as an upperclassman, Pavlenko had more experience. Ryan lost and ended up finishing just out of the medal round.

Ryan went on to great academic achievement, studying chemistry at the U.S. Air Force Academy. While there, he scored among the highest on his fitness exam, top five out of fifteen-hundred students. Thanks to grinding out four years on the mat, Ryan and many of my other athletes would admit that their future successes were no doubt a result of lessons garnered from wrestling. He is now a dentist and blessed with a beautiful family.

People at North, and the entire wrestling community in Arizona, were watching us, even if we weren't fully aware of it. One day in class, a kid looked me up online and blurted out, "Robert Shegog! You're gay!"

My mind went blank for a moment. *Oh no, this could be bad.*

"What makes you think that?" I asked.

"You placed silver at the 1986 Gay Games." He was right, but I couldn't come out to my class.

So I replied, "Do you know how many Robert Shegogs there are?" Which is true. Googling my name brings up dozens, probably hundreds of Robert Shegogs. Then I looked away, continued with my lesson plan, and nobody pressed the issue. I was good at diverting people away from my truth, still needing to maintain the status quo.

⚕

On the wrestling side of my life, we were winning and doing it in an honorable way. Our track record motivated more and more kids to come out for wrestling and inspired teachers to talk to their parents and students about wrestling. Wrestling was more than a sport. It was a place where students strove for more. As a team, we supported each other, bled, sweated, and sometimes cried together in glory and defeat. We were a family.

In 2003, I started taking North kids to Prescott for a wrestling retreat. We had plenty of room at our house for the kids to camp out in the living room. Many of our wrestlers grew up in central Phoenix, in a rough area known as the "Barrio." Prescott was unfamiliar to them, and some kids had a hard time sleeping the first night.

I asked, "Why can't you guys go to sleep?"

One answered, "Because it's too quiet. There are no gunshots."

It was a startling reminder of where these kids came from and how vital wrestling can and will be for them.

During the retreat, I passed out Mitch Clark's book *Make It Happen*. Mitch was an Ohio State NCAA champion. His story confirmed for my wrestlers that great things happen by growing out of failures and hardships. These kids had everything to gain, and it was my pleasure to use wrestling as the tool that would teach them these important lessons.

There were also incredible off-the-mat success stories with my wrestlers. Zeke Gutierrez was a junior but only had sophomore-level credits. He had not focused on his studies because he was "chasing all the girls," as he put it. I sat down with him to come up with a plan. We decided he would take a full schedule. In addition, he would sometimes leave practice early for after-school classes. Then I made him a teaching assistant (TA), which helped him earn a credit and provided extra study for his classes. Finally, he took summer classes.

By the end of his senior year, Zeke had earned enough credits to graduate. He made it to state as a wrestler, but most importantly, he made it to graduation. A much higher honor in my book. I am proud of the mature man Zeke has become. He runs his own construction business and, best of all, is raising a loving family.

In January of 2004, Tino Kehagias and I flew to Pennsylvania to watch his brother Nick wrestle in the national duals team tournament. Nick was an All-American the year before. He'd finished eighth in the nation at 125-lbs and was looking to improve on that record. He lost his first match by seven points, then won his next three matches by one point each, going 3-1 for the tournament. Later, I learned that just two days before this tournament, Nick tore his lateral collateral ligament (LCL) in a dual meet. This ligament connects the thigh bone to the lower leg, preventing the knee from bending outward. Any tear in the tissue destabilizes the leg and triggers pain and swelling. Nick realized after his first match that he couldn't spring off his left leg like normal. He had to wrestle his next matches very conservatively, hence the low scores. Nick was so happy we had come to watch him that he didn't want to disappoint us. Impossible. I was already more proud of him than he could imagine.

The three of us went to Arby's after the tournament. That's where I told Nick and Tino the truth. I told them I was gay and had lived with HIV since 1986. They hugged me and told me they felt honored that I was comfortable telling them the truth. They also laughed a little because some things now made sense. Such as, when they called me and heard Robert on my answering machine, "This is Robert Orlick. Please leave a message."

They also apologized for their and others' past insensitive gestures and thoughtless comments. For example, wrestlers often made fun of said Robert Orlick recording. During wrestling practice, they'd sarcastically ask, "Coach, who's Robert Orlick? Your gay lover?" I would numbly laugh it off like I learned to do over the years and falsely assert that Robert was my roommate. Nick and Tino showed love and self-reflection because they knew they could be better than how they grew up. It felt good knowing that more of my ex-wrestlers supported me.

🤼

In 2004-2005, North's team enjoyed a resurgence. Jeff Warmath was the head coach. A state runner-up in Alaska, he was energetic and knowledgeable. Kelly continued to coach the team until he had to leave mid-season for his Mormon mission to the Philippines. Tino also continued coaching while balancing his demanding ASU schedule. As a bonus, Nick had just graduated from the University of Chicago and was looking to give back to the team.

North had about ten seniors hungry for glory. They were experienced and even cocky at times, posing for the camera while holding their opponents in pinning moves. I knew that I had to reel the team back to focus.

I told them, "You guys are good, but you're each doing your own thing. You're not acting like you're leaders."

It was a reality check that motivated the team to be better. As a result, they started to mesh, primed for success rivaling the 2002 class. We won numerous tournaments as a team, won regionals, and qualified wrestlers in, if memory serves, eleven out of fourteen state weight classes. Notable wrestlers who qualified for state include Joe Kuczora, Adam Galgamez, Danny Barrera, Adam Banda, Eric Sanchez, Jeremy Taliman, Jonny Barnes, and Luis Rivera.

Although many of the seniors took part in captain tasks, Adam Banda set the tone for the team. Over his four years, Adam wrestled at North, transferred to Maryvale, and then transferred back to North for his senior year. Kind of opposite to John Moraga's move three years prior. Adam excelled at wrestling on his feet, a fit specimen with unmatched endurance and mental strength that allowed no room for butterflies as he sought out challenging opponents. His efforts led to the entire team toughening up, which made North an exciting team to watch heading into state.

North placed three wrestlers during the state tournament, more than in any of its prior seasons. Adam Banda finished third, Eric Sanchez fourth, and Jonny Barnes took sixth place. Jeremy Taliman was one match away from placing at state. An impressive feat since he was battling a fever and a shoulder injury. Joe Kuczora was also one match away from placing. Some time later, I introduced Joe to Embry-Riddle Aeronautical University in Prescott, where he wrestled and graduated as an electrical engineer.

Adam had one of the greatest matches I ever saw in the All-State round. In that round, the winner is guaranteed a medal. The possibility of carrying home that prize usually results in a higher level of wrestling.

Adam's opponent was a tough kid from Dobson High. It was back and forth with nobody getting a takedown in the first period. Then Adam picked the down position, escaped, and went up 1-0. At the beginning of the third period, the Dobson opponent picked the down position. Adam's mental game was brutally tough and crushing when he was on top. Constantly grinding, Adam worked to turn his opponent. His opponent fought with everything he had and got to his feet, knowing that a single escape would tie the match. Adam squeezed harder, used excellent technique to lift his opponent, and with a combination of grace and force, slammed his opponent to the mat. There were no calls for stalling, no warnings, and Adam won 1-0 through pure grit, determination, and will. He was in the semifinals, guaranteed a medal.

Adam lost his next match in the semifinals to a three-time runner-up (I believe), Kareem Abdullah. If he had faced Kareem earlier that year, Adam would have had the confidence to beat him. Nevertheless, he roared back and eventually took third place in the state—the sign of a true champion. I'll never forget his spirit. And now I've preserved that indomitable heart in this book.

Eric Sanchez was 34-0 heading into the state tournament and attained the number one seed. He was kind of like Rocky Balboa during the entire season. He routinely chose down position in matches. His opponents used up all their energy wrestling him, then Eric hit them with an unexpected throw from the neutral position for the win. The Jaurequi throw.

Eric learned this move from an older Maryvale wrestler named Gabe Jaurequi. Gabe even used it on Eric once in a match. By his senior year, Eric had perfected it. Using this throw, his opponents ended up on their backs in the third period, too tired to mount a significant fight. Eric pulled out many wins by pin despite being behind by points.

Battling tougher opponents in the state tournament and dealing with mounting shoulder injuries, Eric had a harder time executing his throws because his opponents were studying him and making adjustments. He went on to finish fourth place, a proud accomplishment. Eric proved that specializing in one move can get a wrestler so far, but as the level of competition increases, it is essential to have an expanded repertoire.

Jonny Barnes had lost to his Deer Valley opponent during the season and was now losing to him again in the All-State match at state. From the top position in the third period, Jonny used the Superman move while riding legs. He wound up, jumped forward, and willed his opponent onto his back. Jonny held him there for the pin, securing a state medal. It was an exciting competition—one of my proudest moments as a coach.

It was only a few years earlier that I had nudged him in class when he was acting like a goofball.

I told him, "Look at me. You're the youngest in your family. Your family is smart, and they do well in school. Don't be acting dumb like you can't do stuff."

So at the end of his high school career, four years of hard work culminated in his All-State performance. I watched an unsure kid emerge into a confident and vibrant young adult. Jonny Barnes went on a Mormon mission, became a cardiothoracic (CT) surgery perfusionist, and now lives in Kansas with his growing family.

·_·· ____ ···_·

1946: My parents' wedding. Dad Charles and mother Amanda in the middle with grandpa Dave Kemp on the right.

1958: Me in second grade, eight years old.

Black friendly business information when traveling across country.

1969: Albion High wrestling
state qualifiers in blue.
Me on bottom left.

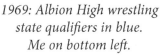

1976: My mother's high school
graduation diploma.

From left: My aunts Lillie Brown, Mary Kemp,
Estella Johnson, and Mother on right.

1972-73: Ronnie Bates, a freshman, on the left. Me on the right, a junior, at Olivet.

1970-71: My freshman year wrestling at Olivet.

1972-73: Me sweaty after losing weight in practice junior year.

*1973: Me beating Griggs of Albion College 3-1
to become the MIAA champion.*

*1974: My senior year. Me getting beat by
Yerrick of Calvin College 10-6 in the MIAA finals.*

1972-73: Olivet College 20-0 wrestling team: Front row left, Phil Britton, Carl Connin, Jim Wencel, Dale Traister, Jack Felton. Second row, Larry Boyer, Ron Bates, Dave Elliot, Larry Jones, Me, Rodger Smith. Top row Marty Curtis, Norm Thomas, Doane Renshaw, Doug Burland, Don Goetzinger, Steve Felder, and assistant coach Curt Wall.

1973-1974: Journal documenting the season's thoughts of me, Dave Elliot, and Dale Traister.

Kreiner family.

Frat Party: From left, Dave Fleet, Tom Kliman, Tom Barberie, me, Greg Morrison, Mark Millis, and Dan Dieterle.

Athlete of Week

Two Hartland High School cross country runners are this week's area High School Athletes of the Week.

Senior Tim Howell and sophomore Dan Skinner have led Hartland to its best record ever in cross country — a 9-2 dual meet season and a second place in the Genesee Suburban Conference.

In doing so, both Skinner and Howell tied in setting a new Hartland record of 15:58 earlier this year.

Last week, the pair led Hartland to second place in the Suburban Conference meet. Skinner finished third and Howell was seventh in that meet.

Also last week, Skinner qualified for the right to compete in state Class B tournament action, finishing seventh in a regional competition with a 15:59 clocking.

Hartland tied for 10th place in the 17-team regionals.

TIM HOWELL

DAN SKINNER

Hartland Finishes Best Season Ever

Hartland High ended its best cross country season ever last week with a second-place finish in the Genesee Suburban Conference Cross Country Meet.

Lake Fenton beat out the Eagles by only eight points, 38-46, to take first place in the loop. Hartland placed six runners in the top 16, paced by Dan Skinner, who finished third.

Dick Lanning took a sixth place for Coach Bob Shegog's runners and Tim Howell came in seventh. Taking 14th through 16th places were Dan Waterman, Howard Daulton and Ernie Sweeten.

Hartland ended the season with a 9-2 overall mark and a 7-1 league slate, best in the school's brief cross country history.

"We outscored our opponents, 291-437, averaged 24.6 points in meets and averaged six people in the top 10 of each race," first-year Coach Shegog said proudly.

In the league meet, Hartland's jayvees fared extremely well, taking first place.

Article showing our cross-country success at Hartland.

1975-76 Hartland Wrestling team: Jim Takacs on top Left, Me on top Right.

10/25/1980: With Rich Levitte at Olivet.

1979-80: Beecher Varsity wrestling team.

Young Russel before we dated.

1984: Moving to Phoenix.

Minert family.

Russel in seminary school clergy robes.

1985: Russel as Santa

Russel at our home working out.

1986 Gay Games in San Francisco. Russel and I resting. This picture resembles the image on Louanne's quilt, yet she didn't see this picture until after she made the quilt.

August 1988: Russel and my holy union. Before Civil Unions were legal.

Louanne's Name's Project quilt for Russ Fetters.

Robert Orlick and me.

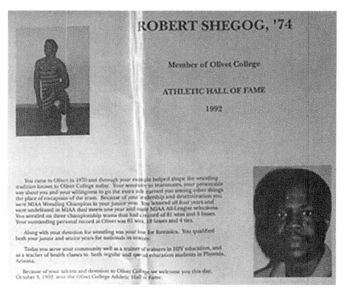

1992: My induction in the Olivet College Athletic Hall of Fame.

October 1988: In memory of Russel.

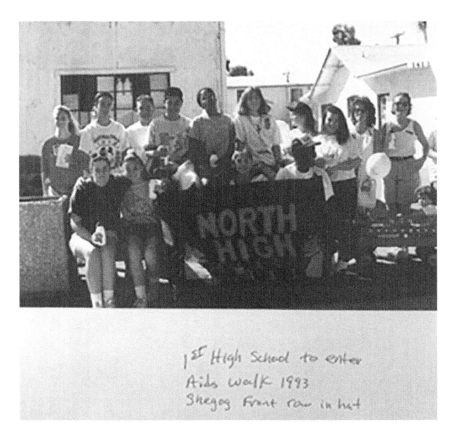

1ˢᵗ High School to enter
Aids walk 1993
Shegog front row in hat

1993: North High students who participated in the Phoenix AIDS walk.
1st high school to enter.

1996: North Family of Leaders (NFL) participants.

Anthony (Chief) Myhalov pinning his Trevor Browne opponent.

1995: Jared Burdick greeted by Coach John Brigham, Nelson Curly, and other teammates after beating his South Mountain opponent.

1994-95 North High varsity wrestling team: Notable names include me on the top left, Michael Nerini 5th from the top left, Coach Brigham on the top right. Middle row: Mark Lewis left, Jared Burdick 4th wrestler from the left, then Chief Myhalov, Nelson Curly, and Gary Barnes. Bottom row second from the left we have Andrew Valenzuela, Jeff Taliman, Robbie de Roock.

Coach John Brigham on my right and Coach Mike Garcia on my left.

Mark Lewis Metro Region Champion and multiyear state qualifier.

Mark Lewis pinning his opponent.

Ted Faz and me in Payson at their Rim Country Duals (RCD).

Me with Doc Eitner fixing Dominic's bloody nose during a match.

Mike Nerini riding his opponent in Payson at the RCD.

1998-99 North High varsity wrestling team: Top left Me, then two from the left Alfredo (Freddy) Jimenez, followed by Dan Wing, Richard Cachola, Roger Long, Michael Phasely, Ruben Rico, and Coach Wright. From bottom left Dustin Robinson, Alan Barnes, Dominic Martinez, Antonio Sandoval, Nick Kehagias, Jon Sarager, Chris Alday, and Gary Hargus.

1998-99 North High wrestlerettes.

Roger Long in Payson at the RCD.

Freddy Jimenez in Payson at the RCD.

1999-00: North High varsity wrestling team finished 11th in State: Me top left, then Nathan Phasely, Roger Long, Dan Wing, Jared Lapadura, and Coach Wright. Middle row left Freddy Jimenez, then two to the right is Rafael Amavizca, followed by Chris Hightower, and Zeke Gutierrez. Bottom row left Justin Makekau, Kenny McAllister Nick Kehagias, Tino Kehagias, Kelley Barnes, and Antonio Sandoval.

2000: Nick Kehagias senior year state champion.

2000: Andy Charlie places 2nd place in state.

2001: Saturday morning practice hiking Piestewa Peak (Formerly known as Squaw Peak). Featuring Coach Wright, Freddy Jimenez, Kenny McAllister, Antonio Sandoval, Dan Wing, Nathan Phasely, Sam Phillips, Shawn Turner, and Zotero Amavizca.

2001: Kelley Barnes is a Metro Region Champion. He went on to place 3rd in state.

2001: Karl McAllister places 4th in state.

2000-01 North High varsity wrestling team: Champions in Apache Junction at the Glenn McMinn Tournament. Coach Mark Lewis top left, followed by me, Zeke, Karl, Jose, Dan, Chris, Moises Sandoval, Nathan Phasely, and Coach Wright. Bottom left you have Tino, Justin, John, Antonio, Kenny, Zotero, Rafael, and Kelley.

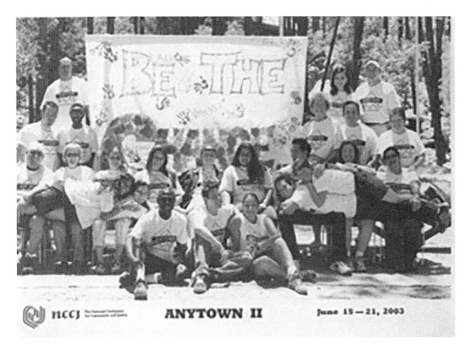

2003: Anytown gathering in northern Arizona.

Toni Miserantino in the neutral position and then pinning her opponent. She was a 2X state qualifier in the boys division.

2003-04 North High Varsity wrestling team: Me top left, Neimeyer four to the right, then Ryan Gustafson, Eric Sanchez two to the right, Coach Antonio Sandoval. Middle left is Toni, then two the right is Jeremy Taliman, Johnny Barnes, and Jesus Guzman. Second from the bottom left we have Danny Barrera, Adam Galgamez, then two to the right is Adam Banda, and Joe Kuczora.

2008 Steve Isaman and me at our commitment ceremony in Prescott, AZ.

Steve and me with Nick and his wife Marie.

Marriage Certificate for Steve and me. We were legally married in San Diego, CA.

My nieces: Angel (Nickki) on my right and Patricia on my left.

My prim and proper mother.

2016: Ruben graduating from Olivet College. Featuring his girlfriend Gloria Aros with her kids, and mother Marta Rodarte.

Winners of the Bradshaw Mountain High School Connection Speech Contest pose April 5 at the school. From left are senior Kevin Moore, third place ($50); junior Leigha Campbell, second place ($75); junior Aaron Bowman, first place ($100); and Robert Shegog, HUSD substitute teacher who co-sponsored the contest with BMHS Connection. (Sue Tone/Tribune)

2011-12 Camp Verde Tournament: The Bradshaw Mountain Middle school wrestling team.

Substitute teacher brings speech contest to high school

Speaking in front of group a valuable skill to have

By SUE TONE
Prescott Valley Tribune

Robert Shegog, substitute teacher for the Humboldt Unified School District, noticed the high school offered no basic speech classes. The only way students got practice speaking before a group of people was if they joined the drama club — some can't make that time commitment — or if a teacher required an oral presentation, he said.

"I complained for a while and finally said, 'If no one's going to do something, I will,'" Shegog said this past week, April 5, at Bradshaw Mountain High School.

He offered a contest with $100 as first-place prize, and found five judges from Prescott and Prescott Valley Toastmasters clubs. Following a March 28 workshop, students had a short amount of time to prepare for the contest. Nevertheless, judge Margie Crider said the students' "strong, clear voices" impressed her.

Nine contestants signed up for the contest and five appeared to speak on this topic: Pick one person in your life for whom you admire their positive leadership skills, and write about the traits that make them special and how they have influenced you in some way. They had to speak for 3.5 to 5 minutes.

The time requirement disqualified one student, sophomore Kaylin Harris, for coming up short with less than 3.5 minutes.

Judges looked for minimal use of "filler words" such as "like" and "um," gestures, clear voice,

See **SPEECH**, page 8

Sports

Bradshaw senior Jacob Kidd places 2nd in D-II state meet

2017: Article about Jacob Kidd placing second in DII Arizona State wrestling tournament.

Article describing the speech contest I started at Bradshaw Mountain High as a substitute teacher in retirement.

217

2021: After having lunch to discuss the book: From left to right Ruben, Gloria, Marie, Nick, Jerry, Me, Monique, Ted Faz, and Mike Tighe.

CHAPTER 9

When to Say Yes, When to Say No

Volunteering

After the 2006 season, I decided it was time to retire. It was a difficult decision to leave so many up-and-coming younger wrestlers. Said Martinez, in particular, was an extreme talent. He was one match away from placing in state as a sophomore. Mentally strong, he would go on to place second and then fourth in state his junior and senior years.

I toyed with the idea of working in administration but realized early on that I wanted to influence the students directly. So at the end of thirty-three years as a teacher, I took the school district's retirement package and moved to Prescott. After retiring, I discovered I couldn't stay away from wrestling. So I became a substitute teacher and volunteer wrestling coach with Prescott Valley's Humboldt Unified School District. But that didn't feel like enough. I had time now to reach beyond the education system to make a difference.

It is hard for me to say NO in most situations because I learned I should always help others. Saying NO means I have no responsibility, no labor, and no loss of time. Other people often assume retired people have more free time and can take on more tasks. To avoid overcommitting, I learned to play it safe by saying NO, understanding that I might miss out on wonderful experiences.

My new ability to say NO doesn't prevent me from saying YES to my passions. I believe that service to humanity is the supreme work of life. That's why I acted as caregiver for my eighty-six-year-old neighbor, Burt, for the last three months of his life. He knew the real me, about my partners, and how I helped take care of them at the ends of their lives. He was a conservative gentleman but saw me as a helpful friend. Before he died, he told me, "Bud, as long as you're happy."

It was easier for me to be free and open with people once I retired. I didn't have to worry about losing my job, angering a parent, or arguing with my partner over secrecy. I enjoyed my time with Burt, getting him up in the morning, and settled into bed in the evening. On December 14, 2018, while teaching, I got word that Burt had died. Caring for him was one time I was glad I had said YES in retirement.

My neighborhood has many senior citizens who walk the streets each day. Some need occasional assistance with small things like snow removal or lifting heavy boxes. I enjoy helping when I can, especially with my next-door neighbor, Penny, who recently lost her husband. Penny supports me too, with rides to the doctor, and by cooking for my partner and me. She makes killer banana nut bread. When we're out of town, she watches our home and vice versa.

I spend time with Northland Cares, the HIV clinic for northern Arizona, helping with their community events. I also volunteer at the Highlands Center, a natural history resource. They promote lifelong learning and the conservation of all living things. I acted as a docent, teaching fourth-graders the center's various programs. These two places get my time and money, but wrestling is still my greatest passion.

Retirement offered a new adventure—substitute teaching. The school system plugged me in everywhere, so I taught everything from math to history in core and Special Education (SPED) classes. It was easier to talk freely with the other faculty because I no longer faced losing my job.

Greg Staley was one of the SPED teachers for whom I subbed. He made it easy to open up and talk about myself. His uncle died in the early 1990s from AIDS-related complications. That loss may have contributed to his genuine empathy for my situation.

Maureen Conway (Mo) also worked in SPED as an aide. We worked together frequently when I subbed at her school. She is such a genuine person. Mo spent time working with Alzheimer's patients and job skill transition students. Together, we organized art, plant, or holiday projects. One such project involved decorating holiday wreaths. We raffled them off and used the proceeds for other projects and school trips.

According to Mo and Greg, the kids loved it when I filled in. The classroom was my element, and I commanded the room. I brought my own lesson plans and supplies. The school gave me a dedicated cabinet to fill. It didn't take long for it to overflow.

Substitute teaching was the perfect way to ease into retirement. Many faculty members and coaches would comment that they learned a lot just watching me teach and coach. Every time I cash a check from a school district, I am grateful. I tell myself, *I could be digging a ditch*. I think of this path of service as a blessing, and my upbringing taught me I need to share my blessings.

In November of 2021, I celebrated my seventieth birthday. After shaving off all my white hair, I look very youthful. So it was no surprise that when Mo found out I was gay, she said, "Bummer, Robert. That means I can't marry you."

I replied with one of my old sayings, "Black don't crack."

We laughed and smiled over shared memories. Then when my partner died, she was very supportive and helped me through my grieving process.

I am deeply grateful for all the opportunities I've received and for the new relationships I have fostered in Prescott.

Back on the Mat

Even in retirement, I had to be involved with wrestling. As a volunteer coach with the Humboldt Unified District, I helped on the mat and made annual Arizona tax-deductible donations. I sponsored kids for summer camp, bought wrestling shoes and T-shirts, and purchased school insurance for those in need. The same contributions I had made at all my previous schools for the wrestling programs.

I worked with coaches Jeff Brown and John Vick in the practice room. Jeff and I coached opposing schools for years. Originally from New York, Jeff wrestled for the University of Buffalo and has coached in Arizona since the mid-'90s at Bradshaw Mountain High. We ran into each other at tournaments like Payson. It was not uncommon for me to instinctively demonstrate a technique to rival school wrestlers after their matches. Jeff has a specific memory of me doing this with his kids. I got down on all fours in the wrestling position to show the athlete what he could have done in the match. Shocked and slightly possessive of his wrestler at first, Jeff and I first met as he asked, "Who are you?"

Jeff realized that, for me, it wasn't about winning at all costs. It was about elevating the sport and pushing the envelope of what each wrestler could attain. That's why I took my kids to wrestling camps like the one at Embry-Riddle in Prescott. While there, the kids worked together. They learned that you get better by teaching, not by just whaling on a less experienced opponent.

In my retirement, I felt no need to hide my sexuality. I didn't flaunt it either but was happy to discuss it if asked. Nobody asked, but I did receive the occasional comment.

While coaching, I noticed myself falling back on old sayings. "Teacher! Teacher!" "Pee on the ceiling!" "Plug the hole!"

My exhortations got a different reception in Bradshaw Mountain's wrestling room than in North High's. The Bradshaw coaches and parents started gossiping that I might be gay.

Coach Vick suggested maybe I shouldn't say things like "plug the hole" anymore. The wrestlers knew the technique I was talking about, but it made the other coaches and some parents uncomfortable. I said okay and refrained from using certain phrases.

At the season-ending banquet, I spoke to all the parents and socialized the same as I did in previous years when coaching at North. Coach Vick, the head wrestling coach, pulled me aside and said, "You can't talk honestly to everyone because they aren't as understanding as I am."

Dumbfounded, I could only answer, "Okay."

I continued to ask myself what he meant by "not as understanding." That I was gay? How did they know? I mean, now that I was retired, I was more open. Or, more accurately, less protective of the fact that I was gay. I didn't worry anymore about being seen in public with my husband. I was cautious to some degree about who I talked to, but not like when I was at North. I came to terms with my sexuality decades ago. Discussing my sexuality is dependent on whether the person I'm talking to can handle it, not whether I can handle it.

I was encouraged that it didn't take long for the parents to respect me and not care much that I was gay. This was evident in my invite to the subsequent year's wrestling banquet. The envelope was addressed to "Coach Shegog and Significant Other." I smiled and felt more comfortable than I had in a while. I could attend an event without worry. Steve Isaman was my partner at the time. The happy details about our courtship will be revealed later in the book so you'll have to stay tuned. We had a civil ceremony in 2008, even though all fifty states had yet to legalize gay marriage. It would not be legalized until June 26, 2015, during Obama's second term.

⚇

I am comfortable with my sexuality and have no problems talking about it freely. That still doesn't stop me from being slightly nervous when seeing an old friend for the first time in decades or mentioning it to one of my wrestlers for the first time. Again, it has to do with how they're able to process the news.

I remember when Alfredo Jimenez, my ex-wrestler Marine from North, visited me. He and a friend were running a marathon in Prescott and slept at my place the night before the event. After their race, I was slightly worried as I told him the truth about me. His characteristic large grin appeared as he said, "Coach, I've got lots of friends who are gay." He made it easy.

Just last year, an old friend from Olivet, Jeff Therrian, mentioned that he would be in Arizona to golf and that we should get together.

Yes, I thought. *That would be nice.*

Then my brain toiled. How would I introduce Michael? As my friend, partner, significant other? As far as Jeff knew, I was a straight, macho male.

I know that I shouldn't still be nervous, but because I hid my sexuality for so long, it still feels like a minor confrontation every time I tell someone new. Unraveling the truth is like continuously untangling a ball of yarn.

But there is so much more to me. My sexuality is just a small part of my character, yet it has the potential to strike such a strong chord in people, in society. With each conversation, it does get easier and, as the years pass, I feel more acceptance. I can more easily be me.

I've stayed in contact with a significant amount of my wrestlers. I've gone to their weddings, Eagle Scout ceremonies, college graduations, you name it. I've coached entire families. Two Kehagias brothers, three McAllisters, three Talimans, and the four Barnes siblings, to name a few. I remember talking with the youngest Barnes, Johnny, at Tino Kehagias' wedding. He mentioned he felt sad that I had his siblings' number on my phone but not his. I laughed, promptly added his number, and years later attended his wedding too.

Ruben Rico had an academic resurgence. In his thirties, he went to college and graduated from my alma mater, Olivet. I helped him become an RA and assistant wrestling coach to pay tuition. Ironically, he had my same economics teacher, Dr. Homer. The professor was still saying, "If you're early, you're on time. If you're on time, you're late." I quoted the professor often, and now Ruben does. He works in the insurance industry and still sends me cards on Father's Day. A true honor.

While at Bradshaw Mountain, I helped coach another stellar student, Jacob Kidd. Jacob was a great wrestler who placed in the

Arizona state tournament. He was an even more brilliant student, graduating high school early to attend Olivet College. At Olivet, he enjoyed success his freshman year, winning more than half his matches. Then tragedy struck.

Jacob succumbed to the toll of major depression and took his own life. There is no way to console parents when such a loss occurs. Their grief struck me to the core, and I made sure I was there for his family. We created the Jacob Kidd Scholarship fund. In his memory, many students will have the opportunity to further their college education.

I seek out teaching opportunities as a substitute teacher, coach, or even Sunday School lecturer. I involve myself with community events, pass out fliers, or volunteer when I hear of a need. I am vocal for important causes because I notice that getting out there makes a difference and leads to progress.

Don't get me wrong. It is important to set boundaries and say NO occasionally, but it is vital to continue to follow your passions. When passion is the root driver for activities, there's no stopping the flow of energy through your body and into the universe. It becomes contagious, attracts others like a magnet, and the world slowly becomes a better place.

The week of March 12, 2020, was spring break at Bradshaw Mountain. No one imagined when we left that we would not be allowed to return. I was putting together plans for the wrestling program, doing lesson plans for SPED classes, and making travel plans to Michigan. I had a wedding to attend there, plus a wrestling tournament where I planned to purchase cheap wrestling goods. COVID-19 stopped all this and sent me, along with the rest of the world, into a lockdown.

On a scale of one to ten, I'm probably a two when it comes to technology savvy. Because I had commitments, I forced myself to learn Zoom. Through Zoom, I continued to work on the Martin L. King celebration for 2021 and on my church Sunday School class.

My current partner Mike Tighe and I decided to channel more money into home repairs. We spent hours online purchasing items for our remodel. I grieved the loss of substitute teaching and volunteering with wrestling. Even though I couldn't be there in person, I continued to financially support wrestling and found other socially distanced work.

We waited out the pandemic and got vaccinated. Now Mike and I have been venturing out slowly. I've had a few health issues, all related to old age more than anything, and my viral load is undetectable. My thoughts are turning to getting back into the wrestling room.

After all these years, I still feel a thrill of excitement when involved with wrestling. I feel fully alive when wrestling or working with young wrestlers. It gives me purpose. It has saved my life. It gives me life. Like the sun gives strength to Superman, wrestling invigorates me. I will likely be on the mat until my dying day.

•_•• _____ •••_•

CHAPTER 10

Friends with Unconditional Support

I'd like to talk about some very important people in my life. Friends who shaped my character and set the example of how to be supportive and loving.

Years after college, during my ten-year reunion, I told Paul Kreiner, Ed Jamison, and Jimmy Wencel the truth. They were nothing but supportive. Ed even told me I was one of the most influential people in his life. I didn't realize it at the time, but as I reflect on it, I see how I must have changed Ed's initial fear and bias toward Blacks and other marginalized groups. Ed, along with many of my teammates and other friends with whom I've connected over the years, was able to see me for myself and discern my character. That superseded the misinformation he and others grew up learning.

Some friends have not been supportive, breaking off communication. You will learn of one example later in the book. For them, I continue to hope they will eventually focus on my substance, the genuine part of me they befriended, instead of the superficial aspects of my life.

Two angels in my life are Al and Peg Minert. Al coached at Beecher while I was at Hartland. When I was unable to land employment in the fall of 1978, it was Al who contacted me about an opening at Flint Beecher. Thanks to him, I got hired as a permanent substitute teacher and head wrestling coach.

Unfortunately, when seeking a place to rent in Flint, I came across the same racism I had dealt with in Hartland. It only took one rejection from a landlord to realize I had to play the game if I wanted a rental. Al Minert and I decided he would visit the same property to view and see if he could land it. He got it and made sure I signed and secured all the documents for the place.

While in Flint, my relationship with Al and Peg matured. Their family is one of the most giving and selfless I know. As devout Methodists, they practice what they preach. The couple routinely volunteers in programs for the homeless, both domestic and abroad. I'm known as the Godfather in their family pictures, and I'm not the only Black guy. They have an adopted Black son who is fifty-one years old now.

Al coached the middle school kids, and Ray Chapman was my assistant at the high school. I credit my success at Beecher to these two men and the other staff they recruited. When we hosted wrestling tournaments, Al and Ray recruited math teachers, English teachers, parents, and football coaches to work the tables and concessions. After the tournaments, I gave an award to these wonderful people to show them how much I appreciated their willingness to help. I continued this practice throughout my coaching career.

At the time, I was single and often had dinner in the homes of Al or Ray. Al and Peggy started a tradition of hugging me and saying, "WE LOVE YOU." The first time they hugged me, I froze. I was speechless. I didn't grow up hearing those words. As time went by, I looked forward to those hugs and hearing, "WE LOVE YOU."

I began doing this with my mother and friends, and it felt great. The first few times I hugged Mama, she fell silent. Love from my mother was implied with the food, shelter, and clothing she provided. The physical and verbal expression of love was different. Soon, however, she responded in kind.

My friend Miles replied to my salutation with, "I'm not going to say that."

I started this practice in 1985, and today, Miles and most of my family and friends reply with love. Even when we were apart, we had a special signal of LOVE. They would call me, let the phone ring one time, and hang up. That ring said they were thinking of me and that they loved me, without having to accrue any long-distance charges.

In the early 2000s, there was a movie titled *I Love You, Man*, and people started using the phrase. I feel it is crucial to say it to the people I love. With my partners, I have learned to say, "I love you." I make a point of saying it when one of us leaves the house since we don't know if we will see each other again.

I organized a wrestling tournament called the Minert Invitational because my friendship with the Minerts was no "minor" miracle. When I announced to the Minerts that I was gay, they embraced and supported me more than ever before. When my partner Russell and I visited them, it felt liberating to be my authentic self with good friends. They also joined the group Parents, Families, and Friends of Lesbians and Gays (PFLAG) in their community and actively participated in the organization's events. The Minerts protested for gay rights, wrote editorials, and sat for newspaper interviews. They are now members of the United Methodist Church, a Methodist branch that accepts LGBTQ+ members.

At the time, I was in the closet to protect my job and my passion. Meanwhile, Al and Peggy were my advocates. They sustained and encouraged me when I made life-altering decisions. When my mother was in failing health, the Minerts stood by me every minute of her final days. I was blessed to have them to hold me up during dark times. I am thankful for all the angels in my life.

Miles was one of my first friends who learned that I was gay. It was in 1981. I was helping him move apartments and run errands after his recent divorce. I wanted him to hear it from me first. I was hopeful our friendship would supersede any biases but feared my news might challenge Miles' conservative upbringing.

After I told him, he looked at me and said, "How do you know you're gay?" To him, I was the hunky guy who dated the beautiful Char.

I told him about how I had gay feelings from a young age.

Then he said, "Shegog, God put us together for some reason. We treat people the way we want to be treated. You're not going to do this drama thing on me?"

We looked at each other, laughed, and continued our errands. Our friendship didn't skip a beat. I was free to be myself and eventually introduced Russell, Robert, Steve, and Mike during visits to Miles' house. Miles even saw me when I was very sick from pneumocystis pneumonia and was nothing but supportive. He has had his health battles, too, and I made sure to be there for him.

Years after that conversation, I lent an ear to Miles when his adult son came out as gay. I had suspected it when the boy was thirteen, but I let time take its course. Some moments should not be rushed. Miles claims he learned more from me than I ever did from him. But there's no denying he showed me what a family is supposed to be. One of the greatest compliments I have ever received was Miles' statement that I'm the kind of person he would want his kids to be.

Nancy Kloss, the talented North High School principal and amazing human being, grew up in a small town just south of Chicago. Her father was a carpenter. And her mother was one of the nicest, most inclusive, and nonjudgmental people you can imagine. Kloss attended one of the most diverse high schools in the country during the late 1950s, called Bloom Township High School.

Here, she had friends who were very wealthy as well as friends who lived in the projects. The neighborhoods were segregated. But the Brown v. The Board of Education Supreme Court decision made the schools melting pots of kids from all areas. (As an aside, Jerry Colangelo, owner of the Phoenix Suns, also attended Bloom and graduated a few years before Kloss.) Her experiences in high school were so positive that she went back to teach and was the dean of students at Bloom from 1966 to 1978.

In April of 1968, a confirmed racist assassinated Martin Luther King Jr. Intense riots ensued the following day. Kids ran around all over campus, missing class, and some teachers and students at Bloom got stabbed. The school closed for two weeks. When it reopened, law enforcement officers stood in position every fifty yards to ensure order. These were intense social and racial times with almost yearly riots.

As the dean of students, Kloss dealt with these issues firsthand, even participating in all disciplinary meetings. This frontline educational experience, combined with top-notch leadership, propelled North into being a one-of-a-kind student-centered campus of excellence.

Bev Bostrom and I met during our summer Phoenix Union school district workshops. This good friend was outgoing and tended to look at projects holistically. I focused more strongly on individual aspects. We complemented each other and instantly hit it off. Both of us are gay, so we understood the fragility of our job positions.

Bev was an early advocate for setting policies and teaching HIV-related material. She even flew to conferences in San Francisco to gather information. Through her efforts, and those of many others, the district became a more informed and tolerant place. It was definitely less hysterical than most of the state and country at the time.

We were even able to reach the Spanish-speaking students at North with HIV education material. Zita Robinson taught biology in Spanish as part of the bilingual IB program. Her students jumped on the opportunity to learn not just about HIV, but other sexual education aspects like STDs, safe sex, and how to protect themselves from abuse. In fact, her students were so inspired they invited their predominantly Spanish-speaking parents for evening classes. On those nights, the students assumed the role of teacher to their parents. I don't know of any other school districts where their students learned to teach their own parents. What we were doing was truly revolutionary, but above all, it was effective. An entire community became knowledgeable and safe, literally overnight.

I couldn't tell Coach Garcia what was going on in my secret life, but there were a few people at North in whom I could confide. Diane Escalante was one such person. A civil rights advocate since the 1960s, she taught English.

I remember, not long after my conversation with Garcia, telling Diane, "I guess you can tell I've got HIV since I've lost a lot of weight."

She gave me a sincere hug and continued her supportive and trusting friendship. Diane made it easy for me to be positive and upbeat. It was always a happy time in her presence. The ability to talk to her and a few others like Monique Mendel, Jerry McCarty, and Zita Robinson was a needed release.

In 1992, Olivet College inducted me into their Wrestling Hall of Fame. When I spoke with the school about the ceremony, they asked if Char would be one of my honored guests. I hadn't spoken to her in decades, but the college still remembered us as an item. I said to myself, *Why not?* After all, at one point, I was ready to marry her. The school gave me her contact information, I called her, had a great conversation, and she accepted the invite. So Char, my mother, and my aunt were my honored guests.

At the ceremony, my aunt kept saying to Char, "I really wish you would have been part of our family."

Mama just chuckled because she was one of the few family members who knew I was gay, having met Russell.

Char also picked up on my mother's reaction and asked me, "Why did your mother laugh every time your aunt suggested that we should have been married?"

I grinned. "Take me out to dinner, and I'll tell you."

Intrigued, she did.

That night I told Char everything. That I was gay. Having had no idea, she sat there puzzled. Then she asked, "Did my breakup cause you to be gay?"

Calmly, and with a slight laugh, I told her, "No, there were experiences in high school and college before we dated. I really did love you, and it hurt when we broke up."

I described how men have always been attracted to me and that I was interested in exploring relationships with them, too.

While wrestling at Olivet, there's no way I could have come out as gay. The team and fraternity would have ostracized me. I would have lost my scholarship and likely forfeited my degree. With my secret finally revealed, Char was supportive, reflecting the traits that make her the wonderful person she is. She wished me well, and I wished her the same.

·_·· ____ ···_·

CHAPTER 11

Friends with Benefits

Our life experiences shape who we gravitate toward in our relationships. Growing up, I was roughed up and abused by a few Black kids in the neighborhood. My earliest negative experience took place in elementary school when I played Little League baseball. One of the kids forced me to the ground, laid on my face as if he was humping me with his clothes on, and ordered me to surrender my baseball glove. This happened at each of our games that season and I had to use one of the worn-out gloves provided by the Parks and Recreation Department. I did not welcome this treatment, so I quit the league.

In seventh grade, I was still a novice to wrestling. There was a student who roughed me up and took my lunch money. During one of these encounters, he got an erection and forced me into a janitor's closet. Thankfully nothing else ensued after he got my money. After that, I hid my lunch money in my shoe. When he couldn't get money from me, he stopped the assaults.

Another experience took place a few years later when I worked my paper route. One of my married customers was a nudist and answered the door naked as a jaybird. He asked me to step inside while he went to get the payment for his paper. The next thing I knew, we were having sex at the front door. He, too, was older and White.

I recounted, in Chapter Five, the story around a local business owner who offered me a ride home whenever he saw me walking home from school or work. He was White, plump, and kind. Then one day, he asked me to give him a blowjob. Mama taught us we should never take rides from strangers, but he wasn't a stranger. He was an adult. I didn't expect his behavior, but I didn't resist. I complied. I thought, *Do I have a sign on my forehead making me an easy target?*

Unlike the two Black students, these two men were gentle. This went on for several months and then suddenly stopped when I started running home. I knew it was wrong but I was confused. Questions rolled through my mind. Did I like it? I think I liked the attention and I liked pleasing him. This is going to sound weird but I didn't feel endangered by this man like I did with the Black students.

I noticed that I missed the attention I was getting from men. I didn't know what to call this feeling. I was a minor. What they did was sexual assault, but I did not want to report it to anyone. I had mixed feelings about these men and didn't want them to get into trouble. I didn't want to shame their families. And how would I face my family and friends?

These experiences helped form my internal attraction to older White men. Everyone learns that they prefer certain types of people as sexual partners. Some people are attracted to tall, short, or big people.

In Phoenix, there was a nightclub catering to big women. Women who fit that description entered free and received drink tickets. Men attracted to big women had to pay to enter. Sir Mix-a-Lot recorded *Baby Got Back*, a song about the love of big booty women. Leonard Nimoy, who starred in the original Star Trek series as Spock, published a photo book called *The Full Body Project*. His work recognizes a wider range of attractive female body types.

My point is that attraction is extremely unquantifiable. Some folks are attracted to blue or green eyes, dimples, or a big smile. I am attracted to mature, big, White men. My church told me that this was a sin. When I was growing up, my neighborhood described any non-mainstream attraction or non-heterosexual tendencies as "kind of funny." Over time, the term "gay" became the word of choice. In the meantime, I kept these thoughts to myself. I believed I would someday grow out of these feelings and marry a woman. That's what young men were supposed to do.

As a senior in high school, I did have that one long-term relationship with a slightly older woman. The librarian and I would have married if my mother hadn't intervened. I dated two other women prior to my sophomore year in college. By then I had a car, making it easier to date. But no relationships stuck.

Then, still in my sophomore year, there was a White male student at Olivet College with whom I had a secret relationship. His girlfriend attended Michigan State University (MSU). I was familiar with MSU from summer camps during high school. In exchange for gas, I agreed to drive him and his girlfriend to and from MSU. When it was just us guys in the car, he often talked about his girlfriend. He was frustrated that they were only having oral sex to avoid a pregnancy. These conversations got very graphic, and before I knew it, I was giving him a blowjob.

I knew it was a sin to be with a man, but how could something sinful feel so good? I didn't drink or smoke at the time, thinking they were worse, more sinful acts. I figured I would eventually marry and have kids like society dictated. Right then, I just wanted to have a little fun with men before settling down.

Soon this student was demanding service on campus, making me very nervous. He demanded attention even in front of other students. His tone toward me was controlling but not sexual. I was afraid the other students would notice and wonder what was going on between us. I had anxious flashbacks of the Black students in Albion who treated me rough when I was young.

One day he showed up to our open mat session before practice and wanted to wrestle me. He thought because I was servicing him, he could dominate me. He wanted to show it on the mat as well. I warned him against sparring with me since he had no wrestling experience, but he insisted. So we wrestled. I had no pity and literally wiped the mat with him. That was the last time he came to wrestling. Lucky for me, he failed to return to college the following year, so the issue resolved itself.

Years later, I ran into him and learned that he had married his Michigan State girlfriend and had four kids. I was no longer insecure about my sexuality. I proposed to him that we could be intimate on the side. Nothing ever happened between us. Even though he was married, I justified a relationship with him because, at that time (and even today), gay people got married and had kids to satisfy societal norms, not their own wishes. As I've matured, I realized that cheating is cheating. One should not be in a heterosexual relationship in the first place if they prefer to be in a homosexual one. If they are, they should respectfully end the first before pursuing the one they desire.

After my sophomore-year college fling, I didn't want or pursue any relationships for a while. I feared being outed. That is, until my senior year, when I saw one of the most beautiful women that I have ever met—Char.

Char and I had a traditional relationship. As you know, we were together for over two years. We broke up during my second teaching year at Hartland, Char's junior year at Olivet. She had received a B in a class, her first ever, and went into emotional shock. Char had plans to attend law school, become a corporate lawyer, and nothing but perfect grades would do for her. I drove from Hartland to Olivet to comfort her. But it was too late. Her focus had shifted to her studies, her future career, and there was no room for an "us" anymore. I would not see Char again until 1992, during my induction into the Olivet Wrestling Hall of Fame.

The following year, I enrolled in a dating service. I knew I was a great catch as a handsome, college-educated, Christian, Black man with good values. I dated multiple women over the next few years, sharing anything from a cup of coffee to our beds, but not one connection could compare to what I had with Char.

I traveled around Michigan for graduate classes and wrestling events. It had been years since I had been with a man, but the interest and excitement never left me. I tried to do what society demanded of me—meet a nice woman, settle down and marry—but it wasn't happening. What if I did find another Char, got married, and had kids? Would I still be cruising other guys? In other words, would I still be seeking sexual encounters with other men? I toiled with these thoughts. I really only had a handful of experiences with men. So I set out to learn more.

I began at the adult bookstores, looking for the gay section. Early on, I remember being afraid to even pick up any of the gay magazines.

What if someone saw me? On the cover of one magazine was an ad for a gay bar in Detroit. I memorized the address and repeated it in my head until I was safely in my car, where I could write it down.

My next free weekend, I put twenty dollars in my pocket and drove to that Detroit bar. I told myself that when the money was gone, I'd simply drive back home.

At the bar, I was quiet, keeping mostly to myself, watching everything around me. I noticed some people dancing, others kissing and making out. Some were cruisy as they walked around giving thumbs-up or thumbs-down for potential sex. Then, out of the blue, the bartender placed an empty shot glass in front of me.

"What is this?" I asked.

"Someone just bought you a drink."

Intrigued, I accepted without knowing from whom. It wasn't until I was about to leave that an older White man started a conversation with me. He purchased two more drinks for me, and we talked for a few hours.

I asked him a thousand questions. Where are the other gay bars? How do you know if a bar is for gays? He mentioned that there were also different types of gay bars. There were cowboy-themed bars, drag queen bars, leather bars, bondage bars, bear bars where the men were larger and hairier, and twink bars where younger, skinnier men often met older men. In time, I had the chance to explore each of the bars, realizing that my previous experiences with older men shaped my preference toward the bear bars.

I learned that when the lights flashed on and off, it meant the police had entered the bar, and everyone was to stop public displays of affection (PDA) or risk harassment or arrest. I noticed that some patrons also wore whistles around their necks. Yes, the whistles shrilled jubilantly on the dance floor, but initially, they were used for safety when harassed by strangers or the police. We have come a long way now, but during the mid-'70s, tolerance was the exception rather than the norm.

After a while, the man suggested that I follow him back to his home. He wasn't single but had a lover who also happened to be Black. The three of us had sex well into the next day. That was the first time I received anal sex. The Black guy was not gentle with me. The next day, I had a hard time walking and had blood on my underwear. This experience reinforced my younger feelings that my partners of choice were older White men. There's even an organization that I later joined called the National Association of Black and White Men Together (NABWMT). At their conventions, the NABWMT share stories about joy, loss, you name it, while helping couples foster relationships. There are groups for almost everything you can imagine.

⚕

In the 1977-78 school year, I was teaching at Cassopolis, a small farming town in the far southwest corner of Michigan. There were no traffic lights. The closest large town was South Bend, Indiana. I was unhappy at this school and put in my notice toward the end of the year. While finishing at Cassopolis, I had a lot of free time, so I traveled to South Bend looking for the gay scene. I was not living with anyone and not in a relationship. I was what you would call "door trade," free to move from one sexual experience to another. Some of the experiences turned into relationships, although none lasted long.

I did meet and date a nice older man named Vince. We seldom went to the bars. Instead, we stayed in at his house, being sexually intimate, cuddling, and talking. My weekends with Vince were the highlight of each week. He was a computer engineer under consideration for a promotion with his company. A promotion meant he'd possibly have to relocate to another city. I assessed my priorities, reasoning that I could get a teaching position in any city, but I was not willing to move farther away from my mother. Vince and I talked a lot about the possible move. In the end, I decided to end the relationship.

When spring arrived, I decided to move back to Hartland and seek a position with the district. I shared a house with two teachers who were also Olivet alumni and fraternity brothers, Dan Mischler and Tom Barberie. From Hartland, I often traveled to Lansing to visit gay bars. One night, I met a handsome Black man who was gentle and loving. He was a teacher who lived in Flint, Michigan. I had been unsuccessful at landing a job in Hartland, so I expanded my options to include Flint. Soon after, I secured a job at Flint Beecher, got my housing arranged, and gave my handsome Black lover a call. He immediately wanted to meet with me. We shared coffee while he informed me that he was married with a son. He wanted to continue to see me behind his family's back. I wanted a one-on-one relationship. At the same time, I felt so overpowered by his caring and loving ways that I agreed to his request.

He was the first Black man I met who knew the difference between rough sex and loving intimacy. I was willing to do whatever it took to spend time with him. That included leaving or ending wrestling practice early and paying for a motel room. Compromising wrestling practice was not something I take lightly, but I was just so taken with him.

We were both discreet since we had a lot to lose between our jobs, his family, and the risk of becoming social outcasts. Once, he was unsettled because I reserved a room in an unfamiliar town. He also failed to show up for some of our trysts. These were red flags that preceded his demanding attitude for more sex.

In addition to teaching, this man was a church deacon entrusted with keys to the building. He invited me into the church basement, where we had sex. He wanted me to become a member of the church and invited me to his home, where I met his wife and son. Whenever he was home alone, he asked me over for sex in the basement. If his wife or son came home, we quickly dressed and turned on the TV to a football game.

On two occasions, we traveled to East Lansing to watch Michigan State play football. He drove, but I paid for the tickets and the motel room to prevent a paper trail for him. We continued like this until the beginning of the wrestling season in November.

Once wrestling started, I didn't have much free time. It was clear I could not be in a relationship with a controlling, married man and do my job. Again, I reviewed my relationship needs and fell back to my preference of being with an older, single White man who didn't demand control of the relationship. I ended it with the teacher.

The following Christmas season, I met Lee Dear. He was an older White man with four children, one still living at home. Lee was out to his children, and they were supportive. He ran a financially sound and strict home. I love children in general and especially enjoyed giving Lee's kids small gifts, often denied to them by their dad, like candy or a small toy. I spent a lot of time with the Dear family, even meeting extended family members.

That summer, I went to Albion and spent time with my mother. When I returned to Flint, Lee broke up with me. As I write this, that was forty-two years ago. Lee has since passed, but I am still in touch with his children.

When he was dying, he asked them to spread his ashes at every truck stop from Michigan to Florida. So his daughter Juanita and other family members honored his wishes and made the road trip. We often talk about their dad and how we wish the relationship had lasted. I do not think it would have lasted forty-two years because he was another man who wanted to control me. I cherish the memories of times with Lee and his children. I try to see Juanita when I visit Michigan. I also send her yearly holiday cards.

Shortly after that breakup, I met and dated Gary in the summer of 1978. Gary was my age, slightly rotund, and sported a red beard. He worked at the Flint Buick factory, had served in the military, and lived with his parents for several years. His parents did not charge any of their children rent so long as they saved most of their paychecks. Gary had saved enough money to purchase land and build his own home for cash once he decided to move out. Together, we had no mortgage, two incomes, and our utilities were the only expenses. I spent a lot of time and money on the Beecher wrestling program. Gary and I had financial freedom, and life was as great as you can imagine.

We held lots of wild parties with a seemingly endless flow of guests, alcohol, and herb. I remember salad bowls filled with rolled joints. On his four acres of land, Gary grew his own marijuana crop, hidden within his cornfield. He kept about two years' worth of harvest at any given time. It was high grade, definitely attracting party goers who got blitzed and swore, "That's some good pot, man."

Michigan laws were relatively conservative. Stores weren't allowed to sell alcohol on Sunday mornings. Seven and Seven was our drink of choice, and it wasn't unusual for us to finish multiple bottles of Seagram's Seven Crown during a party. We just had to plan ahead to make sure we had ample supply. Some guests did other drugs like coke.

I even got into an argument once when partiers tried to get me to do a line. I told them, "I draw my line at a line."

The partying all came to a halt one night when the neighbor noticed helicopters flying over Gary's property with a spotlight. I made it safely to my neighbor's house, but Gary was stuck at his house, confronted by police. It wasn't clear if the crop overgrowth or a snitch had caught their attention. They arrested him and pulled all the weed from his yard and hauled away six truckloads of marijuana. Gary eventually paid the bail and got away with a slap on the wrist. Talk about a clear case of White privilege. He seemed to get away with everything. If I had been caught in the house, I likely would have rotted in prison. After that, we still had parties, but they were lower key.

Professionally, I was still nervous and not openly gay. Losing my teaching job, and worse yet, being banned from coaching wrestling, was my big concern. Because of this, I asked Gary not to attend wrestling events for fear of being outed. Even though Gary knew where I was after school, he still paged me regularly and questioned my whereabouts. To reassure him, I hosted a gathering of senior wrestlers at our house so he could meet them and the team could discuss their plans for the future. That didn't satisfy him. His questions became more intense and led to a lot of arguing. I refused to argue for long, so I often left the house and went to a local bar.

During this time, I even joined the bar softball team. The time I spent away from home with wrestling, the bar, and the softball team was not good for our relationship. We talked about it and decided to plan some personal vacation time together.

However, the arguments and overbearing questions remained and forced me to move out of the house. Two times I moved out. And two times, I sent the wrong message by returning after his family pleaded with me. They said, "Bob, you got to go back with him. He's nasty to everyone. Even to Mom and Dad, he's nasty. He was never like that when you were with him."

Because nothing changed after I returned, the tension continued to build and became so high again that I moved out a third time. Gary started following me around town, even showing up at wrestling meets. One of the kids noticed Gary on the balcony and asked who he was. I just brushed it off, saying he was a friend, but thought, *Okay, this is how it is?*

Then he showed up at the school office cursing at the staff and demanding to see me. They called me to the office and mentioned that Gary was being rude.

I calmed him down and persuaded him to leave by promising I'd be at the house right after school. I moved back in but kept my apartment, just in case.

Not long after, Beecher eliminated my teaching position. I couldn't live on coaching alone. Luckily, the adjacent Mt. Morris Schools hired me as a long-term substitute teacher and head wrestling coach.

Some Mt. Morris wrestling parents didn't want a Black man as the head coach, so they dug into my background for dirt. One of my supporters warned me that these parents had once followed an unpopular superintendent everywhere he went. A few days later, I noticed someone tailing me as I drove around town. The stress of the situation made me uncertain about how to proceed with the job.

To make matters worse, Gary continued his controlling ways. One night at the bar, the bartender told me that Gary sucker punched a guy just for talking to me.

Disgusted, I drove to Gary's house to talk about it and ended up telling him, "We are not going to be an item."

At the end of our conversation, he stated that if he could not have me, nobody could.

I was terrified. It was like the movie *Fatal Attraction*—only that would not come out for another five years. The words to Patti LaBelle's cover of Michael McDonald's song "I Keep Forgetting" kept playing in my head. I mentally checked out of my three-and-a-half-year relationship with Gary.

With a growing sense of urgency, I returned to my apartment, loaded my truck with essential goods, and notified my downstairs landlord that I was moving out. Immediately, I started driving toward Los Angeles, stopping in St. Louis to call and resign my Mt. Morris job without explanation. There was no notice for family or friends. I had sensed the inevitable fallout with Gary for some time. I had received a credit card from a guy in L.A. with whom I had been corresponding via a gay magazine ad. Without knowing what to expect, I knew I had to leave Michigan since both the school and my ex-partner threatened my life.

Soon after I got settled into his home, the L.A. man showed signs of wanting to control me. This time I asked myself, *Do I have a sign on my forehead attracting these controlling men?*

I had requested my Michigan State Retirement funds by mail. While waiting for the payout to arrive, the L.A. man opened a $500 bank account in my name. When my check from the Michigan Retirement System came, it was for less than the expected $10,000. The school districts withheld some of my retirement funds, took back some of their matching funds, and applied an early withdrawal penalty. I received just over $1,800. As soon as I got the check, I left the L.A. man's home. I had been there, under his control, for three weeks.

I drove my truck to get food and hygiene items, then parked outside the bank. I slept there overnight, and as soon as the bank opened, I closed out that $500 account. I had enough money to get a small apartment for one month, but what would I do after, having drained all my money? I decided to live on the streets of L.A. for the next month, moving from place to place to avoid being robbed. I learned the L.A. roads and washed up in the restrooms of fast food restaurants. Many of the gay bars had free food at certain times, so I planned my days accordingly. Then, almost through divine intervention, I ran into Dan Cheverette, a friend from Flint, Michigan, in one of those bars.

Dan managed a Sizzler restaurant. He let me sleep on his couch for free while I looked for a job. I did what I could to contribute, including cleaning the apartment. One day, Dan called me from work, told me to put on some black pants, and drive to the Sizzler. He had just fired an employee, and I was the replacement. Dan was an angel in my life at this time.

Soon after, I secured a second job at North Hollywood High School as an educational aide. I worked there from seven-fifteen until two-thirty in the afternoon and then at Sizzler from six until midnight. Often after work at Sizzler, I dropped into a gay bar until half-past two in the morning. The bars in L.A. stayed open until four in the morning, but I left before closing to get some sleep before the next day's work.

I met a construction worker in one of the bars. No, he wasn't one of the original Village People members. He worked on movie sets and hired me as extra labor on weekends. I was not a union worker, so he paid me each day in cash. If a union rep showed up on the worksite, I had to hide in the truck. With three jobs, I had reverted to the constant on the go schedule I had maintained in Michigan.

While living at Dan's house, I often saw TV stars. Sometimes I ran with Charles Haid at a nearby park. I recognized him for playing Officer Andy "Cowboy" Renko on *Hill Street Blues*. He mentioned that he liked the pace I set and seemed to look forward to running together.

Eventually, I got my own place and wanted to get back into my passion—teaching and coaching. My Michigan teacher certificate wasn't valid in L.A., so I started the necessary community college classes and studied for the California Teachers Exam. To get involved with wrestling, I volunteered as a coach at the Harvard Boys School from three in the afternoon until a quarter after five.

In addition, one of the gay bars had a sign about a gay wrestling practice. Intrigued, I checked it out. The gay wrestling club competed on weekends with other clubs as far away as Chicago. Only a few of the men had any real experience. With my experience, I was a standout in the room, and eventually took second-place in the 1986 Gay Games.

Church involvement was always a big part of my life. I attended the local MCC and even dated a few men in the congregation. None of them was the one for me. In integrating myself into the L.A. scene, I did establish some true friends from church and the wrestling team. My life was full with my busy work schedule, trips with the club team, and noteworthy after-parties. Partner-wise, I didn't have what I wanted, that being a long-term relationship with one special man.

One weekend, while in a gay bathhouse, I noticed an attractive older attendant. I knew he worked there because he was the only person wearing clothes. I followed him around until I got his phone number. Later that night, I followed him to his apartment and had the most wonderful sex of my life.

His name was Scott Goulet, and he owned the bathhouse. If you were wondering, you guessed right. He was a first cousin to the famous singer Robert Goulet.

Scott took me shopping for nice clothes. Then I escorted him to Hollywood galas and parties. I had to learn to contain my awe and excitement in rooms filled with Hollywood royalty.

During these events, I stayed close to Scott's side. He liked showing me off to his friends. I was thirty-two years old with a twenty-eight-inch waist, a distinct six-pack, and a big, black butt. I wore boys' clothes when I went out to the bar because they fit tight to my body. And I never spent more than ten bucks on drinks as other bar patrons always bought drinks for me.

While I got lots of attention and flirtatious glances, I only wanted to be in Scott's arms. We dated for almost six months. I didn't mention my desire to be his one and only love. I didn't want to scare him off.

One weekend, I stayed with Scott on his twenty-acre horse ranch in the hills of Hollywood and met his brother. I took this extended time together to let Scott know how I felt about him. He wasn't happy to hear that and asked why I wanted to be with him, mentioning our twenty-year age difference.

Sadly, after that weekend, he curtailed the time we spent together. I continued to explain my feelings and pursued him whenever possible. But there were long periods when we did not see each other. This on-again, off-again relationship continued until the spring of 1984. That's when I met Russell Fetters of Phoenix, Arizona.

⚘

I've already described our electrifying first meet (Chapter Six). What I didn't share about that first night was what happened after we left the bar. We spent the night in a wild romance, accidentally breaking our friend's bed. Russell graciously offered to pay for a new one.

He was in L.A. for the weekend to attend a church convention at the very church I attended, the MCC. The next day, I took him to the airport. I didn't leave until his plane lifted off. I was already missing him before the aircraft cleared the boundaries of the L.A. area. I had asked him to call me once he was safely home. Russ called, and we talked for over two hours. After that, we talked every day, sometimes twice a day. We shared everything about our personal histories. I no longer found excitement in the bars, and I told my wrestling friends about Russ. On multiple occasions, while Russ was on my mind, he would call. Once, he even knocked on my apartment door just as I was thinking about him. In less than two weeks, we were making plans to live together. Twenty-two days after Russ flew home, I was packing to move to Phoenix and saying goodbye to friends.

My wrestling friends were skeptical because we were moving so fast. They said they would miss me at practice, but more importantly, they were worried about me because they didn't know Russ.

Russ took a week off work to help me pack, get to know my friends, and move me to Phoenix. Before we left L.A., the wrestling club threw a going-away party at a local restaurant owned by wrestling club members. My friends grilled him with all sorts of questions. When we left the party and started the drive, Russ stated that my friends were very nosy. I replied that they were just concerned and with good reason.

A lot of gays had gone missing over the years. In one horrible example, Jeffrey Dahmer confessed to killing seventeen men. Most of them were Black men he picked up from gay bars between 1978 and 1991 before he was caught and convicted. My departure fell right in the timeframe of his killing spree. Gays everywhere were looking out for each other.

And I did have that airline ticket purchased by my teammate, John Buse, should I have any trouble in Phoenix. The truth is, we had talked so much that I did not anticipate any problems. I was walking in the clouds over being with Russ.

Life with Russ was more than heaven on earth. For the first eighteen months, we never argued about anything. In social gatherings, we often used the same words, made the same choices, and defended each other in public. He earned over $300,000 a year as a mortgage loan officer. I was working two jobs to bring in fourteen thousand.

Over time, this became a problem, especially when we purchased another home. Russ wanted me to stop working and go to graduate school. He wanted me to get my master's so I could qualify for higher-paying positions in education. I resisted and had flashbacks to past partners who attempted to control my choices. We both cared for our relationship and decided to see a marriage counselor.

The counselor pointed out that if I had five jobs, I would still not make as much money as Russ. We learned what it meant to be in a loving relationship. One of our assignments was to write down all the things that would make us leave the other person. In the next session, the counselor asked Russ for his list.

Russ affirmed there was nothing I could do to make him break up.

I held back tears as I looked at my page, filled on both sides with reasons I'd leave. When the counselor turned to me, I hid my notes and claimed that I, too, could not list anything.

Russ' response to the question made me realize how much I was loved. One of the greatest gifts anyone has ever given me. I learned an important life lesson that day. So long as we were together, no problem would be insurmountable. I began focusing on joys, not obstacles.

In Plato's *Symposium*, he discusses how Thebes was triumphant over Sparta because of their Sacred Band military unit. The Sacred Band unit was composed of one-hundred-fifty male couples. Plato describes them as "an army of lovers and their beloveds, fighting side by side, [who] though few in numbers, might defeat nearly the entire world." Russell and I were a loving and powerful couple. There was nothing that we couldn't handle together.

I missed him when we were apart and couldn't wait to see him again. We planned little spontaneous trips around Arizona and would fly to L.A. just for dinner. In the 1980s, a Southwest ticket to L.A. was only thirty-five dollars one-way. Russ noticed I was missing my West Coast friends, so he surprised me with a four-day trip to the City of Angels. On my birthday, I had to work at Pizza Hut. He ordered a sheet cake and dropped it by the store.

Russell's thoughtfulness knew no bounds. The truck I had driven from Michigan to L.A. and then to Arizona was on its last gasping cylinder.

Russell noticed, smiled, and said, "Let's go buy a new truck."

When we showed up at the Larry Miller Dealership, we saw three Mazda trucks lined up at the entrance, all different colors. Russ knew my preference, my need, and all I had to do was pick the color. When I decided on red, he smiled, knowing that's what I was going to choose. We were on the same page and reaffirmed that we were an old married couple every day.

We were so happy and so in love.

·_·· ——— ···_·

CHAPTER 12

Life-Changing News

The Diagnosis

Russell and I were very intimate, and we made a habit of showering together. One day in September of 1986, while in the shower, I noticed Russ had a bruise on his hip. I joked, "Nobody's allowed to spank you but me." I rubbed it and noticed it was deeper under the skin, not like a normal, superficial bruise. Not sure what it was, we scheduled an appointment with Dr. Fisher. Test results identified it as Kaposi's Sarcoma, a lymphatic cancer of the skin and other organs seen in patients with AIDS. The only approved drug at this time was azidothymidine, known as AZT, which Russ started taking along with some experimental drugs.

Dr. Fisher looked at me and stated, "If he has it, then you have it too." Our safe sex was that we did not cheat or have any outside contact. But together, we did not use condoms.

I remember seeing HIV information at bars and community centers back in L.A. There was even a group called the "Blood Sisters." They were a group of lesbians who volunteered in hospital wards, donated blood, and cared for AIDS patients in the fearful early days. When I first heard about them, I remember saying, "Far out."

So we knew about HIV but still kind of ignored it, never thinking it would happen to us. There was no ignoring it now.

I was in shock. I just wanted Russ to get better. I had left Pizza Hut and was working full-time at the Phoenix Union High School District. The next school holiday I would have off was Veterans Day, nearly two months after Russ' diagnosis, so I scheduled an HIV test for then. It took three weeks to get the results. Three weeks of hell! Every cough or bump was suspect. When the results finally came back, they confirmed that I, too, was HIV positive. How would I be able to take care of Russ? How would this affect my teaching and coaching?

We accepted our diagnoses without accusations, blame, or guilt. We loved each other immensely. Russell remained positive, and it rubbed off on me. He reveled in these situations, analyzed the problem, and came up with productive solutions. These talents first emerged when he worked at his dad's wholesale business supplying grocery stores. During this time, Russell won the "Mr. Peanut" award for his food displays. After a falling out with his dad and the loss of his job, Russell collected cans, volunteered at both the local church and thrift stores, and still thrived at life on unemployment. Now, he approached HIV in the same way, volunteering for the HIV hotline. Over time, he became its executive director, organizing bar functions, fundraisers, and participating in many clinical trials.

Dr. Fisher himself was openly gay. We went to him as our primary care provider before either of us knew we had HIV. During the epidemic, Dr. Fisher made it his mission to stay on top of the leading research to provide the best care for his patients. In the late 1970s, doctors noticed that many gay men were developing skin cancers and pneumonia. The illness was first termed the "gay plague" followed by "gay-related immune deficiency" (GRID). *Milk*, the movie about Harvey Milk, the first openly gay American politician, touched on GRID.

By 1979, health officials estimated that ten percent of gay men in San Francisco had the virus. Two years later, in 1981, it was called AIDS, and an estimated twenty percent of gay men in San Francisco had it. As the medical community began to understand the disease, they noticed its prevalence in other populations like intravenous (IV) drug users, hemophiliacs, women, and children. The disease's name properly reflected the reality when it changed to human immunodeficiency virus (HIV) in 1982.

In 1983, with the virus identified, there were tests to detect it, and an estimated fifty percent of the gay population in San Francisco had it. Researchers understood that transmission occurred via blood-to-blood contact, sexual body fluid exchange, breast milk, and pregnancy. It did not spread from sweat, saliva, or skin-to-skin contact.

San Francisco General Hospital created the first AIDS ward in 1983. Some non-AIDS patients didn't want to go to hospitals if they also served AIDS patients. Many nurses and physicians didn't want to treat AIDS patients. If they did, medical personnel didn't recognize the patients' partners as family and often excluded them from conversations. Sadly, this lack of recognition persisted in the 2010s with my partner.

Initially, only volunteers staffed these AIDS wards. Thousands of volunteers spent tens of thousands of hours caring for AIDS patients. The lesbian community was especially committed and courageous. Hundreds of drug studies were conducted, often with poor results, and not uncommonly, all of the AIDS participants died.

It was an extremely gloomy and scary time for those with AIDS and their loved ones. Seeing malnourished, wasting bodies spotted with Kaposi's Sarcoma lesions exacerbated the horror in a gay community so used to public displays of beauty and fitness. Parents of dying patients often revealed their lack of grief over the deaths. One brutally remarked, "It's harder for me to find out that my son's a fag than to find out he's dying soon."

Public hysteria set in. Legislatures began their panicked response. In 1985, discussions proliferated about quarantining HIV positive communities. Creating identification cards and tattooing HIV-positive patients almost became a dystopian reality. HIV-positive immigrants were denied entry to the US. People were fired from work and even tested against their will if were suspected of being HIV positive. There was no cure, medications were ineffective, and the only plan was prevention. Health agencies promoted safe sex, condoms, and testing of high-risk individuals. The patients and community persisted as they enrolled in more clinical trials, and donated their eyes and bodies for research upon death, all in the hope that their lives had meaning in finding a cure.

Blood transfusion products underwent testing only after many recipients succumbed to the virus. Ryan White, a young hemophiliac, became famous because he got HIV from a blood transfusion. He just wanted to go back to school, but the district wouldn't allow it. Rumors spread that he would bite kids, spit on vegetables at the grocery store, and pee on the walls in the restrooms. People noticed the poor treatment the young boy endured. Soon his story began to change public opinion. In 1986, he was finally allowed back into school. He died four years later at the age of eighteen.

Massive protests took place to raise awareness and pressure the government to invest in treatments. Princess Diana publicly shook hands and hugged an AIDS patient. Adored and respected celebrities like Liberace, Rock Hudson, and Freddie Mercury passed away from AIDS. Activism paid off, and Congress adopted the Ryan White Act in 1990. Government funds were directed to victims, research, and treatments. By 1995, AIDS was the number one cause of death for those aged twenty-five to forty-four in the U.S., with nearly 1,500 deaths in San Francisco alone. Treatments improved. Deaths were finally on the decline.

The AIDS Coalition to Unleash Power (ACT UP) activist group used civil disobedience and confrontation to promote awareness. They threw red paint on politicians who voted against HIV research or funding. ACT UP also pressured pharmaceutical companies to lower drug prices with their protests on Wall Street. AZT went from $10,000 per patient per year to under seven thousand.

They also outed numerous gay individuals who were influential members of society. Protesting outside the offices of wealthy executives, legislators, and even teachers, they shouted, "Come out, come out, wherever you are." I understood the importance of coming out of the shadows so people could see that gays are contributing members of society too and nothing to fear. Sadly though, this direct approach often led to job loss or ostracism. That was my fear. As a result, I stayed far away from anything that had to do with ACT UP. The country was just not ready to hear my story.

In 2005, the world reached a peak number of deaths from AIDS. Patients who had created their bucket lists could start planning for the future again. Sadly, though, in 2017, complacency set in, condom use declined, and those under twenty-five years old now account for twenty percent of new infections.

In 2020, just under forty million people worldwide were HIV positive. More than thirty-five million people have died from the virus since the start of the pandemic in the late 1970s. In Africa, one in twenty-five people has the virus, with rates as high as twenty-seven percent of the population in Swaziland (now officially known as Eswatini). HIV has taken millions of lives. Remembering this history is imperative if we are to prevent a resurgence. Then, in the future, possibly rid the world of this scourge, once and for all, with a vaccine.

Dr. Fisher was one of the earliest providers in Phoenix who treated HIV patients. The more immune-compromised patients he treated, the more referrals he got from other primary care providers. In time, eighty percent of his practice was HIV patients. The life expectancy of patients with AIDS was only twelve to eighteen months in the 1980s. Dr. Fisher was helpless to save so many and grieved each loss of life.

Despite his feeling of powerlessness, caring for large numbers of HIV patients provided extraordinary insight and a deeper understanding of clinical results. Dr. Fisher was able to run trials on new treatments and weed out the ineffective. He implemented treatments that showed promise long before they gained momentum nationally. He wasn't on the cutting edge. He *was* the cutting edge. For example, he started patients on steroids months before national researchers and *TIME Magazine* published papers and articles confirming the morbidity and mortality benefits. For this work, Dr. Fisher became a world-renowned voice and educator about HIV, speaking at global conferences in Germany and Africa.

I remember waking up one morning with my entire body stiff as a board. I couldn't move my neck, back, or even walk. I feared this was a complication of HIV. Russell picked me up, placed me in the car, and drove to Dr. Fisher's office.

After Dr. Fisher learned that Russell and I had spent the night before engaging in passionate lovemaking, he looked at us and said, "Girlfriend, when your husband weighs two hundred and fifty pounds, you need to be creative. Rediscover the kitchen sink."

We used our imagination to figure out what he meant. Once I recovered, we tried the kitchen sink. Sure enough, it worked.

The Journey to Loss

As Russell's health declined, Dr. Fisher placed him in clinical trials for new treatments. AZT was the only somewhat effective medication at the time. I chose not to be in trials because I wanted to guarantee that I got AZT, fearing an alternative might be ineffective. Russell had a different view. I still have a VHS recording of when the popular New York newsmagazine television show, *West 57th*, interviewed him and Dr. Fisher. During the conversation, Russell said he would do whatever he could to help advance HIV knowledge and treatments, like the other thousands of clinical trial participants. If his participation helped save lives, then it was worth it, even if his own could not be saved.

All that is true and noble, I thought, *but I would still rather have him.*

Russ worked as long as he could until the mortgage company let him go. Despite many hospital stays, Russ maintained his optimism and still fulfilled his AIDS hotline and MCC commitments as best he could. I accompanied him to all his conferences as moral and physical support. When he was too weak to attend, I flew to Albuquerque and read his final MCC conference report in his place.

His night sweats were intense, often soaking the bed sheets. The home health nurses helped more than they knew, teaching me how to lift and roll Russell, change his soaked bed sheets, and dry the mattress with towels.

For two to three hours before going to my classroom each day, I helped Russell get to the bathroom, wiped him, bathed him, fed him, rubbed lotion on his swollen legs, cut his toenails, and groomed him. During my prep hour at school, I drove home to check on him. We had a host of friends who regularly checked on him as well. He was my lover, my partner, and I wanted to care for him as best I could. We were lucky to have compassionate health care staff working with us on his care. For that, I am profoundly grateful.

To be gay and dying from AIDS was a recipe for some of humanity's lowest sorrows. Society called people like us evil, sinners, and monsters. Blame was often placed on us, alleging that we got what we deserved or that God was punishing us. Family members were afraid to reuse plates or use the same toilet as HIV patients and often abandoned their loved ones at their sickest moments. I can name ten friends who died from AIDS. Some had family support, while others did not.

It was not uncommon for partners to leave their dying lovers. They couldn't handle the emotional time and energy required to care for them, especially when most needed. I was there for Russell, through and through. I loved him immeasurably.

The MCC church in Phoenix was instrumental in combating the loneliness that many AIDS patients experienced at the end of life. Led by Reverend Charlotte Strayhorne, our church discussed the truth about HIV and educated its members against the nation's mass misinformation.

Early on, many gay members feared HIV to the point where they were in denial and ignored signs of pneumonia or Kaposi's Sarcoma. Others remained silent and refused to seek medical attention until the disease had progressed. The same was true for heterosexual men. They were afraid to seek help because they didn't want to be labeled gay. It took time for these barriers to fall. Sadly, even to this day, many of these same fears still exist, albeit in a lesser form.

Reverend Strayhorne met Russell and me at a national MCC conference. We persuaded her to move to our Phoenix chapter from Cincinnati, Ohio. She had battled her own family's expectations. Her father, a Baptist pastor, told her the ministry wasn't for women. When she made the decision to come to Phoenix, her father told her he would never worship with her and that all her followers were bound for hell. Despite the lack of support, Reverend Strayhorne followed her heart and became the voice that I, and the rest of the Phoenix MCC community, needed. Although not a member of our church, Dr. Fisher also worked with the MCC to form the Community AIDS Coalition. He would say to Rev. Strayhorne, "You know I'm your favorite Druid." His potions were his HIV treatments. I can attest to their effectiveness.

At this time, I began to reflect on my past support systems and the people I cared about. So I decided to meet with Coach Klein in Michigan to tell him the truth. He could see the worry in my face as I sat on a park bench waiting for him.

"Bobby, what's wrong?" he asked.

I choked up as I told him, "I'm having a hard time. I have to tell you something. I'm gay. I have HIV."

Coach Klein hugged me, and like any loving father, said, "You've got to be careful who you're running around with."

I filled him in on Russell and how sick he was.

Coach continued hugging me and said, "Be yourself and love yourself. Nobody understands you better than you."

Then he said he loved me. I told him I loved him too. At first, it felt weird hearing this, but I soon realized the power in expressing that emotion. Coach Klein remains a beautiful person in my life. I am grateful for all his teachings and support in my life.

⚔

When Russell passed, the MCC was there for me, and I continued to devote my time to the church. Rev. Strayhorne and I were on the MCC board. We were Servants of God and unafraid to get on our knees in devotion. One afternoon we noticed the office floors were dirty. Rev. Strayhorne and I got on our hands and knees and cleaned them just like our parents taught us. Nothing was beneath us because we didn't look at things that way. As a servant, you do what needs doing. Leading by that example led to the MCC's success as a beacon of hope against discrimination for everyone. Rev. Strayhorne's father even noticed this humble piety.

A year before her father died, he visited the MCC in Phoenix. Rev. Strayhorne was relieved and elated to see him in attendance. Respectfully, as was the tradition in Baptist parishes, she recognized him as a fellow preacher and asked if he had any words for the members. He stood up, spoke beautifully about his daughter, and blessed her congregation. It was another example of how people can change, be better after self-reflection, and acknowledge that someone's truth, although different than yours, is equally real and valid.

Over the years, many members of our gay community succumbed to the disease. I remember visiting my friend Glen James, who was dying of AIDS in the early 1990s. His partner Charlie Dirennzo was taking care of him until his own sudden death due to the disease. When Glen saw me, he immediately started playing with himself, "whacking his meat." I redirected his focus and covered him up. As you can imagine, actions like that deterred many visitors, but I realized that he wasn't being inappropriate on purpose. It was AIDS-related dementia compounded by loneliness and his need for physical contact. This was when he needed people the most, so I made sure to visit him regularly until he passed.

Another friend, Jamie Wilson, also had a partner who left their relationship when he was dying. I helped him with errands and even bought him a smaller car because he was too fatigued to get in and out of his massive truck. He passed in 2004. I hope that I was at least a beam of light during my friends' most lonely moments.

I constantly asked God why they died and not me, Did I start medication before symptoms? Was my previous excellent physical condition enough to get me through? Was it my faith?

On three occasions I was sick and febrile with Pneumocystis Jirovecii Pneumonia (PJP). This bug was responsible for taking many AIDS patients' lives. Each time I had PJP, it was during the summer when school wasn't in session. Luckily, I always turned the corner. I felt that God was protecting me from missing teaching and wrestling. Whenever my fever broke, I would say, "Thank you, God, I got one more year at North! We're gonna have the best damn wrestling team ever because it might be my last one!"

I once got sick in May toward the end of the school year. To save energy, I slept in the wrestling room. I just had to make it to the summer where I could rest and get better. I did, recovering from PJP for the fourth time. *I got one more year*, I thought.

When Russell had to be admitted to the hospital, the staff at Phoenix Baptist got to know us well and extended us many courtesies. They provided a rollaway bed so I could spend the night. When sleeping there, I made sure to bring a change of clothes for the next school day. Russ' health waxed and waned. Then it crashed on October 14, 1988.

After Love and Loss

The forecast for the day was cloudy skies and a chance of light rain. In the early morning, it started raining and didn't stop. It came down so hard local streets became rivers. Bethany Home Road, where Phoenix Baptist Hospital is, flooded, trapping cars on the street and in the parking lots. The severity of the downpour resulted in school closures. Radio and television stations announced cancellations of other events scheduled for the day.

A dear friend, Maratha, called me at six-fifteen that evening to say that Russ had just visited her kitchen. That's the moment Russ transitioned from the earth. Many of our friends believed that the rain was Heaven washing out to make space for Russell.

I was so melancholic my heart felt like someone ripped it out and trampled it on the ground. Had it not been for the support of friends, I would have dropped to the floor, paralyzed with grief and shock.

Russell was supposed to be my one and only, my long-term partner. I learned, over the years, that many gay people do not have one lifelong partner. The enormity of societal pressures, subsequent abuses (substance, domestic, and emotional), coupled with the AIDS epidemic, have made lifelong gay couples the exception to the rule. I also noticed some of my gay friends, who lost their partner, decided to stay single and became asexual. Instead of committing to another partner, they immersed themselves in other activities like church or civic volunteering. Each person navigates these hardships in their own way. I personally did not want to think of anyone or anything else but Russell. I wanted nothing to change. I wanted to keep the life we had together.

Bill Medley and Jennifer Warnes captured the emotion of the four years Russell and I shared when they sang "(I've Had) The Time of My Life." They released it in 1987, one year before Russell's passing. The soft-rock band Bread's song "Everything I Own" had me in tears almost every time I listened to it. I truly would have given EVERYTHING to have Russ back with me again! Music that mirrored my emotions in this way helped me sleep at night and navigate my grief.

My friends were so comforting. They reached out and sent cards in support. Some mentioned metaphysical occurrences, almost mimicking some of the experiences I had been having. One friend said they saw a light come down across their swimming pool around the time Russell passed. At the same time, another couple was on a road trip driving over a mountain when a sudden unique feeling passed through them. Finally, Russell's masseuse, who frequently helped with his lower leg edema by rubbing a crystal on it, heard a loud bang one night. She found the crystal split in two. She told me that had never happened to one of her crystals before.

Nobody knows what happens after death, but it's interesting to hear all these accounts. Maybe Russell was saying goodbye. Perhaps they were each friends' way to process his passing. I wasn't the only one grieving.

I couldn't let go of Russ in my thoughts or daily activities. I continued to work and made arrangements for his celebration of life. But I didn't socialize or go to wrestling. Louanne, Russell's sister, and my mother stayed with me and were my rocks of support. Russ had been so active in real estate and church that we had to hold the service outside to accommodate the many folks who came. Louanne spoke at his celebration of life, telling the gathering of Russell's friends and associates that she had "never seen such support" and that our congregation was "more a community than his own family."

Adding insult to injury, I had no say or right to make decisions under Arizona state law. Louanne, Russell's blood relative, had to sign all the county and state papers.

In addition to the ceremony at the MCC, I planned a service outside Albuquerque, New Mexico. Louanne didn't repeat the words she'd spoken about Russell's Phoenix friends because she didn't see the same level of support. In fact, she saw the opposite. Russell's family wrote an obituary for him but were more concerned about what to include, what not to reveal, and who would see it than honoring his life. Also, because many unreasonably feared his ashes could spread the virus, a group of us hiked to his favorite spot on earth, the Sandia Crest, to disperse them. We released balloons in his honor. It was magical, and some guests who didn't make the hike but flew home early claimed to see the balloons from their plane.

Today, Louanne is one of my closest family members. She and her two boys have always been a part of my life. Her son Steven once asked me to go to school with him when he was a sophomore in high school. Thinking I would only visit in the morning and then leave, I agreed. I ended up staying the entire day, meeting all his teachers and many friends. He introduced me as his Uncle Robert. That is just one indication of how close we were and still are.

Louanne and my mother stayed with me in Phoenix for over a month. When they left, sadly for me, on the same day, I felt so alone. I continued to isolate myself. My grief was so intense. I had lost the greatest love of my life. The man who loved me unconditionally and taught me how to love wholeheartedly in return. Russell was supposed to be with me forever. He left us, he left me, way before his time. I grieved for him and for the love that we had. I shut myself in the house and stayed there until friends Jamie, Kenn, Charlie, and Glen forced me out.

⁂

I went to my regular checkup with Dr. Fisher. He noticed that my CD4 count was low, at 105, indicating that I was in the AIDS range (<200 T-cells in a cubic millimeter of blood). Any other physician would have prescribed a cocktail of antibiotics, antivirals, and steroids. But Dr. Fisher took a "let's wait and see" approach since I didn't have any symptoms. He knew the level of my emotional stress after losing Russell. My low CD4 count reflected that. I just needed time. Time for my CD4 count to rise. Time for my sorrow to subside. Both eventually did improve. I give Dr. Fisher credit for that decision to wait. There's a good chance it saved my life.

After Russ passed, I learned that he had paid for a Mexican Riviera cruise for our fifth anniversary. The cruise line would not reimburse the money. I had to use the trip or lose the money. The cruise wasn't during a regular time off from school like spring break or a major holiday, so I needed an administrator at Trevor Browne to approve the leave. But who would approve the paperwork knowing the leave had to do with my late partner?

Arizona, as a state, was very homophobic, and it was no different at Trevor Browne. I knew I had to be upfront with the administration regarding my HIV status should an accident happen while teaching or coaching. By notifying the school district ahead of any incident, maybe I would be at least a little protected during this time of public hysteria.

In 1986, many states still had laws making it attempted murder if an individual accidentally infected someone with HIV. In the early 1990s, inflated worries over transmission myths were still rampant. HIV does not transmit via sweat or saliva. It only spreads through blood, semen, vaginal and anal mucosa, and breast milk. Yet in the National Basketball Association (NBA), Karl Malone was outspoken about refusing to play alongside HIV-positive players. That's one of the main reasons for Magic Johnson's retirement.

The national debate stirred by Kimberly Bergalis' alleged infection by her dentist led to further discrimination against HIV patients and even transformed politics. Laws forcing health care workers to take HIV tests, and laws testing patients for HIV without their consent, were approved.

I was already in a dentist's chair, only to have them refuse me service after I revealed my HIV-positive status. The dentist just didn't want to deal with any backlash if the public found out they treated me. If their office was practicing standard sterile techniques, like they should be for other blood-borne viruses like Hepatitis B and C, treating me should have been a non-issue.

I was blessed to find Dr. Richard F. Martin, DDS, to be my dentist. Such a loving man and provider. He often gave free services during medical missions in Mexico. When Steve and I had our commitment ceremony, Dr. Martin and his wife Judy attended. They were a bright spot during dark times.

Even within the gay community, gays discriminated against other gays who were HIV positive. I was ostracized, as were many of my HIV-positive friends. People were afraid to hug or touch us. It made me retreat, be less open, and more cautious with all my friends, both straight and gay. It reinforced my decision to separate my straight friends from my gay life, letting me avoid most conflict.

So with extreme caution, I selected the one administrator at Trevor Browne who seemed extremely honorable and full of integrity to whom I'd explain my situation. Linda Goins was the first female athletic director at Trevor Browne and dealt with constant gender discrimination. After telling her I was gay and had HIV, I was overwhelmed with fear about how the district would react to the news. Was that going to be the end of my teaching and coaching career?

Linda came up with a plan that allowed me to take leave, continue to teach, and volunteer with wrestling. With helpful information from Dr. Fisher, Linda began implementing HIV education for all Phoenix Union High School District schools. North High even made the news for its two-week HIV education session for faculty. Despite immense pressure from higher-up administrators to reveal my name, Linda refused, telling them the policies were important, not the person.

I learned later that Linda's younger brother was gay. He passed from AIDS-related illnesses in 2006. A former mental health counselor from Kentucky, she had learned to value and respect all people. In me, she saw someone who was driving across town to do his passion, wrestling. Linda herself would say she rooted for me, the committed, hard-working, talented, caring, and good-hearted underdog. I earned her respect, which returned peace, faith, and love in my heart. She reversed the darkness that society pushed gay, Black, HIV-positive men, including me, toward. Linda is, without a doubt, an angel in my life.

·_·· ___ ···_·

CHAPTER 13

Living and Loving Again

New Love

As I tried getting back to normal, I sang along to a song from the movie Dirty Dancing. "I've . . . had . . . the time of my life." Russ was my soul mate, my sustainer, and a model partner for a loving relationship. Russ and I had been in a bowling league, and I returned to our team, initially trying to mimic the life we had together. Many of the members were kind and supportive. It took me about six months to open up to the possibility that my life could begin moving forward again. That's when Robert Orlick, another bowler, expressed the desire to have dinner with me.

At first, I refused Robert's advances, still clinging to memories of Russell. Plus, I had a rule about not dating friends. I didn't want any awkwardness should things go south. Maybe because he was persistent, perhaps because I was lonely, I finally agreed to dine with him. Even then, I was slightly abrasive, telling him, "Don't call me, I'll call you." I called him a lot. It felt good to talk to someone who understood what I was going through. He was very nurturing during my grieving process.

Robert also had HIV, but we never discussed the details of how we each got it. It didn't matter. At that time, I had already known

Robert for about three years from bowling, social parties, and church events. On his birthday, the ninth of April, we decided to become committed partners and move in together. He told me, "This is the best present ever."

To help with closure after Russell's passing, his sister Louanne made a quilt in Russell's honor for the ongoing Names Project. You can find it under Russ Fetters #1268. It is absolutely beautiful with gold and silver fabric, showing Russell in a wrestling singlet, with me lying next to him. Remarkably, it is almost identical to a photo I had. Louanne hadn't seen the picture, which imbued the quilt with an almost supernatural quality. Also stitched on the quilt are verses from Bob Dylan's "Blowin' in the Wind," very fitting in capturing the sentiment of those affected by the epidemic.

The Names Project, originated by Cleve Jones, started as a 1,000-pound quilt consisting of 1,920 smaller quilts, each representing an AIDS death in the United States. This work of love toured the country, debuting in Washington D.C. on October 11, 1987. In April of 1988, the quilt arrived in Phoenix. Russell and I received training on how to handle, walk with, and open the quilt to protect the delicate ornaments that lined the various pieces. Russell was chosen to read some of the newly added names. By this time, there were about 8,000 small quilts. The Names Project received a nomination for the 1989 Nobel Peace Prize. By 2020, the quilt had grown to approximately 108,000 pounds (fifty-four tons), with nearly 50,000 panels representing the lives and deaths of over 105,000 Americans.

Now Robert Orlick and I, the oral Roberts, as we used to introduce ourselves, playing off the famous TV evangelist Oral Roberts, were a pair. We continued bowling at Squaw Peak Lanes on 30th Street and Indian School Road. The place took its name from the local urban mountain now called Piestewa Peak (while researching for this book, I discovered the facility closed in 2013). Every Monday night, we joined our gay friends and packed the house. It was almost like another gay bar. There were raffles in which the prize money often reached $1,300. If nobody claimed the prize, it rolled into the next Monday's pot. People bought extra tickets in a drunken frenzy, hoping to win. "That girlfriend's spending her rent money," we joked.

One time, a straight guest complained to the manager. Something about them wanting separate lanes because they were uncomfortable with us, with all the "gayness" going on.

"Do you know how much money these people spend? Are you out of your mind?" The manager staunchly refused.

Money talks. And it definitely spoke in our favor during those Monday raffle nights.

On the personal side, Robert was a self-trained Computer Assisted Design (CAD) designer of municipal buildings and water treatment plants. He had taken classes at Purdue University but dropped out in his junior year. As the CAD field grew, Robert attended workshops to update his skills. Despite not having a degree, he was a valuable employee because he could use current and old techniques to complete tasks. His Type-A work ethic made him a top member of project teams.

At home, Robert was a handyman who purchased the latest tools and could do almost any job. That was a blessing since Russ left me five houses that needed work. Robert was a perfectionist, often bringing that attitude home, which caused many arguments. I wanted him to leave that mentality at the door.

When we disagreed, my first reaction was to stop talking. This approach increased Robert's anger, which resulted in me leaving the house. One day, his anger caused him to destroy an item in the house. That's when I knew we needed professional help.

We scheduled sessions with the same counselor I had previously consulted with Russ. I had learned techniques for building a good relationship but wanted Robert to hear them from another person as validation. Robert's perfectionist and aggressive attitude manifested not only in our home but in the bowling league, where he was known as the Junkyard Dog. His tantrums at the bowling alley were hurtful and embarrassing. During our heightened arguments, I often said nothing. Instead, I handed him a handwritten letter and walked away. When I returned, it was easier to have a receptive discussion with Robert when he would say, "I didn't know you felt that way." Over time, he learned to respond less aggressively and more lovingly during our disagreements.

Another source of conflict revolved around wrestling. I made extra efforts to spend more quality time with Robert to make up for the long hours spent with wrestling. It did not help that I didn't allow him to attend any wrestling events. I couldn't truthfully explain who he was to people, so I didn't want to introduce that uncertainty into my career. Also, he was still prone to temper tantrums, and I couldn't risk that. I had experienced such events in the past with my previous partner, Gary. I didn't want history repeating itself.

Some of our worst fights were over me not being home when I said I would be. The length of time it took me to get home after a wrestling event varied because I stayed at school until everyone got picked up or I took them home. Also, in the middle of the night, twice that I can remember, I drove to pick up and help a wrestler in need.

Robert didn't understand that the wrestlers and wrestlerettes were my kids and that I needed to do what a reasonable parent would do. On this point, I could not compromise, and Robert could not win any argument with me. I did what was needed to keep the kids safe.

Through counseling, Robert understood more of what wrestling and teaching meant to me. It lessened our arguments when I came home late, and he later donated money to the wrestling program. But looking back, I should have figured out a way to include Robert in my wrestling life. Even if he sat in the stands as a random spectator, he would have seen me in my element and witnessed my passion. It would have connected us on a more intimate level. I was not courageous enough to overcome my fears. I still regret that.

A few friends from Michigan knew about Russell, but none had met Robert. As it happened, my ex-wrestler and fellow Adelphic Olivet alum Rich Levitte had been trying to reach me for a few years. His persistence finally led him to call my mother. She gave him my updated contact information, and he called me.

I didn't answer the first time because I honestly wasn't sure what to tell him. He was one of the first wrestlers I had coached and called my kid. Could I tell him the truth? I wrestled with the idea for a while. Then he called again. This time I answered. It felt so good to hear his upbeat voice. He told me about his two daughters Regan and Paige and filled me in on important life events as he had done in years past. I was supportive, happy that he had called, and humbled yet again that he valued me so much. I did not reveal my truth to him then. I think it's because I wanted to tell him in person. So Robert and I made a trip to Michigan to see family and friends.

When we visited Rich and his wife Sue, it felt like a warm hug. Rich would tell you it was an initial shock to learn I was gay, but I didn't notice any change in his demeanor. He was just as accepting and loving as before.

Jovial and more relieved than anything with their acceptance, I could be myself with the people I cared about.

Rich and I are close friends today, and we're both very involved with Olivet alumni events. Rich tells me all the time that he is so grateful I grabbed his arm and suggested he come out for wrestling that fateful day at Hartland. Since then his life unfolded on an amazing course with wrestling, meeting his wife at Olivet, having two beautiful daughters, including one graduating from Olivet. Rich loves every minute of life.

He told me, "It's not what you've done. It's what you've helped others do. You are the finest human being I have ever met."

I am humbled and honored to have been able to echo my own experiences through Rich, for I too received my introduction to wrestling through a mentor/coach who grabbed my arm in the school hallway nearly twenty years before I encountered Rich. A coach who reached out just because he believed in me.

Anyone who knows Rich will tell you that he is one of the finest and most honorable human beings himself. The two of us are born out of similar experiences.

⚶

In 1993, Robert and I had a commitment ceremony with family and friends. We sustained each other in times of sickness while maintaining our jobs and homes. I was blessed to only get sick in the summers, so I didn't have to miss any school. In the summer of 1996, I was severely ill with Pneumocystis Jirovecii Pneumonia (PJP). It's the same infection that took Russell's and so many others' lives due to HIV. Robert tended to my every need, including carrying me to the restroom, hand-feeding, and bathing me. With only weeks left before the start of school, my fever broke, and my strength slowly returned. I made it back to teach and coach. Nobody at the school knew how close I had been to the grave. Robert's unconditional love and care, my passion and dedication to wrestling, and God's grace got me through it.

By the end of 1996, my new HAART HIV regimen was working. My CD4 counts normalized, and the virus was undetectable. For the first time in a decade, Robert and I could start planning for our future. I pursued my master's at Northern Arizona University. We sold all our houses except the one where we resided and looked at retirement homes in places like Payson and Wilcox before settling on Prescott, where we purchased a lot in the Park Avenue district. We wanted 1,400 square feet with no stairs. We learned that the slope of the land on this lot would require stairs to separate levels. We didn't want the extra hassle, so we decided to sell it for a $35,000 profit and purchased a different house. Over the next few years, we continued to work in Phoenix, renting an apartment, and stayed in our Prescott home on the weekends.

In Prescott, we made new friends. Marriner Cardon was one of the first. Marriner is an older White man, a lawyer with a vast knowledge of world religions who seems to know everything. I view him as a mentor I can confide in during difficult decisions. He helped orient us to the different churches and places where other gay men socialized, such as Bistro St. Michael in the historic hotel. He also told us of the many diversity camps held in Prescott. Anytown Leadership Camp was one. Ourtown was another camp that Marriner helped spearhead in conjunction with his congregation. These were the camps we mimicked when we formed NFL at North High.

In 1997, we attended one of these diversity camps in Prescott. It was Robert's first such camp since only North faculty and students could go to the NFL camps. I was still worried about people knowing my sexual orientation and explained to Robert that we would sign up as two individuals. That didn't last long.

In one exercise, everyone lined up and performed the "privilege walk," also known as the "culture walk." The instructor yelled, "If you had a family vacation as a kid, take one step forward. If not, take a step back." The exercise continued with all kinds of scenarios. At the end of the exercise, we noticed one kid was far back compared to everyone else, a single step from the edge of a ravine. He was blind and couldn't see that his life was at risk. It was a powerful moment, literally and metaphorically. We are all blind to our upbringing and privilege. Only with self-reflection and community discussions does one realize the hand one's dealt. Once discovered, the necessary life changes to overcome one's challenges can be made.

The diversity camp was so effective that, by the end of the first day, I publicly announced that Robert and I were a couple. Even though he was gay, Robert was quite conservative. That didn't stop him from soaking in the atmosphere of the camp. It was a welcome sight to see Robert meet a ska-punk, purple-haired, atheist high school student named James Rivard.

Despite different backgrounds, they became instant friends. Robert's hard shell cracked, and he embraced new perspectives and open dialogue. He realized that even though James didn't seem like someone he'd normally befriend, they had more in common than initially thought. They connected on a deep level that superseded superficiality.

Word got out that Robert and I were about to celebrate our commitment ceremony anniversary. As a surprise, the camp brought a cake for us. By far, this was my best and most relaxed weekend in quite a while because it was one of the first times I could be openly gay around straight people.

Over the years, I saw James at many diversity camps. He once paid me a beautiful compliment.

"You've made an impact on many of my friends' lives even after only meeting them a few times. Not many people can do that. That's, for lack of a better word, Christlike."

I was speechless.

As Christians, our goal is to act like Christ. To be loving, selfless, serving, and humbled. I felt a sense of serenity and pure happiness to know I made a difference in peoples' lives. I genuinely try to empathize with everyone I meet. By sharing my experiences, I am often able to help someone navigate through a difficult time. I embrace serving my neighbors. Service is in my nature. It has also been ingrained in me by my religious upbringing, my work as a teacher and coach, and by my amazing mother. It's what brings me the most joy while invigorating my spirit.

The Journey Once More

In 1999, Robert's health started to fail, and I needed to spend more time at home. After caring for Russell, I knew the type of care Robert would eventually need. I reduced my time with the wrestling team to be with him. Coach Wright and I bumped heads on more than one coaching decision, thus making it easier to commit more time to Robert. Robert's employer, Carrollo Engineers, was also very supportive, allowing him to work half-days while keeping him on full pay. We did not have any financial troubles since our combined income was over $175,000.

Over the next few years of Robert's declining health, I ran between school, doctors, the pharmacy, and the hospital. It was difficult but necessary. As his mental decline progressed, Robert often yelled out vulgarities and even pulled out his Foley catheter. Sadly, this forced us to use restraints. Despite these events, the hospital staff was understanding when they dealt with Robert and me. I shared Robert's health and my need to be with him with my small support system at North High.

When Robert was bedbound, Monique Mendel, one of my life's angels and teacher at North, said to me at school one day, "What are you doing here?"

She escorted me to the office, and I checked out for the day. She was a Jewish mother to me.

I applied for family leave. This meant the school district would hold my teaching position, but I wouldn't get paid. I listed Robert's name on the paperwork. Soon after, I had a meeting with an official and learned they had denied my request. The district questioned why I asked for family leave to care for someone who was not a family member. It was clear to me that Robert and I were a family, but the district did not recognize gay couples or commitment ceremonies.

In my nearly twenty-five years of teaching, I never missed a day of school. Since I couldn't get family leave, I went the medical leave route with a note from Dr. Fisher. On medical leave, I got paid my daily rate, and the school paid for a substitute teacher. The total for both was over $300 per day. Lack of compassion actually cost the school more. But what mattered the most, I was able to be there for Robert.

With the help of good friends, we cared for Robert in those final days. I decided not to coach during this time and drew back from all social commitments. Robert and I talked a lot about our relationship, what he wanted at his celebration of life, and what I should do when he was gone. These were difficult conversations. I wanted him to live.

I remember holding him out by our pool. His head was on my chest. He said, "You know, I'm okay if you want to go to the bars."

Lovingly, I looked down at him. "Why would I want to go to the bars? You're my partner, and I love you. What if something happens to you? I'm here till the end because that's who I am."

I just held him, cherishing every last moment we had together.

On February 28, 2002, Robert Orlick transitioned from this world. Mama stayed with me like she had done after Russell passed. She told me that Robert had called her every week just to talk, mostly about me. I think these talks helped him understand my passion for wrestling and made our relationship all the more loving.

Robert and I had a tradition of gifting each other teddy bears on special days like birthdays and anniversaries. We amassed over sixty bears. I spread the bears throughout the church pews and asked the people sitting next to bears to please take them home as a memory of Robert.

Robert's sister, Donna, flew in from Chicago to help with the paperwork. After all this time, the state of Arizona still did not recognize us as a married couple, so I could not sign anything about what to do with his body. Thankfully, Donna was more than willing to help. Robert and I lived together for over thirteen years, yet we had no rights in the eyes of the law. The law has since changed, and I'm glad to say that same-sex couples no longer have to endure similar restrictions.

Donna wanted to have another ceremony in Chicago with the rest of Robert's family. She asked if I could separate his ashes into smaller urns for them. My grief was so intense that I could not do as she requested. Instead, I met her in Chicago to pass on the entire urn.

During my trip, one of the airport security personnel suspected I was transporting cocaine. Before I could protest, he had sampled the ashes with his finger. When I told him it wasn't cocaine, but human remains in the urn, he became expressionless. With haste and without further delay, they let me through security.

Upon my arrival in Chicago, Donna informed me the family didn't want me to go to the ceremony. I was hurt. I did not have a deep relationship with the rest of the family but had stayed with Donna on more than one occasion when Robert was alive. I was disappointed she didn't stand up for me. I gave her the urn and went to visit my family in Michigan to occupy the next few days. On my return trip through Chicago, I retrieved the urn from Donna and made my way back to Phoenix. Sadly, I have not kept in touch with Donna or any other member of Robert's family.

⚘

Shortly after Robert died, I entered another extreme depression. I wanted to leave everything and isolate myself like before. I even felt suicidal. Why would God allow me to fall in love with two wonderful men only to take them away? John caught me in the bathroom with water and a handful of pills. That's when my friends set up teams to spend time with me. One of those friends was Richard Bradley.

When Robert and I first met Richard at the MCC in Phoenix, I told him, "It'll be easy to remember our names because we are the oral Roberts."

After Robert's passing, Richard moved into our Phoenix apartment to help watch over me. We talked a lot about God, the blessings in my life, and what Robert would want me to do. Richard worked for the government as a public health advisor, had degrees in religious studies and philosophy, and knew firsthand the effects of the AIDS epidemic. If not for Richard Bradley living with me, I might have chosen suicide.

That was the only time in my life I contemplated such an act. I did not see a future for myself and felt death was the best option. The societal pressures against being gay, HIV-positive, and Black were nothing compared to the grief of losing not one but a second life partner. I kept my mind occupied during the day, but nighttime was a different story. It was hard to sleep. I watched the movie *Sleepless in Seattle* over and over and related to the emotion in it. Like Tom Hanks' character in the film, I purchased oversized pillows to hug and listened to radio stations that played nature and rain sounds.

Kevin Sharp's song "Nobody Knows" struck me to the core. How did this stranger know what was in my heart? How could no one around me see I was dying mentally and emotionally? I carried a portable cassette player and played the song on repeat. After a while, the tape jammed in the recorder. I took that as a sign it was time to move on. Still, if I hear the song while driving, I must pull over and stop for fear of losing my composure.

With the passing of Russell and Robert, I learned grief is not something one just gets over. I found myself going through the entire gamut of emotions. Little things triggered flashbacks. For example, I remember shopping in a mall and noticing a man in front of me walking with the same gait as Robert. Grief came over me so abruptly I had to go into the nearest restroom and cry. Other times, while alone at home, I heard my partner call my name from the other end of the house. When somebody loves you, the way they say your name is different from anybody else. I knew it wasn't real, but for a few seconds, I hoped I would see him.

The grief counselor comforted me, explaining that it was okay to cry when grief overwhelmed me. The hardest part was when grief overcame me at school during class. I asked my students to please stay in their seats as I stepped outside the classroom to get myself under control.

Later, I learned I was experiencing AIDS Survivor Syndrome. I was not alone in having such strong emotions. I was never alone. Knowing that helped me heal.

No Escape from a Widow's Fate

I started dating again, but from 2002 until 2007, no relationship lasted longer than six months. I did not meet anyone who might be a potential long-term partner. In 2006, I retired from North High and permanently moved to Prescott. I attended the Unity church as it is open to gay and lesbian members. But I missed my home church in Phoenix and often drove down for Sunday service.

One Sunday in Phoenix, the usher said there was a visitor from Prescott. That visitor was Steve Isaman. We exchanged phone numbers so we could carpool to future services in Phoenix. The next Saturday, I called to arrange the ride to church. Steve asked why I had not called during the week. I sternly replied that because of my past relationship history, I was only interested in sharing a ride. I gave him many reasons we could only be friends. The most important reason was my HIV status and that both my past lovers died of the disease.

Steve didn't care about any of these reasons. I felt comforted and relaxed hearing such a nonjudgmental response. Maybe I could lower some of my psychological barriers. He was also an older White guy, which fit the mold of my preferred partners.

We dated for about eight months before he moved in with me. On May 3, 2008, we had a commitment ceremony at Goldwater Lake, just south of Prescott. We planned for 180 guests, but more than 200 showed up, including around twenty former wrestlers and wrestlerettes. It was like a coming-out party. My kids knew my secret now, and it meant the world to have them there in support.

Steve was a gym rat who worked out almost every day. We practiced safe sex and he got tested frequently for HIV. It was essential to both of us that he remain negative.

At this time, I was a volunteer coach at Bradshaw Mountain and Steve supported my passion as long as we checked in with each other during the day.

We went on many trips around Arizona and southern California. I still remember when Steve removed his shirt at the beach and showed off his heavenly body. I enjoyed holding his hand and cuddling up to his massive muscles. In L.A. I surprised Steve with tickets to see Patti LaBelle. Her song, "On My Own" reminded him of his mother who had passed just three years prior.

On another trip, we drove from Prescott and toured through San Francisco and the Russian River, all the way to the Redwood National

Park. Bodega Bay is one place we stopped, the site where Hitchcock filmed his classic horror movie *The Birds*.

Life was good. I added Steve's name to the deed of the house. We made plans to improve our home and cleared space for his growing garden and chicken coop. We had no issues, no significant fights, and it reminded me of the days with Russell.

Then in May of 2010, I received another high honor. Nick Kehagias graduated medical school and included me onstage with his mother, aunt, and grandmother (who had flown to Arizona from Greece) for his hooding ceremony. He thanked me, saying he would not have gotten to where he was without my positive influence, hard-working example, and love. That I, along with his family, was one of his most powerful role models. It is no surprise to me today that he spearheaded this telling of my story. I am truly grateful.

༰

Back in Prescott, Steve was my rock, especially when my sister Orpah passed away on August 19, 2010. Her passing made me extremely sad. Of all my family members, she was my stoutest defender when others made snide comments about my sexuality. She got into four shouting matches, that I knew of, with my dad on the subject.

Orpah worked as a peer educator on HIV and even passed out clean needles to help decrease the spread of bloodborne diseases. Her daughter, my niece, Angel Nicole, whom I call Nikki, took on the role of my protector when Orpah died. My family is very important to me, and I make an effort to contact them via phone or a card on their birthdays and holidays. I encouraged them to pursue education, and I even helped with tuition if needed.

This influence came all the way down from Grandpa Kemp, the family's original settler in Albion. My cousin Pat Brown Paul reminded me of what Grandpa used to say.

"Get God, get an education, and nobody can ever take that away from you."

With God's grace, I embraced these habits and applied them to the wrestling program. The wrestlers and wresterlettes are also my kids, my family.

I try to be there for my family yet notice that awkwardness sometimes exists when I'm around. It's more noticeable with the men in my family. At family get-togethers, it's common for the women to socialize in one room while the men are in another room talking and watching sports. I remember walking into the loud and boisterous room on multiple occasions when the men were trash-talking, laughing, and yelling at each other, only to be met with awkward silence.

I mean, come on, guys. I like sports too and can trash-talk with the best of them. Just because I'm gay doesn't mean I only have stereotypical gay interests.

That is a huge misconception that anybody with at least one gay friend recognizes. I'm the same person my family knew growing up. They just can't see that. Despite having less contact with the men in my family, I still want them to know I love them and am there for them. I will be there for my nieces and nephews if needed. That is a family rule I have and try to abide by.

There was only one exception to the family rule—my dad. My dad didn't pay much attention to us after we moved to Albion. So I wasn't surprised he broke off communication with me after he learned I was gay. We never talked again. I didn't even go to his funeral. I wish I had enjoyed a better relationship with him. Sometimes circumstances just don't work out that way. My mother was the perfect role model and father figure. She filled any void my dad left.

ॐ

Just when life was as perfect as it could be, tragedy struck. In the early morning of March 8, 2011, Steve suffered a heart attack. The EMTs arrived along with the police and transported him to the hospital. The police looked around the house with flashlights and were reluctant to leave. I got angry because I wanted to be with Steve in the hospital, so I demanded they leave our home. They finally left, and I called a few friends who met me at the emergency room.

The staff at the hospital initially prohibited me from seeing Steve since I was not a blood relative. Only after my friends protested on my behalf did they allow me to say goodbye to Steve.

It was devastating.

To make matters worse, the county sheriff and coroner's office questioned me as if I caused his death. The hospital failed to treat me with respect since they did not recognize us as a couple. Yet they didn't have a problem sending medical bills to the house in MY name.

I ignored the bills.

Unlike Robert and Russell, who had been sick for quite some time before passing, Steve's passing was quick and unexpected. Like a zombie with stoic movements, I took care of necessary arrangements. Internally, my despair was further rooted in the thought that nobody should have a funeral home on speed dial or know which florist to contact for such occasions. And I couldn't even sign my husband's documents because, yet again, our relationship was not recognized by the state. Had it not been for supporters like Debbie Davey, I could easily have broken down. I met Debbie through Steve. Talking with her reminds me of him to this day.

Steve's sister Cheryl assisted with the funeral planning. Friends filled the visitation room to overflowing. The children of our friends were a big part of our family too. I routinely send cards for Christmas and birthdays. To them, we were Uncle Robert and Uncle Steve.

Many members of the Unity Church came together to form the Steve Isaman Scholarship fund. We raised enough money to give several scholarships of $1,000. It is still active today.

Months later, I continued to grieve and longed for companionship. In August of 2011, I joined an online dating service. I had lost multiple partners with whom I had committed to spending the rest of my life. Was I cursed to never find life lasting love? I didn't have to wait long because, on September 18th, I started talking with Michael Tighe.

I learned that Mike had three adult children with his ex-wife. When he had visitation with his children, he often had to clean them up, shampoo their heads to kill the lice, and buy new clothes. I like the fact that Mike was a responsible parent. He was up-to-date on his alimony and continued to pay until the youngest child was almost twenty years old. To do this, he sold his car, moved close to the public transit, and worked two jobs. He had periods of unemployment, but even then, his priority was the care of his children. Mike has nearly twenty years of sobriety and strictly follows the Twelve-Step program. He is committed and dedicated, characteristics I admire in a long-term partner.

Mike came with me to a Bradshaw Mountain track meet. I introduced him as a friend, and they put him to work.

I don't worry anymore about what anyone thinks about my sexuality, and I talk openly about it. Prejudice still exists, and I don't force my views upon anyone. I have noticed less bias over the decades, so I am optimistically hopeful. Everyone has a past and being able to persevere and bloom despite difficult times is what matters.

·_·· ____ ···_·

CHAPTER 14

Words of Faith and Love

Spirituality and Sexuality

In the Bible's Old Testament, Jeremiah 1:4-5 (International Children's Bible) states, "The word of the Lord came to me saying: 'Before I made you in your mother's womb I chose you. Before you were born I set you apart for a special work.'" Everyone is born for their special work and has the ability to make a difference in the world.

I have a Bubba Gump T-shirt that reads, "My mama says I'm Special." That could easily read, "God and my mama say I'm Special." I'm special just the way God made me. Some people argue that my sexuality is a choice. Those people don't understand that there are different ways of loving. I believe in God and feel that my spirituality and sexuality are one and the same. Learning to love myself in the face of early religious teaching that told me I was damned and going to hell was a challenge. With maturity, plus a lot of prayers, I might add, I learned to follow my heart, to follow my truth. I love myself just the way I am.

I attended the Metropolitan Community Church (MCC) in Flint for the first time in 1978. The MCC promotes the belief that God is love and encourages people to break free of doctrines that try to separate a person's spirituality and sexuality. Opponents of this belief ask that we return to traditional family values as illustrated in the Bible. Look at family values in the Bible and compare them to today's standards to see many questionable examples. Cain kills Abel. David kills a man to have sex with his wife. Ruth secretly sleeps with a rich man. Women caught in the act of adultery are stoned to death. Herod kills hundreds of boys under the age of two to find Jesus. People with leprosy were killed or banished. We can go on and on. Which of these family values should we follow? Where are compassion, love, and understanding? If Jesus had interacted with gays, lesbians, bisexuals, and transsexuals, what would He have done?

Leviticus 18:22 (New King James Version) says, "You shall not lie with a man as with a woman; it is an abomination." Then Leviticus 20:10 (New American Bible (Revised Edition)) states, "If a man commits adultery with another man's wife both the adulterer and the adulteress are to be put to death." So anyone who ever cheated on their spouse should be killed? Today, it's obvious that this is an extreme response. We can go on for pages worth of these Old Testament rules. That raises the question—which verses are we to pick and choose for how we should live life?

Luckily for us, we don't have to worry about that because many New Testament verses tell us to leave the old rules and follow the new teachings of Christ. Romans 7:6 (English Standard Version), for example, states, "But now we are released from the law, having died to that which held us captive, so that we serve in the new way of the Spirit and not in the old way of the written code." Another example, Hebrews 8:13 (ESV), says, "In speaking of a new covenant, he makes the first one obsolete. And what is becoming obsolete and growing old is ready to vanish away." I feel there is no better verse than Hebrews 8:13 to catch the view of an ever-changing modern world. Not just for the Christian view on homosexuality, but for all topics in the search for truth and justice.

I believe Jesus would live up to John 3:16 (ESV), which says, "For God so loved the world that he gave his one and only Son that whosoever believes in him shall not perish but have eternal life."

"Whosoever" means everyone gets included and treated with love. Those who are against gays often say they love us but hate our sin. How can they love us if they want to deny us employment, housing, promotions, safety, and happiness?

Like Martin L. King expressed in his "I Have a Dream" speech, I too want people to judge me on my character, ethics, and work, not on the color of my skin or who I love. If you love me, you will celebrate me being the best me I can be.

The pivot point is how we love one another. The kind of love described in 1 Corinthians 13:4–8 and 13 (NIV). "Love is patient, love is kind. It does not envy, it does not boast, it is not proud. It does not dishonor others, it is not self-seeking, it is not easily angered, it keeps no record of wrongs. Love does not delight in evil, but rejoices with TRUTH. It always protects, always trusts, always hopes, always perseveres. Love never fails . . . And now these three remain: Faith, Hope, and Love. But the greatest of these is LOVE."

Love is boldly proclaimed to everyone. It provides opportunities, not roadblocks. Love builds bridges, not walls. Love is freedom. Love may not act or look like you. Love is giving your best to another. Love knows that we are better together. Love is a story that must be told and must be heard. Love is what it is, not based on any one person's morals and values.

I grew up believing some people would be saved and some would go to hell to burn in eternal fire. We were taught to fear the wrath of God. As I got older, I began to test some of these values. I learned about the grace and boundless love of God. I did not have to be limited to a set of conditions. I encountered people full of fear who claimed to be acting on behalf of God. They preached this fear and often declared that God wants us to act a certain way.

I decided I would wait for God to speak directly to me. The Bible is a blueprint for getting to heaven, and if God is love, then we can all go to heaven. If you want to see a Christian, listen to my words and watch what I do.

Galatians 5:22–23 (ESV): "But the fruit of the spirit is love, joy, peace, patience, kindness, goodness, faithfulness, gentleness, self-control; against such things there is NO law."

Mama Said

Mama passed away in May of 2012. Yet she is still with me today. It was a blessing to have family in Albion routinely visit my mother when she was in declining health. This included my cousin, Chrissy Pressley, and God-brother, Frank Cooper. They made sure she was fed, bathed, attended church, had groceries, and took her meds. Chrissy even met Mike during my frequent trips to Michigan.

She tells me, "If everyone in the world could model ourselves after you, the world would be a better place. Despite all you've gone through, you're still positive."

I thanked her for those kind words and reiterated how blessed and grateful I was for her care of my mother. Every Mother's Day, I send Chrissy a thank you card, even though she never had kids of her own. I do the same for Frank on Father's Day.

Josh Groban sang a song that helped me cope with Mama's death. We played "You Raise Me Up" at her memorial service. I used to say I never wanted to be like my mother, yet I see her in things I do and say. I am proud of the example she set for our family.

As I got older, I realized how hard it must have been for her to raise our family. We boys were certainly aware that the majority of young Black men growing up when we did ended up in prison. My mother raised three boys on her own and made sure we did nothing that would send us there. My oldest brother did get into some trouble. When the police called to inform my mother, her response was, "Keep him overnight." He never got into trouble again.

Mama had a way of doing things and speaking that kept us in line. I find myself delivering some of those same decrees to my teams. Things like, "You leave here together. You come home together." That was her rule when we went to football games as teenagers. We had to be home by 10:30 p.m., not 10:32 p.m. I now understand she wanted everyone in the house before she left for work at eleven. We couldn't make plans with our friends because Mama didn't give us permission until the last minute.

"We'll see," she would always say.

When we ventured away from home, there was always a lecture on how to behave, a demand for a phone number where she could reach us, and a time she expected us home. If we were near a fight, we had to leave and run in the opposite direction. Otherwise, she'd comment, "If you stand around to watch a fight, you are just as guilty as the ones fighting."

Her rules included:

- Do not talk back to adults if you think they are wrong. Bring it home, and I will handle the issue.
- If it does not belong to you, keep your hands off it.
- If you borrow something, return it in clean and working condition.
- You cannot clean the floor with a mop. You must get on your knees.

Before we left the house, my mother inspected our clothes and hair and rubbed lotion on our bodies if needed. She told us we represented not only ourselves but also our home.

"Don't embarrass yourself or your home. What happens at home stays at home."

She frequently shared affirmations to build our character and self-esteem. Her example made us strong and resilient.

I tried to be as strong as her, but when Russell and Robert died, it was hard. I've described how my mother visited me in Phoenix and stayed for a month after each death. She was with me as I took care of all arrangements. When grief overtook me, she grasped my hand and said, "Be strong."

I didn't want to be strong. I just wanted to cry.

Yet there were so many things to complete during those times. I appeared resilient, when in reality, I was hiding in those distractions. I busied myself with a multitude of tasks during the day so I would be exhausted by bedtime. I was my own personal *Sleepless in Seattle*. When Mama returned to Michigan, I missed her so much I cried.

Her words of wisdom comforted me then and still do today. There is a Mama-shaped story behind each of them.

- You are no better than anyone, and they are no better than you.
- Treat people the way you want to be treated.
- Don't let anyone steal your joy.
- If you don't have anything good to say, don't say anything.
- Let your answers be yes or no, then stop talking.
- Don't be a messenger; let people go to the source.
- Do it today. Tomorrow is not promised.
- The tongue is the smallest member of the body, but it can cause the most trouble.
- Vote with your feet.
- Life isn't easy—get used to it.
- Always do your best.
- Pride goes before a fall.
- Look at what you have, not what you don't have.
- It's better to be early than late.

Our home life stressed that we should always do our best. When my mother gave up working as a domestic to work at the County Hospital, two of her clients requested that she continue cleaning their homes. One was Dr. Ralph Cram. He cared for our family with house calls and often deferred payments. The other was Ms. Margorie Sautyer. She lived by herself. When Ms. Margy was in failing health, my mother also provided home health care for her. Ms. Margy later went to a nursing home. When we visited her, she said to me, "Your mother is my best friend."

My mother had integrity and always did her best.

During one visit to Phoenix, Mama joined me during the school day at North High. When some kids got out of line, all I had to do was give her the "Okay, they're all yours, Mom" look, and she took care of it. She motioned the unruly kid aside, opened her Bible, and began preaching. My mother had this way, not just with us but with others.

"Your word is your bond" was another value passed to us from my mother. She often purchased items on credit at stores and reconciled her debts on payday. Sometimes that meant walking nearly three miles round-trip just to make a ten-dollar payment. She had no extra money but was rich in her words and honor.

I sent my mother monthly checks to help with living expenses. These checks were accepted and returned stamped by the bank. Which made one experience in Albion that much more puzzling.

Once while visiting Michigan, before the advent of automatic teller machines, I ran out of cash. I went to my mother's bank to cash a check and noticed that the teller was an old high school classmate. Despite that, the bank refused to honor my check because it was from Arizona.

I protested, "You cash my checks from Arizona every month."

After the teller talked with the manager, they requested that I bring a note from my mother before they would honor the check. I was in my 40s and still in the shadow of my mother. That's okay. I didn't fight it. I would be under her influence, in some shape or form, for the rest of her life and mine.

Since I always helped Mama with her living expenses, one way she thanked me was to send me more than thirty dozen cookies for Christmas.

I protested, "Mom, I can't eat all of these."

Her reply was, "Then you know what to do."

I bagged up the cookies and handed them out to the school faculty. The staff at North got so used to the goodies that they asked for them first thing before saying good morning. One of my friends was unhappy with his bag of cookies for some reason. He called my mother to complain. She sent him a new box of cookies. Even when one of the PE teachers retired and moved to San Diego, I still sent him his portion of the treats.

"You always have enough to share," was Mama's firm belief. She baked the utmost delicious pound cakes. When one was almost gone, we children fought over who got the last piece. Mama solved the issue when she took the last piece and sliced it so thin you could read through it, ensuring that we all got a piece of cake.

These lessons from my mother, and even more than I've mentioned here, guided my actions and reasoning when engaging others. The greatest work in life is service to others. When we think of miracles, we often envision a choir of angels singing through parting clouds. In reality, miracles are the work we do for others. Mama taught me the actions and thoughts that help me create even minor miracles in people's lives.

$$\cdot\_\cdot\cdot \quad \underline{\quad} \quad \cdot\cdot\cdot\_\cdot$$

CHAPTER 15

Legacy of Service and Love

I send Father's Day cards to some of my friends who have kids. One card said, "We all go about our lives doing good deeds for others and then we go on to another chapter in our lives not thinking about the good seeds of the past. Then we notice the beautiful flower from the good seeds we've sown. I know this is true because one of those flowers is me."

To grow flowers, you need sunlight, good soil, water, and sometimes plant food. Metaphorically, these are the people who sustain me in life and are the reason for my success. When I think of these family and friends, I know they are my silent place. They come to sit with me, and in that sacred space, they raise me above my worries and sorrows. Then I reach for their hands so we can rise together.

Over the last few years, I have given dozens of talks about diversity for our church and our schools, and accepted an invitation to give a TED talk. The teachings I share are not new or creative. They were passed down to me from my mother, influential teachers, friends, my coaches, and even random people I met during my life journey.

For my wrestlers, one of my earliest coaches, Floyd Marshall, influenced my practice of not letting finances or transportation issues deter one's ability to wrestle. Coach Marshall learned that from one of his mentors, who learned it from his mentor, and so on. These lessons transcend time. I am honored to have had the opportunity to pass the torch. Wrestling was my passion, and I gave my heart and soul to it.

When most people hear about HIV, AIDS, COVID-19, or other diseases, their first response is to brush it off, to ignore it. Only when they face a significant emotional event with someone they know, someone they love, who has the disease or dies from it, does it become personal. Some say my story creates a hero for anyone who faces similar challenges.

At all times, I tried to project myself honorably, respectfully, as a loving friend, in the hope I would be judged and accepted based on my merit. When people learn my truth, the truth I have been wrestling with my entire life, I hope they see through their prior prejudices. I want them to see the decent person who tried to do good deeds in this world. Not just for my sake, but for the sake of the next Black, or gay, HIV positive, or other historically marginalized person they encounter.

The world is moving closer to this reality every day. Because of this, more and more people are living their truth and refusing to stay in the shadows. The influential politician Pete Buttigieg, NFL player Carl Nassib, and actor Kal Penn all risked their careers when they became open about being gay. Yet their vulnerability was met with societal support. Now they are thriving in their endeavors.

The truth will set you free. With the emotional journey of release I experienced in writing this book, I now understand firsthand the full meaning of that promise. I let go of things that weighed on me for years, shaping who I am. I didn't shy away from taking myself to task for matters I regret. I wrote my truth, and that changed my life energy. It was because I took this journey that I experienced this catharsis. The catharsis is part of the journey. Creating this book came about so others could understand they have the power to find their path to the freedom of being themselves. I hope everyone who reads my story will find opportunities and courage in their own lives to experience the same sense of freedom.

We all have more power and influence than we realize. The question is, how are we going to use it? Are we going to lift people up? Or break them down? I've answered as many of these questions as I could. As the stitched words on Russell's quilt remind us, the rest of the answers, my friends, you'll find blowing in the wind.

·_·· ___ ···_·

Acknowledgments

Telling Coach Shegog's story has been an absolute pleasure. It would not have been possible without the support of so many people. I want to thank his family for their insight into his early life. I thank his friends and colleagues who shared their stories and common experiences of personal growth. Thank you to all his former wrestlers and coaches who reminisced about lessons on and off the wrestling mat. Gideon Richards, thank you for your creative title. Thank you, Seth Stuart, Tiffany Davis, and Tino Kehagias, for your initial reviews and critique. Thank you, Diane Escalante, for your thorough review and multifaceted assistance. Thank you, Suzanne Gochenouer, for your calculated edits and seasoned consulting. You are a true hero of this project. To the North High NFL crew, Jerry McCarty, Monique Mendel, and Zita Robinson, thank you for preserving our coach's truth so his positive influence could prosper and shine through to so many of us. Thank you, Louanne Fetters, for your beautiful quilt and even more beautiful character. Alex Kun, thank you for your vivid photos. I want to thank my talented wife, Marie, for her design creativity and endless support. Thank you, Mike Tighe, for joyfully sharing and living this fleeting life together with Robert Shegog. Lastly, I thank all the readers who support us. I hope Coach Shegog's story gives you the courage to live your true self-life.

The Authors

ROBERT SHEGOG

Robert Shegog grew up in the small Michigan town of Albion. He is the youngest of four children raised by a single mother. Robert fell in love with the sport of wrestling at an early age and wrestled at Olivet College, where he was later inducted into their hall of fame. He coupled his love of wrestling with his passion for teaching to become a teacher and coach.

His first teaching job out of college, in 1974, was at Hartland High. As the only Black teacher, and one of only a handful of Black residents in Hartland, Robert had difficulty securing an apartment to rent due to racist housing policies. With the support of the Hartland High administration, he secured temporary housing with a local family. When friends encouraged him to file a lawsuit, he refused, saying that he anticipated these types of roadblocks and made the commitment to work through them so he could focus on teaching and coaching his students. He took this approach for the next thirty-three years before retiring.

Even in retirement, Coach Shegog volunteers as a wrestling coach and substitute teacher, inspiring a new generation of wrestlers and coaches. But his journey was fraught with social as well as health issues, and his dream almost failed to become a reality. As a gay man in the 1970s and '80s, it wasn't feasible to be open with his peers. To continue teaching and coaching a hands-on sport like wrestling, Robert knew he had to be selective with whom he brought into his circle of friends. His diagnosis of HIV in 1986 not only complicated the matter but added significant emotional weight to his psyche. He lost multiple partners to the disease and had his own brushes with death.

At North High, he coached a highly successful team. He trained his first state champion in 2000. Two years later, the wrestling team won every tournament they participated in and were on the hunt for the state title. Robert couldn't wholeheartedly support the team toward the end of the 2002 season when they needed him most because his time and focus were on taking care of his dying partner at home. The team did well but fell short of a team state title.

Despite these challenges, Robert's perseverance through social and health challenges did not harden him but instead softened his heart. He has been involved with the sport of wrestling in some shape or form for nearly sixty years. With his demonstration of love and compassion, coupled with the relentless pursuit of his passion, Robert motivated countless mentees to pursue their highest aspirations.

NICK KEHAGIAS

Nick Kehagias grew up in Phoenix, Arizona, after originally living in Chicago, Illinois. He is the oldest of four, raised mainly by a single mother. Nick played many sports as he grew up. In high school, he became a four-year starter in baseball and wrestling. Small and stocky, Nick was recruited to wrestling by the freshman football coach, Mike Garcia. Coach Garcia also worked alongside Coach Shegog as the head wrestling coach.

In his first-ever wrestling match as a freshman, Nick pinned his opponent. He was hooked and slowly fell in love with the challenging nature of the sport. He qualified for the state tournament his freshman year but didn't win a match. The higher-level pressure of the state tournament was too much. By his junior year, Nick had improved dramatically. He made a name for himself that year when he finished the state finals as runner-up in his weight class. During his senior year, he had only one objective—winning the state championships. He wrestled hard in practice and put in extra hours of running outside of practice. His efforts paid off, and he won the state championships.

Nick also had significant academic success, graduating as salutatorian in his high school class. He attended the University of Chicago, became a four-year letterman, and placed eighth in the nation in wrestling his junior year. His senior year, he was undefeated in Division 3 wrestling during the first half of the season. Unfortunately, a cervical radiculopathy injury kept Nick from placing his senior year. However, these wrestling experiences helped shape his future.

After college, in 2004, he partnered with Coach Shegog and Coach Warmath to help coach at his old high school, North High. North did exceptionally well during his first year with the team and developed three state placers, the most in North's history. After two years at North High, Nick started medical school at the University of Arizona in Tucson. He stayed with University of Arizona affiliated hospitals to complete his anesthesiology residency.

Throughout medical school and his internships, Nick tried to get into the wrestling room whenever he could. He volunteered in both Tucson and the Phoenix area. He continues to coach and plans to do so well into his golden years should health permit. There is no greater joy than helping someone find their purpose in life. That is only one of many truths he learned from one of his greatest mentors, Robert Shegog. Helping Coach Shegog immortalize his story was a labor of love and a monumental honor for Nick.

Nick resides in Chandler, Arizona, with his loving wife, Marie, and their dog Daphne.

Additional Resources

Support Organizations

Someone is ready to help, whether it's you or a loved one in need. You are so valuable, you make a difference in this world. Please reach out.

National Suicide Prevention Lifeline

https://suicidepreventionlifeline.org/

800-273-8255

If you are reading this after July 16, 2022, please call **988** for help.

AIDS Survivor Syndrome

https://www.sfaf.org/collections/beta/what-is-aids-survivor-syndrome/

A community forum providing information about the specific trauma suffered by people who survived the worst periods of the AIDS epidemic.

Gay & Lesbian Alliance Against Defamation (GLAAD)

https://www.glaad.org/

Focused on ensuring, fair, unbiased, and accurate information shaping the narrative around sexual diversity.

Metropolitan Community Churches (MCC) AIDS Information

https://www.mcchurch.org/world-aids-day/

Global health day providing education and resources for the fight against HIV.

Parents, Families, and Friends of Lesbians and Gays (PFLAG)

https://pflag.org/

Offers peer support, advocacy, and education for LGBTQ+ people, their families, and friends.

The Well Project

https://www.thewellproject.org/hiv-information/long-term-survivors-hiv

Serving long-term survivors of HIV.

Shegog's Favorite Charities

Northland Cares HIV Specialty Care Clinic

https://www.northlandcares.org/

Highland Center for Natural History

https://highlandscenter.org/

Jacob Kidd Scholarship

https://humboldteducationfoundation.org/projects/jacob-kidd-scholarship/

Anytown

https://anytownleadershipcamp.org/

History of AIDS/HIV

American Psychological Association

https://www.apa.org/pi/aids/youth/eighties-timeline

CDC - Epidemiology of HIV/AIDS—United States, 1981-2005

https://www.cdc.gov/mmwr/preview/mmwrhtml/mm5521a2.htm

National AIDS Memorial (Incorporates the Names Project Quilts)

https://www.aidsmemorial.org/

https://www.aidsmemorial.org/quilt

https://www.aidsmemorial.org/interactive-aids-quilt Russ Fetters #1268

History of Gay Rights

History Channel – History of Gay Rights

https://www.history.com/topics/gay-rights/history-of-gay-rights

NPR – Discussion on North Carolina Law, 2016

https://www.npr.org/sections/thetwo-way/2016/03/24/471700323/north-carolina-passes-law-blocking-measures-to-protect-lgbt-people

NPR – Discussion on Arizona Law, 2019

https://www.npr.org/2019/04/15/712842522/arizona-teachers-can-now-discuss-lgbtq-issues-without-worrying-about-the-law

History of Civil Rights

African American "Great Migration"

https://www.jstor.org/stable/30036966

African Mosaic

https://www.loc.gov/exhibits/african/afam008.html

Assassination of Martin Luther King

https://kinginstitute.stanford.edu/encyclopedia/assassination-martin-luther-king-jr

Civil Rights Movement History

https://www.crmvet.org/tim/timhome.htm

Malcom X

https://aaregistry.org/story/malcolm-x-showed-a-unique-side-of-blackness/

https://worldhistoryproject.org/topics/malcolm-x

March on Washington

https://www.history.com/topics/black-history/march-on-washington

Pontiac, Michigan School District – Buses Bombed

https://michiganadvance.com/2021/08/30/on-this-day-in-1971-kkk-bombs-empty-pontiac-buses-set-to-racially-integrate-schools/

People Who Made a Difference

CPO John Henry Turpin and other Early American Chief Petty Officers

https://militaryhallofhonor.com/honoree-record.php?id=307635

https://hamptonroadsnavalmuseum.blogspot.com/2021/02/before-chief-turpin-other-early-african.html

MCPO Carl Maxie Brashear

https://militaryhallofhonor.com/honoree-record.php?id=211921

Robert Shegog Speaking up for Diversity TED Talk: TEDxEmbryRiddlePrescott
November 2018

https://www.ted.com/talks/robert_shegog_speaking_up_for_diversity

From History's Perspective

Archaeological Institute of America Feature on Phoenix Indian School

https://archive.archaeology.org/online/features/phoenix/

Mormonism's Negro Doctrine: An Historical Overview

https://www.jstor.org/stable/45226775?seq=1#metadata_info_tab_contents

PBS Features on Indian Schools

https://www.pbs.org/wgbh/roadshow/stories/articles/2020/4/13/early-years-american-indian-boarding-schools

https://www.rmpbs.org/colorado-voices/an-indian-boarding-school/

https://ket.pbslearningmedia.org/resource/arct.socst.ush.wounded12aschoolsa/taken-from-their-families/

https://ket.pbslearningmedia.org/resource/arct.socst.ush.wounded12bschoolsb/the-us-governments-education-of-native-american-children/

https://www.rmpbs.org/blogs/rocky-mountain-pbs/fort-lewis-college-indian-boarding-school-panel-removal/

Phoenix Indian School Visitor Center

https://www.nativeconnections.org/community-development/phoenix-indian-school-visitor-center

Plato's Symposium - The Sacred Band Unit

https://www.neh.gov/article/lovers-and-soldiers

Simon Wiesenthal and the Museum of Tolerance

https://www.museumoftolerance.com/

Sixty Minutes Feature on Deaths at Canada's Indian Schools

https://www.cbsnews.com/news/canada-residential-schools-unmarked-graves-indigenous-children-60-minutes-2022-02-06/

Made in the USA
Monee, IL
16 July 2023

38814739R10184